Praise for *Beijing Welcomes You*

"Wry [and] knowing . . . *Beijing Welcomes You* is a street-level introduction to a city that's at once the world's center and its back office, a place where you can feel 'on the top of the pile and on the bottom, all at once.'"
—*The Christian Science Monitor*

"Part memoir, part urban history, *Beijing Welcomes You* . . . gets us closer to comprehending China. The book Scocca has written describes a city in the midst of radical, contemporary transformation. Scocca renders the physical evidence of Beijing's growth as something monstrously and almost surreally creepy."
—Boston.com

"A spirited portrayal of an old metropolis being turned inside out . . . brought both Twain and Dave Barry to mind."
—Time.com

"A revealing and well-written report on what we should know and understand about twenty-first-century China."
—Gay Talese

"A brilliant cultural study written in a surprisingly poetic style; this is highly recommended to all interested readers."
—*Library Journal*

"Excels at straddling the line between the personal and sociopolitical."
—*Publishers Weekly*

"Blindingly brilliant insights about China, the United States, and the audacity of empire. Scocca writes with grace, texture, nuance, wisdom, and wit. Don't skim this book, savor it."
—Gene Weingarten

"Tracking his experience on the dual planes of resident and journalist, Scocca explodes the dichotomous East-versus-West narrative that's endemic to reports from China."
—*The Onion A.V. Club*

BEIJING WELCOMES YOU

UNVEILING THE CAPITAL CITY
OF THE FUTURE

TOM SCOCCA

RIVERHEAD BOOKS

New York

RIVERHEAD BOOKS
Published by the Penguin Group
Penguin Group (USA) Inc.
375 Hudson Street, New York, New York 10014, USA
Penguin Group (Canada), 90 Eglinton Avenue East, Suite 700, Toronto, Ontario M4P 2Y3, Canada
(a division of Pearson Penguin Canada Inc.) • Penguin Books Ltd., 80 Strand, London WC2R 0RL,
England • Penguin Group Ireland, 25 St. Stephen's Green, Dublin 2, Ireland (a division of Penguin
Books Ltd.) • Penguin Group (Australia), 250 Camberwell Road, Camberwell, Victoria 3124, Australia
(a division of Pearson Australia Group Pty. Ltd.) • Penguin Books India Pvt. Ltd., 11 Community
Centre, Panchsheel Park, New Delhi—110 017, India • Penguin Group (NZ), 67 Apollo Drive,
Rosedale, Auckland 0632, New Zealand (a division of Pearson New Zealand Ltd.) • Penguin Books
(South Africa) (Pty.) Ltd., 24 Sturdee Avenue, Rosebank, Johannesburg 2196, South Africa

Penguin Books Ltd., Registered Offices: 80 Strand, London WC2R 0RL, England

While the author has made every effort to provide accurate telephone numbers,
Internet addresses, and other contact information at the time of publication, neither the
publisher nor the author assumes any responsibility for errors, or for changes that occur
after publication. Further, the publisher does not have any control over and does not
assume any responsibility for author or third-party websites or their content.

First Riverhead hardcover edition: August 2011
First Riverhead trade paperback edition: July 2012
Riverhead trade paperback ISBN: 978-1-59448-580-0

The Library of Congress has catalogued the Riverhead hardcover edition as follows:

Scocca, Tom.
Beijing welcomes you : unveiling the capital city of the future / Tom Scocca.
p.   cm.
ISBN 978-1-59448-784-2
1. Beijing (China)—Description and travel.   2. Beijing (China)—Social life and
customs.   3. City and town life—China—Beijing.   4. Scocca, Tom—Travel—China—
Beijing.   5. Scocca, Tom—Homes and haunts—China—Beijing.   6. Americans—China—
Beijing—Biography.   7. Beijing (China)—Biography.   I. Title.
DS795.S33   2011   2010025341
951'.15606092—dc22
[B]

PRINTED IN THE UNITED STATES OF AMERICA

10   9   8   7   6   5   4   3   2   1

*Penguin is committed to publishing works of quality and integrity.
In that spirit, we are proud to offer this book to our readers;
however, the story, the experiences, and the words are the author's alone.*

For Christina and Mack

And to the memory of Stephen Keller,
who went and saw the world

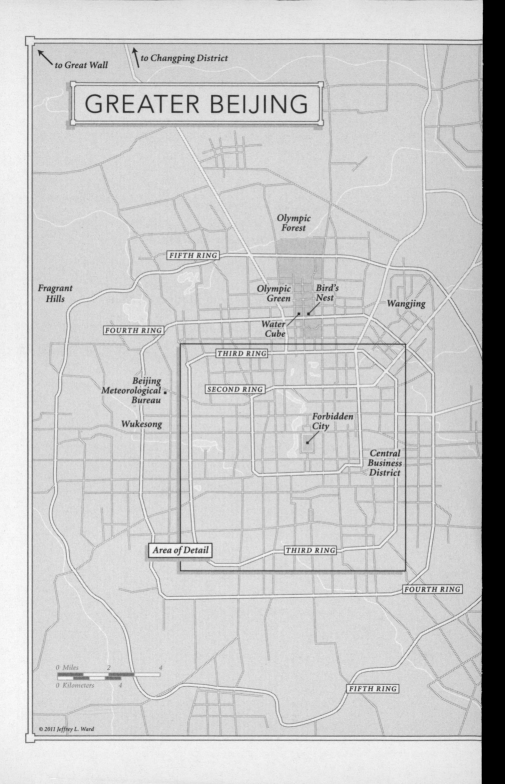

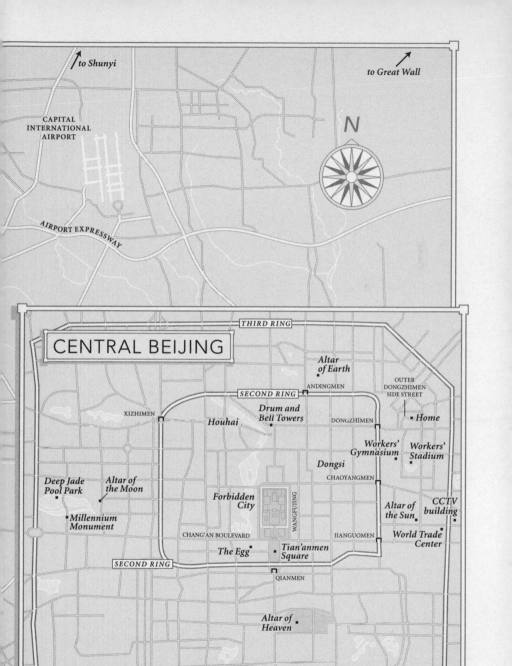

to Shunyi

to Great Wall

N

CAPITAL
INTERNATIONAL
AIRPORT

AIRPORT EXPRESSWAY

CENTRAL BEIJING

THIRD RING

Altar
of Earth

ANDINGMEN

OUTER
DONGZHIMEN
SIDE STREET

SECOND RING

XIZHIMEN

Drum and
Bell Towers

Houhai

DONGZHIMEN

Home

Workers'
Gymnasium

Workers'
Stadium

Dongsi

CHAOYANGMEN

Deep Jade
Pool Park

Altar of
the Moon

Forbidden
City

WANGFUJING

Altar of
the Sun

CCTV
building

Millennium
Monument

CHANG'AN BOULEVARD

JIANGUOMEN

World Trade
Center

The Egg

Tian'anmen
Square

SECOND RING

QIANMEN

Altar of
Heaven

0 Miles   1   2

0 Kilometers   2

THIRD RING

CONTENTS

IX. 胜 TRIUMPH

X. 回家 GOING HOME

I.

京 CAPITAL

1.

城 Walls

The first important fact to know about China is that it has a lot of Chinese people in it. I always knew it, sort of, the way everybody in America knows it. The way we know that Antarctica is pretty cold or Germany is unusually efficient. There's a billion of them, the Chinese: 1,000,000,000. Big number.

The actual figure—I checked—is more like 1.3 billion. That means the rounding error, that stray 0.3 billion, is as big as the entire population of the United States.

But I already knew the numbers, more or less, before I ever got to China. The reality behind the numbers was something else. It began to register with me at the Great Wall, at Badaling. I arrived there in August 2004, my first time on the Chinese mainland. It was almost exactly four years—1,458 days, to be exact—before Beijing was scheduled to host the Summer Olympics. This meant very little to me at the time. Experts were proclaiming or warning that the world was at the dawn of a Chinese Century, and China saw the Olympics as a chance to prove the proclamations true, to demonstrate that its capital city had become a great global metropolis. Though I didn't yet know it, I would be living through that demonstration from the inside. I would become the audience for the display of the New China and a part of the display itself—tied to Beijing by habit and blood, but still a foreign body, for China to tolerate or not.

First, though, I was a sightseer. Badaling was one of the closest stretches of the Great Wall to the capital, in the mountains about an hour north of the city. Tourists in search of the authentic, ancient China prefer to go farther afield, to the more desolate and ruinous parts of the Wall. I was not looking for optimal tourism; I was jet-lagged and baffled by everything around me, and my Chinese-born father-in-law took charge of the project, leading the way to the bus depot and buying a pair of round-trip tickets. I followed.

The global metropolis, where the bus passed through it, was a mass of apartment towers and unidentifiable commercial buildings, tall and bulky but loosely spaced—a bit like Queens, if all the buildings in Queens were doubled in height. Rather than dwindle in size, the clusters of buildings gradually grew fewer in number as we passed out of Beijing's urban districts. The road began winding its way through steep, picturesque hills, past river valleys. Sharp gray patches of rock cut through thick greenery on the slopes; shreds of mist and cloud hung down from the overcast sky. I began to think I understood the national tradition of nature poetry: "the frayed green shawl . . . rocky shoulders . . ."

Then we hit the traffic jam. Between its embankments, the road was clogged with buses, all of them closing in on the Great Wall site. They curved ahead, around the bend and out of view. Our bus stopped and showed no signs of moving again.

We got out to walk. The mist had become a fine but soaking rain, and a man was hawking ponchos right outside the bus for one yuan—flimsy blue trash bags, basically, with hoods. Mine tore almost immediately, and I knotted the sides of the rip together as we trudged past the line of immobile buses, breathing in their exhaust. Water beaded on the impenetrable outside of the plastic, and the inside got clammy.

At last, past yet more poncho vendors, we reached it: the parking lot. Oh, and behind it, up the rise, there was the Great Wall, too. But first there were the buses, and the people getting off the buses, and then rows of stalls full of Great Wall knickknacks and Great Wall books and Great Wall T-shirts, with customers swarming the doorways. The people streamed up into the visitors' center, where they filled a round theater to watch a 360-degree panoramic movie of the Great Wall.

And with only a few exceptions, they were Chinese. High-minded Westerners tend to think of tourism—swarming, grasping tourism—as a vice we carry with us. It is a mobile gravitational force surrounding white people, warping the pure and genuine local culture into a caricature of itself.

But there was no place for Western anxiety or guilt at Badaling. All the available room, psychological and otherwise, was filled by Chinese people—Chinese vendors selling Chinese-made kitsch to Chinese sightseers, all bundled in their clear blue Chinese ponchos. The Great Wall undulated along the ridgeline, softly framed by the mists, and an unbroken mass of blue ponchos undulated right with it, along the top, up and down the wet stone course, and steeply up again, toward the clouds. It could have been a scroll painting.

Beijing is a city of walls. Physically, it is shaped by nothing but itself. It does not harmonize with the natural landscape; it was not laid out along a fertile river valley, for instance, or wrapped around a secure harbor. It was definitely not placed to take advantage of a pleasant climate. The city was raised up, instead, where its rulers more than a thousand years ago saw the need for city walls—at the far end of a hot, dusty plain, at the foot of cold, windy mountains. The winters run long and the water supplies run short.

Emperors favored the site as the capital off and on through the centuries precisely because it was a nonplace: it occupied the spot where the northern frontier of Southern China faded into the southern frontier of Mongolia. From there (with the help, just to the north, of the principal Chinese wall, the most celebrated wall in the world) a ruler could knit together both regions. Genghis Khan seized the city from the Jin dynasty rulers, and his grandson Kublai made it the capital of his Yuan dynasty. The Ming dynasty seized it from the Yuan, and the Qing seized it from the Ming.

So old Beijing was centered on the seat of the emperor—the city's heart sealed off by the towering, dull-red walls of the Forbidden City, built in the fifteenth century. Inside, inaccessible, were the nested halls and courtyards of the palace complex, with only the gleaming yellow-tiled roofs of the buildings showing to the outside.

Those two colors, the red and the yellow of the Forbidden City, were part of the official Beijing 2008 Olympic palette: "Chinese Red" and "Yellow Glaze"—or, in the international language of color, Pantone 186 C and Pantone 123 C. (They were joined by "Scholar Tree Green" and "Blue and White Porcelain Blue.") The East was not simply red, it was twelve parts Pantone Warm Red, four parts Pantone Rubine Red, and one-quarter part Pantone Black.

The Olympic organizing committee also included, last on the color list, the other main shade of historic Beijing: a dead medium-dark gray. Color was for the emperor; that gray—the essence of colorlessness—was for the rest of the city. It spread outward from the palace, on still more walls: low, gray-brick ones surrounding the courtyard houses, or *siheyuan*. Each home sat squarely on a north-south axis, facing in on itself, like a small-scale version of the imperial compound; the windowless outer walls, one story high, ran together in a common gray surface.

The narrow spaces between one common wall and the next formed the old city's lanes and alleys, the hutongs. In the hutongs, the orderly geometry of the courtyard houses was everted into chaos—right-angled jogs and branchings, blind turns and dead ends, parallel lines suddenly swinging perpendicularly away from each other. A labyrinth, meticulously detailed from above and confoundingly featureless if you were inside it.

Many of the courtyard houses, built for single households in Imperial times, had a dozen or more families' electric meters clustered together inside their front gates. On my first trip into the hutongs, this was one of the features the tricycle-rickshaw tour guide pointed out, along with the stones and beams by the doorways marking the original occupants' rank in the nobility. Beijingers' daily life spilled out of the courtyards and into the alleys; people sat out there, gossiping or cleaning scallions or playing Chinese checkers. But the maze was both intimate and desolate at the same time. Walking through an unfamiliar hutong was like playing an old-fashioned first-person video game: one gray box after the next. These are the actual directions I was given to the courtyard house where a friend lived: Take a taxi to the end of the nearest big street, then get out and turn right. Take the first left, then the first right, then the first left, then the first right. Knock on the second gate.

The hutongs, in their own turn, had once been enclosed by the outer city wall, a squarish sixteen-mile circuit, fifty feet high and built of yard-long bricks. There were no elevated prospects within that perimeter, and few significant open spaces. Save for a few protrusions—the gate towers of the wall, the Drum Tower and Bell Tower, the temples—a Beijinger's line of sight and line of movement ended wherever the next wall happened to be.

Is architecture destiny, or is destiny architecture? The history of Beijing is a history of rebuilding projects, at least as far back as Marco Polo's report that Kublai Khan had built an entire new city right next to the existing one, on the advice of an astrologer. The Communists, in their push to overturn the old order, demolished the city wall in the 1950s and 1960s. But they did not obliterate its course. Rather, they built a road, the Second Ring Road, along the pre-revolutionary boundary.

As a result, the ghost of the wall still confined the city, with a band of clogged traffic rather than brick fortifications. The names of its vanished gates—"gate" in Mandarin being *men*—survived as the names of interchanges and the neighborhoods around them: Dongzhimen, Xizhimen, Chaoyangmen. In its new form the wall's influence was echoed and amplified as the city spread—by the Third, Fourth, Fifth, and Sixth Rings, each one a mile or a mile and a half farther out. (There had never been any First Ring, and the reason behind the numbering is lost to history.)

No matter what form renewal took in Beijing, there was usually another barrier. The eight- and ten-lane boulevards, expanded by the Communists to open up the city, were impassable; pedestrians who would cross from one curb to the other confronted not merely a seething mass of cars but a row of metal wickets running unbroken down the center line, fencing off foot traffic. As the old hutong neighborhoods, with their close-in walls, were leveled, developments rose to fill the newly cleared megablocks—as separate and inaccessible as ever, if on a grander scale.

Only in Tian'anmen Square, at the center of Beijing, did open space prevail. There, below the imperial compound's southernmost gate—the Tian'anmen, or Gate of Heavenly Peace—Mao had razed the surroundings to create a gargantuan forecourt for the masses. His monumental portrait still gazed out from the center of the gate, toward his mausoleum and the gray bulk of Qianmen, the surviving Front Gate of the city wall. It was a blank, imposing open space, one that exposed the viewer more than it revealed the city.

And everywhere in Beijing in 2004, there were construction fences. As developers, civil engineers, and star architects frantically tried to get the new metropolis built, the construction fence was the dominant idiom of the cityscape, the latest and most characteristic form of the wall. There were steel-panel fences and masonry ones; plain beige fences; fences painted with inspirational slogans; fences covered with block-long full-color advertising banners for the malls and business parks and luxury apartment buildings to come. There were fences made of mirrorlike chrome facets. One fence was made by filling a framework of wide-spaced red wire mesh with smooth river rocks, to make a loose, unmortared stone wall, with daylight showing through the gaps. The actual building seemed to be in danger of being an anticlimax. The construction walls came right up to the sidewalk, if not to the street. In some neighborhoods, they were all that could be seen—them and, above them, in every direction, the gleaming yellow of the working cranes.

I had never planned or expected to become involved with China. The People's Republic was on the other side of the world from the United States, in symbol and in fact. Though the two countries had begun restoring relations soon after I was born, China remained a symbol of antipodal remoteness: still Communist, still largely closed to outsiders, still aloof from the otherwise irresistible charms of late-twentieth-century American living. When I was seventeen and

Western-style democratic ideals were apparently triumphing over totalitarianism around the globe, China was the exception—a styrofoam Statue of Liberty went up on Tian'anmen Square, embodying the hopes for a unified world, and then the tanks rumbled in, and we and they were two worlds again.

Like most other Americans, I didn't think much about closing the gap. I did not pursue a degree in East Asian studies or a career in low-cost manufacturing. In college, I took one course on the history of the Chinese Cultural Revolution, the period from 1966 to 1976 when Mao had tried to renew the spirit of proletarian fervor by turning the whole country over to rampaging gangs of teenagers. It was a popular course, and it counted double toward graduation requirements.

College was also where I had met my future wife, Christina. Her parents had left mainland China for Taiwan as children to escape the Communist Revolution, but had moved on to upstate New York, where Christina was born. When I met them, they lived in Ohio— the same part of Ohio where my mother was raised. My midwestern mother had married my father, an Italian-American from South Philadelphia, third-generation but unmixed, raised in a house amid immigrant grandparents, foreign language, foreign cooking. That was what people did in America. For our wedding, my mother sewed banners with the Chinese double-happiness symbol.

The actual China was an abstraction. A few of the most serious and hardy souls we knew had gone abroad to study or work in its capital—a grim and daunting city of cabbage, cold water, and coal smoke; of Mao suits and jingling herds of bicyclists. Or maybe it wasn't exactly that way anymore. The news said there was a New China, capitalist and modernizing, interwoven with American (and European, and African) life, by strands visible and invisible:

cell-phone chips, structural steel, movies, contemporary art, foreign debt. We would all reckon with it, sooner or later.

For our household, the moment of reckoning came in early 2004. My wife and I, living outside Washington, D.C., got simultaneous job offers. Mine was a newspaper columnist's job in New York, at *The New York Observer*; hers was with a nonprofit opening an office in Beijing. We couldn't pass up either one. I would move to New York, to start with, and get away to China every three or four months, while she settled into Beijing.

While I waited for my first trip, I had Christina's reports from her travels: In the city of Harbin, she had been to a zoo for tigers and lions where visitors could order live animals from a menu to be served to the zoo's inhabitants—chickens for the budget-minded, a lamb if you wanted to splurge. The lamb hadn't put up much of a fight. In Beijing proper, she had endured wrangling with customs officials and a confounding search for an apartment. The household Chinese she'd grown up speaking, as the firstborn daughter of immigrants, was quickening, spreading to cover professional, technical, and idiomatic language; the manners her parents had pressed on her at boring Chinese-American community functions were guiding her through the rituals of formal banquets. She took taxis that broke down in the middle of the road. It sounded chaotic and harrowing and wholly, satisfyingly foreign.

My own experience of the city began the moment my flight touched down, with the air: a brownish smog over the airport runway, as a summer day blurred into an open-ended dusk. The dimness deepened more by the time I made it out of the terminal and into a taxi on the airport expressway. In a few years, in a transformed Beijing, this would be the old airport expressway, coming from what's now the old international terminal. But it was all new to me, and it seemed only reasonable to make some assumptions about what was passing outside the taxi window. Along the roadway were poplar trees—puny gray-green things, planted in mechanically straight rows, half vanishing as they receded in the ghastly air, a false and futile gesture. So here was the New China: a sprig of baby's breath dropped into a smokestack.

China's pollution problem was what an American would have expected to see. This pollution had deep, mythic resonance in our national consciousness. It was first of all a mark of China's sudden emergence as a rival economic power—both a metaphor and an actual problem, the smoke and dust and chemical vapor of a growing industrial monster (a dragon, if you must) gobbling down ever more of the world's raw materials at one end and squeezing out container ships full of finished goods at the other. The tainted air of China was blowing across the Pacific and into California, like a warning.

Beneath that was the moral panic: the Chinese weren't afraid to poison their own country—even the capital—or the rest of the world, as long as they could keep expanding their factories. Still beneath that, if you cared to keep digging, was the awareness that, after all, these factories were making the iPods and DVDs and socket wrenches and flip-flops that Americans wanted to buy, so that we were maybe more directly implicated in this toxic manufacturing business than we would have liked to have been.

Then, below even that, rarely more than half expressed at home, were the ideas that made up the commonplace Chinese view: that in the West's own pursuit of industrialization, London had buried itself in soot for decades, and the United States had poured waste into its waterways until the rivers caught on fire; and that the wealth we had secured by plundering nature was what allowed us to now breathe clear air and drink clear water and sit in judgment on the environmental and social irresponsibility of countries that hadn't developed quite as early as ours had. And that what really might worry us was the notion that our Western standard of health and prosperity relied on the existence of places that were sickened and poor—that if we did cut the one (point three) billion Chinese in on an even share (or a less-than-even share, former president Jiang Zemin's official goal for the People's Republic having been "moderate prosperity"), the planet and the economy and our own lifestyle couldn't take the shock.

Any and all theoretical discomfort, though, was insubstantial in the presence of the smog itself. The smell of it seeped into the airplane cabin before the plane even opened its doors. It occluded the view of the city. It burned at the back of my throat and left black marks on the tissue when I blew my nose.

Back in New York, I would find the air sweet by comparison. But it was Beijing, foul fumes and all, that would draw me back. Residing there seemed unimaginable—the way New York had seemed unimaginable the first time I climbed the steps out of Penn Station into the roaring whirl of Seventh Avenue. Except in Beijing, the discombobulation did not subside for hours or even days. Hardly anything anywhere even resembled English, written or spoken. I was cut off from text and information—illiterate, deaf, and mute; I felt as if someone had clapped blurry goggles over my eyes and muffling headphones over my ears.

The city was too low-slung and wide to have those tight urban canyons of commercial signage that make a Chinatown look like a Chinatown; still, there was no mistaking it for anything but the Far East. There were tile roofs and winding alleys and carved stone lions and ceremonial archways. There were red-canopied bicycle rickshaws with gold fringe. There were Pekingese dogs, lots of them, and Peking ducks hanging in restaurants. The equipment of modern life was different, too: spiral ramps to pedestrian overpasses, tiny unfamiliar hatchbacks, funny bulging orange domes over the pay phones. Barbershop poles were clear motorized cylinders, as tall and wide as a person, with lurid-colored stripes or radial designs; many of the hair salons were in fact brothels. Red-and-white banners bearing patriotic or inspirational slogans hung across roadways and on guardrails.

It was too much to absorb. We wandered through blocks with bare earth and the open steel forms of unfinished buildings, their rolling and curving profiles all around us. Was this imminent Utopia, or dystopia? We dined in a Sichuanese restaurant down some puzzling sequence of turnings through backstreets, in the feeble monochromatic lighting I remembered from a trip to Havana. Waiters poured hot water from bronze teakettles with skinny spouts as long as rifle barrels, standing off at a distance, the water arriving on target in our little teacups in a ballistic—or, frankly, urinary—stream. There were smallish fish split and skewered and so fire-blasted that their bones were as brown and crunchy as the rest of them. There was a dish of fried bits of chicken gristle sifted in a mound of chopped dried red peppers. The dining room was spacious and shabby and nearly empty. In the middle of the meal, a lightbulb overhead exploded, and glass rained down nearby. This would turn out to be an ordinary experience, the explosion. It was how the ceiling fixture in my study would announce that a bulb had burned out: PWAM! Crunch, tinkle. I never did get used to that.

There was one semi-familiar note: the summer of 2004 was an Olympic summer, and Chinese Central Television (CCTV), the state-run broadcasting giant, was showing the Athens Games on multiple channels at once, day after day: weightlifting, judo, trapshooting, ping-pong. The Chinese athletes were winning.

Only twenty years before, in Los Angeles, the People's Republic had taken a single gold medal, its first ever. In Athens, China captured thirty-two, behind only the United States' thirty-six. In men's track-and-field, where China had previously won nothing and expected less, a twenty-one-year-old hurdler from Shanghai named Liu Xiang stunned the nation with a victory in the 110 meters, in world-record-tying time.

The next games were going to be in Beijing, and over the next four years, Liu would become a national cult figure, like an old Party hero reborn in the era of Coca-Cola sponsorships—the incarnation of possibility. The national sports administration would aim for China to finish atop the Beijing gold-medal count, to demonstrate on its home soil that it was a true athletic superpower. A program called "Project 119" was under way, targeting specific medal-rich sports, 119 medals' worth, in which China had previously underperformed.

Yet there was much more to be won than games. In 1971, a few ping-pong matches had marked the reopening of Chinese relations with the United States and China's reengagement with the West. The Games of 2008 were being designed as a showcase for all the power and development and wealth that had followed. The 1904 Olympics and World's Fair in St. Louis had served to inaugurate the American Century; the spectacle of Berlin in 1936 had been meant to introduce the glories of a Thousand Year Reich.

Now, for the new Chinese Century, Beijing was planning a defining moment of its own—the display of a city and a nation transformed. Throughout China, cities were booming, throwing up new skylines, moving millions of people into urban centers that had been farmland five years before. In the capital, the rush of progress was being funneled toward a single point in time: the opening of the Olympics, on August 8, 2008.

The date, 8/8/08, was a cascade of lucky numbers in China. And over time, the phrase "by 2008" began to seem like a mirror image of "since 9/11" in America—or a photo negative of it, light for dark, an inescapable refrain of hope rather than resignation and dread. While New York argued about what to do with the still-empty hole at Ground Zero, Beijing was spending $40 billion to develop and prepare for the Games. By 2008, everything in Beijing was going to have changed.

By 2008, there would be 2,000 extra police on duty and 1,500 new monitors keeping order on the buses. By 2008, there would be a new $1 billion airport terminal, three new subway lines, an express train to the airport, one high-speed railway crossing the Taihang Mountains to Taiyuan and another connecting Beijing to the port of Tianjin. By 2008, rats, mosquitoes, black beetles, and lice would be exterminated in the area around the Olympic sites. Beijing residents would quit their ingrained habit of spitting in the streets. Thirty-five percent of Beijingers would speak basic English. All rivers inside the city's Sixth Ring Road would be free of pollution, and 50 percent of municipal water usage would employ recycled water. More than a hundred historic sites would be renovated; more than three hundred zones classed as slums would be redeveloped.

Other changes were not in the official goals. The Olympic budget would grow from $1.6 billion to $2 billion. The city's population, listed as just under 14 million in 2004, would swell to nearly 17 million by the end of the Olympic year. Three or four million of those people, by government count, were migrants from the rest of China, without permanent residence rights. They were the ones—living in tents and barracks, burnt brown and red by the elements, clothed in odds and ends—whose hands and backs would build the city of tomorrow.

When the work was done—if the work got done—a once backward and closed-off capital would open up into a national and international showpiece, a city of ample green space and avant-garde architecture, with smooth-flowing transit and traffic, a place that would be civilized and tidy and multilingual. The soot and dust I was breathing were the entropy from which a new creation would arise.

New York? New York would be there in 2009 or 2010, mostly the same. I would have only one chance to see Beijing before it became something else. My two-week visits grew to three and four weeks, the spaces between them shorter. I got a Chinese cell phone and bank card, and I enrolled in a Chinese-language school between the Third and Fourth Ring Roads. If a new Beijing was on its way, I was going to be living there when it arrived.

2.

小街 Alley

Home in Beijing was on an alley, as it had to be. Every story about Beijing depended on an alley. Foreign writers were moving into alley houses as fast as they could, for a taste of Old Beijing and its hutongs before they vanished into the new. They were integral, the alleys.

Every story about Beijing should also include a bicycle, but I messed that one up. The landlord had provided a bicycle, some grim black iron thing with a basket on it, but we left it parked downstairs outside the apartment entry, in the courtyard, in the rain and dust and wind, until we stopped noticing it, and at some point it stopped being there. Possibly someone stole it. It could be that the landlord took it back.

By the time I got there, Beijing was no longer a bicyclists' city, anyway. The bell-jangling herds of bicyclists, iconic in the Beijing of art-house movies and imagination, were gone the way of the bison—not extinct, sometimes impressive, but no longer the rulers of the landscape. There were two million cars on the streets, and there would be more than three million by the summer of 2008. Every time I left the country, the traffic would be visibly thicker when I returned. In 2004, Beijingers' complaints had seemed overblown to a traffic-hardened American, but along the way to 2008, the congestion on the Second Ring would become genuinely world-class, on the level of downtown Athens, the topside of the Capital Beltway, or the mouth of the Lincoln Tunnel.

Most of the drivers were fresh off their own bicycles. This meant that the remaining bicyclists had to be superb riders not to be killed. Encounters that would have maimed a New York bike commuter, or sent one into self-righteous apoplexy, were routine: sharp unsignaled turns; thoughtlessly opened doors; the two-ton drift toward the curb or the alley wall. These drew nothing but a hard, resigned stare from the Beijing cyclists, as they wrenched their handlebars around or stepped off a moving bike to cheat death.

The enduring totem of Beijing, transportation-wise, was not the bicycle but the *sanlunche*, the tricycle, a term covering a whole phylum of three-wheeled contrivances. The pedal-powered rickshaws were the least of it. There were three-wheeled motorcycles, with enclosed cabs, often homemade out of sheet metal, for the driver and one passenger. There were electric commuter tricycles and the street-sweepers' tricycles with garbage bins mounted on the rear. There were tricycles with plexiglass compartments on the back for serving up pots of food to migrant construction workers, and tricycles with tool kits on the back that opened out into repair shops for other tricycles and bicycles. And then there was the cargo tricycle, flat-bedded or with a sunken bed between its fenders, powered by a long, drooping pedal chain or a puttering add-on motor, or both, carrying whatever needed to be carried: fruit or vegetables, wholesale or retail; potted plants; sofa deliveries; twenty-foot mountains of discarded styrofoam; flattened cardboard boxes; Uighur-minority peddlers' candied nut loaves; metal flashing; lengths of pipe; old TVs; used clothes; firewood; coal cakes; new bricks for new buildings and old bricks dug from demolition rubble.

At any rate, there would be no bicycle, or only the ghost of one. We did have an alley, though. The alleys of Old Beijing were endangered, too—caught in a race between photographers and wrecking machinery, memorialized before and because they were being demolished for urban renewal. Ours was not much of an alley, as alleys went. It ran roughly east-west at a sagging angle, failing to quite follow either the narrow Liangma River above it or the broad Outer Dongzhimen Avenue below. There was no street sign, and our landlord claimed it had no name at all. It was three years before we figured out from a you-are-here map out on the main avenue that it did have a name, which turned out to be "Outer Dongzhimen Side Street."

Dongzhimen was the old imperial East Straight Gate—now an overpass, a long-distance bus depot, a subway stop, and collection of ramps to and from the Second Ring. On the inner side of Dongzhimen Bridge, a monumental replica of an ancient three-legged bronze drinking vessel presided over the sluggish traffic. From there, the inner avenue went due west; through a corridor of restaurants, strung with rows of red lanterns and traced in red-and-gold neon, that was called Guijie, or Ghost Street; and on into the low, gray-brick ancient city, past the narrow mouths of hutongs, till it reached the square base of the gilt-trimmed, green-tile-roofed Drum Tower, on the city's north-south axis, where the emperor's watchmen once pounded out the time of day.

But our alley was outside the Second Ring, not in Old Beijing so much as Indeterminate Middle-Aged Beijing. The Outer Dongzhimen neighborhood was a study in Beijing's thrilling, haphazard potential—not unlimited potential, but potential in which the limits were constantly being guessed at, renegotiated, or relocated. If anyone had tried any urban planning there, it hadn't taken. There was sort of an embassy row, running eastward—handsome, tree-lined enclosures for Australia, Canada, Germany, the European Union— but facing or preceding those compounds were aging apartment blocks, new shopping centers, construction pits, massage spas, worker barracks, and office towers. There was a Pizza Hut, and a glittering restaurant specializing in first-quality stewed fish heads, and there were sidewalk vendors frying stuffed pancakes on round griddles or roasting sweet potatoes in ovens made of steel drums.

Though Beijing was a city where prosperity and redevelopment were actively pushing out the poor, it did not have the clearly sorted social geography of Rio de Janeiro, with the rich on the beaches and the poor in their slums on the hills, or the bridge-and tunnel divide of New York. A luxury-apartment tower, thirty-some stories tall, jutted up on the way to our alley, and beyond that was a tower belonging to the national oil company, and on a lane in the shadow between the two towers was the basement shop from which a deliveryman pedaled his cargo tricycle to bring us new watercooler bottles.

The apartment itself was a fourth-floor walkup, three bedrooms, in a six-story building on the alley's north side. The building, a satellite of an aging, unfancy residential complex for Chinese bank employees, was U-shaped around a long courtyard, parallel to the roadway, with our apartment in the outer bend of the U. The doors and most of the furnishings were in caramel-colored wood, with budget-weight wood flooring in the bedrooms and smooth hard tile in the rest of it. The walls were concrete; to hang a picture required brute force and thick masonry nails.

There was a kind of utilitarian Beijing apartment housing that I gradually grew to love: boxy concrete blocks or towers, in clusters or rows, with projecting balconies. These buildings were accented with a three- or four-color paint job—rust-red balconies, say, against a pale tangerine face, with white trim. The balconies had been glassed in individually over time, with different kinds of windows, creating a pleasing overall not-quite-regularity.

Our building—Hujiayuan Small Community, Yard No. 26—was like one of those, only newer and ugly. The façade had been painted in dirty cream and milk-chocolate brown; many of the windows (including some, but not all, of ours) were tinted a heavy marine blue. The stairways were concrete, lit by bare bulbs sticking out from the walls of the landings. The lights were on sound-activated switches, so you had to slap a foot as you approached each new, dark floor. In the mornings, a mute woman came through to mop the steps, and the wash water would raise stale-ashtray fumes from the concrete pores, like the ghost of all the city's pollution returning at once.

Across the street and to the west was the back gate of a compound for well-funded expats, with an imposing old-fashioned polychrome triple archway on the front side and Sino-Californian suburban landscaping on the interior. Next to that, on the east, was a vacant lot behind a wall.

Facing the lot, on our side of the lane, was a collection of buildings that would have been a vacant lot if anyone had bothered to knock them down. Instead they stood, in a skinny jumbled triangle, one or two hundred yards long on the alley side. There were picturesque, ancient gray-brick structures in there, to be sure, toward the back. Down through the years, they had been built over or shored up with red brick, concrete, white tile, corrugated metal. Some of the bricks were up on the rooftops, holding down grimy tarps over leaky tiles. At street level, the buildings served as a retail strip—a long row of narrow stalls and storefronts, many with living space curtained off at the back.

It was an extraordinarily unimportant alley to look at. But take a walk up it, circa 2004. It begins at a T-shaped intersection. As you face west into the alley mouth, to your right is the gateway to the rest of the apartment towers of the Hujiayuan Small Community, with a collapsible metal gate on rollers. Next to the gate is a newsstand, its five-sided counter festooned with local magazines and newspapers, and with a collection of red telephones at the near end where people make long-distance calls. Across the alley, on the left, is the public toilet. Residents of the alley, with no plumbing of their own, come and go from it in their pajamas, and an odor trails sluggishly out the doorway after them—not the worst restroom odor in the world, but not the mild aroma of manure, either. The alley slopes uphill, paved in smooth gray asphalt. Vines grow out of the vacant lot and trail down the blank wall on the left side, toward a dirt margin. To the right, you pass a stall with live chickens and ducks in cages, waiting to be killed, plucked, and boiled on the spot. Then comes a bicycle shop, followed by a tiny storefront full of electrical and electronics supplies—colored and fluorescent lightbulbs, power strips, unidentifiable odds and ends—where a friendly elementary school girl is studying English. Next come plumbing and hardware, dusty and assorted. Then there's a stand selling freshly made fried bread and pancakes stuffed with meat or vegetables, the food passed through the window with floured hands, which also make change with the stained and crumpled money.

Four years later, of those things, only the wall would still be there. The restroom, the bare dirt, the vines, the poultry, the lightbulbs, the shredded-carrot pancakes—gone, gone, and gone. At first glance, and maybe second or third, the alley would look the same.

Getting to know Beijing was like doing archaeology with someone shoveling new dirt and rubbish down into the pit on top of you.
Old Beijing itself was a phantasm—a name for certain elements in
an ever-churning city: hutongs, poverty, eunuchs, public lavatories,
cabbage piles, bicycles. Constituent parts of something inherently
unstable. Two hundred years ago, a courtyard house was an aristocrat's mansion; now, it was cluttered with the possessions of fifteen
families at once. Real, bustling life. Or you could see another house
on another lane, restored, its gate repainted, a garage door set in the
wall for the new owner's Audi. The huddled former inhabitants
moved on. Or you could go to the Wangfujing shopping street downtown and see a replica of Old Beijing, with mannequin inhabitants
and real goods for sale, in the basement of a shopping mall.

The New Beijing was no less a moving target. The first landmark
I learned on the way to our apartment was the Pizza Hut. An ordinary Pizza Hut sign hung from the façade, supplemented by Chinese
characters and red lanterns. It was unexpected but somehow also
seemed foreordained: a perfect emblem of West Meets East, another
chapter in the story of how contemporary global-capitalist American
culture was spreading through the old Communist Orient.

Then they gutted and renovated the whole Pizza Hut again, in
the name of progress. A block away, a man was still stooping in the
dirt by the alley side, carving fake-antique furniture by hand. But
the Pizza Hut had already gotten stale.

A few months after the Pizza Hut reopened, I walked to a local
supermarket I had come to depend on—a branch of a Japanese
grocery-and-department-store company, clean and modern, in the
basement of a four-year-old tower. The familiar entranceway was
dark, with an acrid smell of demolition floating out of it. Inside,
cutting torches flared in the dimness; men toted out sacks of rubble
by hand, stacking them like sandbags. The store was gone. My little

bit of practical knowledge was already useless. I had barely gotten started, and I would have to start over. A rebuilt, improved mall would take the store's place within nine months.

That same night, we took a cab to the Third Ring, to the Beijing Ikea, another relatively recent addition to the modernized city. The lettering from the façade had been pulled down and laid out on the sidewalk, and a yellow-shirted crew was dismantling the interior. Two days later, a replacement Ikea would open out on the Fourth Ring, in a development zone so new the highway ramps didn't all connect with anything yet. It was four times bigger than the old one—the second-largest Ikea in the world, behind only Stockholm's.

Historically, Beijing was not a city where foreign influences were absorbed. It was not corrupted by opium and foreign trade like Shanghai, or colonized by the West like Hong Kong. China habitually describes itself as being 5,000 years old, a continuous civilization transcending and outlasting any of its rulers or governments, or even the lack of rulers. Beijing, as the capital, was the point from which law and culture radiated outward: the emperor's city and the center of the imperial meritocracy, the site where the People's Republic had been proclaimed, the reference point for standard pronunciation and standard time. It was the city of pure Chineseness, save when it was taken over by the Mongolians or the Manchurians—at which point they became the emperors of China.

Now, though, commerce, exchange, and growth were supposed to be part of the national identity. Other Olympic cities had sunk their greatest energies into grand feats of building—threading a modern subway through the crumbling underside of Athens; erecting a would-be retractable-roofed stadium in Montreal—but China had to demonstrate something more elusive. It had enough wealth and labor available to build a new Great Wall, if it chose, but epic Olympic construction projects might be the easy part.

"In China, you can do that in one week," Ma Jian told me. In the nineties, Ma was a star swingman on the national basketball team—an ambitious player who made his way to the University of Utah team and then, without permission from the Chinese sports authorities, into NBA training camp. He ended up barely missing the final slot on the Los Angeles Clippers' roster, which would have made him China's first NBA player. For making the attempt, he was barred from Team China for the rest of his career.

What Beijing needed to do was to demonstrate that it was outward-looking, a participant in the shared global culture, up to the standards of the countries that were already accustomed to prosperity, globalism, leisure sports.

"It's not that China doesn't have the potential," Ma said. "We do have the best potential. The problem is, do we know how to use the potential?" Ma still looked like an NBA candidate: not a human skyscraper like Yao Ming, but a tall, big-shouldered figure with a shaved head, the sort of athlete who in America might have played linebacker while waiting for the high school basketball season to start. He was now a TV commentator and sports entrepreneur, working on an athletic education curriculum for Chinese schools. His plan was to bring sports to young people outside the official sports academies where China develops its national athletic program. Eventually, he wanted to launch a high school basketball league in Beijing.

Could Beijing tell its taxi drivers, Ma asked, "'Go take a shower every day'? Or do they have the facilities to take a shower? . . . 'Can you quit spitting in the street?'"

The Chinese habit of spitting was so well known, it had been startling to realize that it was also true: Beijingers did spit in public, relentlessly and democratically. There was a government office, the Capital Ethical and Cultural Development Office, assigned to control spitting by 2008; it had uniformed volunteers passing out marked paper bags for citizens to spit in. Still, the old and the young spat, female and male, along narrow lanes and modern boulevards, spitting incidental flecks of saliva or big squashy lumps of mucus.

When Ma talked about the Olympic effort, he turned to a basketball analogy. A young player in one of his basketball camps, he said, had asked Ma to teach him some drills so that he could improve his skills. Ma said no. The player was already good enough by himself; what he needed was actual basketball knowledge—how to find open teammates, how to ask for help on the court, how to read mismatches. With that training, Ma explained, the player would become 30 percent better (Ma had acquired the American habit of assigning precise values to abstract athletic quantities), even as his individual skills stayed the same.

Basketball was one of the foreign idioms that Beijing was in the process of absorbing. Before meeting Ma, I had gone to see a Chinese Basketball Association game on the far side of town, in which the Beijing Ducks rallied to beat the Jilin Northeast Tigers. In Chinese, the Ducks are known as Capital Steel, for their sponsor; the word for "duck" is slang for "male prostitute." The star for the Ducks was the hulking Inner Mongolian center Mengke Bateer, an NBA veteran with a championship ring from the San Antonio Spurs. (In a dispute over territorial rights to hometown players, the league would later reassign Bateer to Xinjiang.)

Bateer had been the second Chinese player in the NBA. The first was Wang Zhizhi, a soft-faced seven-footer who had been kicked off the national team after he refused to spend the NBA offseason training in China. In the Chinese league, Wang had belonged to the perennial champion Bayi Rockets, the People's Liberation Army team, which meant that his decision to stay abroad made him not only unpatriotic but technically AWOL from the military. His NBA career faded out, with him bouncing from bench to bench, shadowed by the rumor that teams were afraid their games might be blacked out in China if they signed him.

With the Olympics coming, though, China began to look for reconciliations with athletes who had run afoul of the national sports system. In April 2006, Wang negotiated a contrite homecoming, telling the Chinese media he had made a "big mistake." Television showed him pulling away from the airport in a Buick. By the next season, Wang would be leading the league in scoring, and Bayi was back atop the standings.

Ma Jian said he couldn't stand to watch the Chinese pro league. The players suffered from selfish play and poor teamwork, he said— the same set of complaints that Americans usually hear about American players, compared with selfless foreigners. But as an American-trained college player, Ma explained, he can read nine or twelve options off a pick-and-roll; a Chinese player learns only three or four.

Other aspects of the game experience had also seemed rudimentary. During time-outs at the Ducks game, two mascots in duck costumes would amble around—and then would pull off their costume heads before sauntering off the floor, completely contrary to American mascot protocol. There was a cheerleading dance squad, only loosely synchronized, unable to fill out their metallic-turquoise booty shorts. Their pompoms shed on the court.

Among its Olympic trappings, Beijing would need a motto, something to express its emerging relationship with the rest of the world. "Harmony and Progress," Seoul had declared in 1988, promoting its own leap into modernization. "Friends Forever," Barcelona offered in 1992, a promise for a rising tourist city. "Welcome Home," Athens said in 2004, asserting ultimate ownership of the Games.

Beijing's motto was unveiled on live national television in the summer of 2005, in a special ceremony. I watched it in a provincial hotel room, tagging along with my wife on a work trip. The announcement was accompanied by a video montage of Chinese citizens—young, old, urban, rural—receiving the new slogan as a text message on their various mobile phones. This was not an inaccurate vision. In 1904, to symbolize America's role at the forefront of progress, the Olympics were officially opened by telegraph. In 2005, text messaging was already omnipresent in China, for interpersonal communication and government announcement alike.

"Tong yi ge shijie, tong yi ge mengxiang," the mobile phones said. Officially, in English, the message was "One world, one dream." Or, in an alternative translation, one that sounded less like an aspiration than a statement of fact: "Same world, same dream."

3.

拆 Tear Down

The geographic and symbolic heart of Beijing's plans for 2008, the Olympic Green, was both centered and uncentered: it was being built on the city's north-south axis, aligned with Tian'anmen Square, the Forbidden City, and the Drum Tower, but the site lay on the outer edge of the Fourth Ring, in the zone of pure development, beyond historic landmarks. My first attempt to see the construction, in 2005, had failed; I had told a cabdriver, in rehearsed Mandarin, that I wanted to go to the Olympic Green, and he told me that it didn't exist yet.

I did not have the necessary command of the subjunctive to explain that I wanted to see the place the Olympic Green would be, if it were finished. My formal Chinese instruction had been a few semesters of once-a-week conversational Mandarin in American night school, in a class divided mostly between retirees planning to see more of the world and couples preparing to adopt Chinese babies. Class was led by a woman called Teacher Wang, who had fled the revolution, and whose teaching was extemporaneous and discursive, laced with cryptic anecdotes and parables. The first-, second-, and third-person pronouns—*wo, ni, ta*—reminded her of her aged mother's bemusement, in English class, at meeting a woman named Juanita. Teacher Wang had been back to the mainland, to the capital, which was, in her telling, a rough, heartless city, full of price gouging and deceit and sand, everywhere sand. If you bought food off the street (already a reckless proposition), you could count on a mouthful of grit. She made a face at the memory.

But the capital was where people spoke standard Mandarin, or Putonghua, which was what Teacher Wang was there to teach. Proper pronunciation required a curling and tightening of the vocal apparatus till a hard-edged *r* sound hummed through everything and your tongue was tired after class. I was deaf to the four separate tones of the language, and what few words I had picked up—the numbers one through ten, a few body parts, some food names, and, from Cult. Rev. class, "Long Live Chairman Mao!"—came out with a lax Taiwanese accent. I tried to learn more on my own, but had maybe a hundred words under my belt when I ran aground on the shoals of subordinating conjunctions, which came in confusing mandatory pairs: *because* had to be trailed by a *therefore*; *although* required a corresponding *however*. I settled for copying out characters by hand—the old-fashioned ones still used in Taiwan, not the simplified versions introduced by Mao. So I had arrived in China with surprisingly good penmanship, but all the other language skills of an infant.

Immersion in China had raised my ability level to that of a fairly bright three-year-old. To help guide me around the city, in the spring of 2006, I had recruited an assistant, an abstracted and slightly sardonic Wellesley graduate named JiaJing. Looming digital clock boards, forty-five feet tall, had been cropping up around town—on

Tian'anmen Square, in front of the airport, alongside the ring roads—counting down the days, hours, minutes, and seconds till 8/8/08. The readout for days was down below 900. Over tea in an expat bookstore, JiaJing explained that while she still had her native Chinese passport, she had grown up mostly in Queens. In China, she had done research and handled logistics for American and other international reporters in the past.

So I hailed a taxi, and JiaJing did the talking. I was visiting the city, she said, and I wanted to see the Olympic sites. I lost track of the spiel early on and settled back to watch the scenery, occasionally getting updates from her about what we were saying about our mission. When the cabdriver noticed we were scribbling in notebooks, she told him we were doing research on architecture, which was more or less true. And that we were academics, up from Shanghai, which was not true at all.

However she explained the trip, we made our way to the north side of the Fourth Ring Road, passing complexes of apartment towers—built in the nineties, JiaJing said, and already weeping and mottled on their façades. To the left of the roadway was a building with a swooping, if dingy-looking, concrete roofline: a swimming center left over from the Asian Games of 1990. Then, to the right, came a glimpse of monumental latticework, the exterior of the half-built National Stadium.

This was to be nothing like the twentieth-century stadiums around the world, the grounded flying saucers of the old Space Age. When the National Stadium was finished, it would be an abstract-organic woven bowl—nicknamed the Bird's Nest—a design created in a collaboration among the Swiss firm of Herzog & de Meuron, the China Architecture and Design Research Group, the global Arup engineering firm, and Ai Weiwei, the conceptual artist and godfather-impresario of Chinese contemporary art. At the moment, twenty-eight months before the Games, the lattice was in separate, fingerlike segments, running up the sides of the structure and curling inward at the top.

Soon, after a jaunt through a series of shadowy exit ramps, we were looking up close at a blue, corrugated-metal construction fence. Finding the Olympic site, in the City of Walls, was not quite the same as getting a look at it. Our taxi traced the perimeter of the grounds, driving slowly. Along the west side, over the top of the fence, we could see the rectangular shape of the future aquatics center, the Water Cube. When it was finished, it would be another marvel of engineering, its frame and walls built entirely of polygonal cell-like strutwork, each cell framing an inflated plastic membrane, so that it presented a solid surface of different-sized bubbles. For now, it was a big plain box of scaffolding, swaddled in green mesh.

The fence continued, offering a view only of what could poke above it. The north edge revealed treetops. We drove down the east edge, passing horse carts full of bricks or cinder blocks. There were hills of dirt, draped in green mesh to keep the dust down. Then came the top of the stadium again, and we were back to the Fourth Ring. That was the Olympic tour.

JiaJing guided the cabbie east and south, toward the Central Business District, the other focus of the Beijing-to-be. The district was less central even than the Olympic Green, and it was far from being in business, but it was the place where the city's other principal landmark of the future, Rem Koolhaas's loop-shaped headquarters for Chinese Central Television, was supposed to rise. The angled O of the CCTV building—its top segment hanging some 750 feet in the air, linked to two leaning-tower legs—was to be the definitive example of the everything-goes architectural style.

Until recently, even the new buildings in Beijing had been stolid; Stalinist architecture lingered through the 1980s, then gave way to a mandatory "Chinese" style, in which the mayor decreed that high-rise roofs had to be built according to traditional designs. The result was a bizarre parallel to the most affected American post-modern construction, with chinoiserie rooflines in place of Chippendale ones.

The newest generation of construction, though, was to be aggressively innovative. There were still po-mo decorative schemes going up—Moorish spires on apartment towers, mansard roofs—but the prestige projects were sculptural. The emerging skyline was a collection of improbable shapes: hatboxes, flashlights, sardine cans standing on end, a titanic topiary garden in steel and glass. We drove by a geodesic dome, overshadowed by a mass of concave curves, and a sort of concrete cheese Danish, tipped on end, its center filled with a sheer wall of glass.

The CCTV project was barely visible from the roadway of the Third Ring, its twin tower bases only beginning to rise. In the foreground was an aging masonry wall and behind that a middle-aged five-story apartment building with a red-brick façade and tattered green awnings. The windowpanes were marked in white with a single Chinese character: *chai*, meaning "tear down."

Chai markings were ubiquitous in pre-Olympic Beijing, as ubiquitous as the construction fences, which followed close behind them. Week by week, month after month, new ones appeared on windows, door frames, inner and outer walls. I bought a T-shirt from a rock club that used *chai* as its logo, printed in black on orange. To get there, you had to clamber across a construction trench.

The most common color combination was probably a white or orange *chai*, spray-painted on the old gray hutong brick. Formerly modernized hutongs, covered in white tile in a bygone push for improvement, got black or orange ones. The markings spread through whole neighborhoods at once.

In the interval between the coming of the *chai*s and the closing off of the construction site, views could open up. A few days before the taxi tour, I walked back to our apartment from the expat terrarium of the bookstore. The neighborhood in between, around the old Workers' Stadium, had just been profiled in an English-language Beijing lifestyle magazine as the site of the next residential boom. The streets were lined with new construction fences and old walls that were being repurposed as construction fences.

Through an archway in a wall, I spotted a worn-out pool table sitting in a field of rubble. Beyond the arch lay a neighborhood that was two-thirds, if not three-quarters, demolished. The perimeter wall, along the street, was propped up by iron braces; the houses immediately behind it were gone and cleared away. The rest were smashed where they stood, or half smashed, or still standing, hedged in by the rubble of their neighbors.

Elaborate graffiti, shaded and multicolored like New York graffiti art, had been painted on the exposed white plaster of the walls: snarling orange and blue monsters; a naked man facing a green dog with jaws like a crocodile's, both with chains around their necks, and each urinating toward the other. A man walked by and, seeing me taking a picture, showed the way down a narrow lane to even more graffiti. In black silhouettes on the white, a man with a club and a man with a pistol herded a family through a doorway. The air around them was peppered with ¥'s (the sign for the Chinese currency, the yuan), and big black characters read *"Renmin bi"*—Execute the people—a pun on *renminbi*, "the people's currency" (often abbreviated as RMB).

What was left of the neighborhood was still occupied. People moved about in the shade of mature trees, and children threw chunks of debris at the rubble fields. An electrical box dangled in midair between poles, feeding wires to the standing houses. A barbershop was open, the pole outside lit up. The adjoining building had been knocked down; its front wall was sheared off knee-high.

Back out on the street, a red banner covered the whole length and height of the propped-up wall, with slogans in English along the bottom: "Is one flat per floor a new standard?" "What image? What landmark?"

From the CCTV site, we rode south and toward the city's interior, inside the Second Ring, to the Dashilan district. Dashilan, just below the foot of Tian'anmen Square, was a popular 600-year-old shopping neighborhood; it was also officially a slum, designated for clearance before the Olympics.

Some portion of the existing Dashilan would be preserved and renovated, as a tourist attraction—like other rehabbed neighborhoods, with their bicycle-rickshaw tour guides. The hutongs had become inextricable from the hutong tours. But Dashilan was preparing for much more than a spruce-up. From the main street, most of it was out of view already. I added a new type to my mental list of construction barriers: these were freshly erected sheets of galvanized steel ten feet high, turning the old lanes into mirrored passages. Behind the shiny walls, as customers picked their way around the intruding strutwork and bracework, the stores were still doing business. Bright yellow paper signs announced clearance pricing, while electronic squawk boxes called out in Mandarin, "Emergency teardown—must sell everything—emergency teardown."

Down a side lane, Langfang No. 2 Street, there were fewer steel walls. The buildings were mostly made of wood, with low-ceilinged upper stories; tufts of plants sprouted from the roof tiles. Though it had been weathered into uniform antiquity with the rest of the neighborhood, this section had once been a redevelopment project itself, nearly a century before, under the new and shaky Republic of China. Small restaurants and shops lined the street: Sichuan food, Dongbei food, silk, outstanding leather goods. Vendors squatted by the roadside with their wares spread on blankets. Three blankets held jade carvings and other trinkets, one held assorted cell-phone batteries. A man rubbed a finger around the wet rim of a bowl, making it sing.

Along the lane's wall, the Beijing Construction Company had pasted a notice. JiaJing read it over. It said that a developer had applied for permits to tear down certain buildings in the area, and that residents would have two weeks to submit a written appeal. The notice was dated early March; it was now late April. On Langfang No. 2 Street, the affected addresses would be numbers 1, 3, 5, 7, 9, 11, 13, 15, 17, 19, 21, 27, 39, 41, 43, 45, 47, 49, 51, 53, 55, 57, 59, 61, 63, 65, 67, 69, 71, 73, 75, 77, 79, 81, 83, 85, and 87. Fourteen other streets were listed on the sign, some with fewer addresses and some with more.

One of the buildings on the north side of the street—the odd-numbered side—had an ancient-looking, battered door, with carved and painted words on it, black on a peeling pink background. It was a poem, JiaJing said; it told the reader to value loyalty over profit, and to prosper. Tucked under the right-hand door handle was a business card from a moving company.

A short walk east and north was the Beijing Planning Exhibition Hall, a shiny museum with exhibits dedicated to the city that was to come, the city of By 2008. By the escalators, overhead and to the right as we ascended, there was a giant bronze relief map of the city circa 1949. The old Ming wall ran around the edge, and the Forbidden City sat in the middle, with each hall and palace distinct. And then, filling the space between, were the hutongs—all of the hutongs, with every twist and turn, and all of the buildings in the old city, the whole past cast in metal, clear as a photograph taken from above. I thought it was one of the most astonishingly meticulous things I had ever seen, and it held that distinction for maybe forty-five seconds, till we got off the escalator on the third floor and turned left.

The third floor of the Beijing Planning Exhibition Hall was the home of a model of Beijing that made the bronze 1949 city look like one of those cheapo train sets street-fair vendors sell. It filled a vast room. The floor, around the edges and inward, was made up of large squares of glass-topped aerial photographs, starting at the far outer reaches of the municipality. A visitor would walk inward, with fields and housing developments and golf courses underfoot, across the Sixth, Fifth, and Fourth Ring Roads. Little photographs of buildings disappeared under my shoes. More or less around the Third Ring was a barrier of tight museum rope. On the other side of the barrier was: Beijing. The entire central city, road by road, building by building—only smaller, built on a 1:750 scale, and a few years into the future.

We had arrived just before the half hour, in time for the educational presentation. Louvers in the glass ceiling, two stories overhead, swung shut; colored spotlights came on; and a voice began delivering narration in Mandarin. The spotlights moved around. Tiny blue bulbs lit up to trace the waterways, green ones outlined the parks, and various sets of amber ones marked off the layout of the Ming city or highlighted areas of new construction.

It was after the show that the cityscape had its fullest effect. The louvers opened and the daylight returned, shining on the buildings as they stretched away, the farthest ones blurring together in the shadows of the upstairs observation balcony. The illusion of distance was so vivid my head began to feel like a silent, low-flying airplane. The visibility was too good for the real Beijing.

And there were no cranes to be seen. In the Great Model, 2008 had come; every planned building had been finished. Koolhaas's CCTV tower made its loop in the sky on the east side, lit up from within, surrounded by the rest of the buildings of a fully realized Central Business District. New apartment towers overlooked the low gray patches where the surviving clusters of hutongs held on.

Some of the hutongs were closer to our apartment than I'd thought. I followed the winding blue path of the Liangma River—in real life, lurid green with algae through the summer months—where it left the northeast side of the model, and found our apartment building, disappointingly just over the edge, in the photographic part. At least no new buildings seemed slated to be redeveloped over it.

Then, to the north—

To the north, an arm of the model reached clear past the Fourth Ring. There, by a broad man-made river, was the National Stadium, its lattice complete and immaculate. There was the athletes' village and, across a row of trees, the aquatic center, free of its scaffolding and with shades of blue and white playing across its surface. The Olympic Green sat open to view.

Nevertheless, I wanted another crack at seeing the live version—the pre-completed version. The Beijing Organizing Committee for the Olympic Games (BOCOG) wouldn't talk to me about a tour or any interviews; I was on a tourist visa, with a slip stapled in my passport for good measure that read, "The holder of this visa is not allowed to engage in news report activities in China." Besides, they said, they had just given reporters the only press briefing they would be getting for months.

But where there's one authority in Beijing, there's likely another authority below or beside it. The operations of the one-party state, in practice, were in the hands of various parallel or layered bureaucracies, agencies, and enterprises. So JiaJing tried to book us an appointment to visit the Olympic Stadium Construction Company, an arm of the Beijing Construction Company. That seemed even less promising, especially after an official at the Beijing Construction Company told her that the Olympic Stadium Construction Company didn't really exist. Still, the stadium company had an address—somewhere up off the Fourth Ring, seemingly near the site itself.

A week after our first try, we were back outside the blue fence. This time, we were on foot—we'd arrived in separate cabs, and neither driver had been able to find the right street. It was, JiaJing concluded, inside the construction compound itself. With a mix of purposefulness and genial confusion, an ideal attitude for assuring minor authorities that their authority needn't be exercised, she talked us past the guards at the outer gate while getting them to give us directions.

And then we were inside the wall, walking down an open, office-park-style street toward a second fence and gate, and behind those, the National Stadium. Construction crews were climbing on it and working on the ground below. Through the gaps in the lattice, we could see the stepped interior framework of the seating bowl. A bonging noise of metal on metal echoed from the site.

It was a warm day, with poplar-tree fluff floating in circles on the breeze. Three workers sat by the road, playing cards. They used broken pieces of cement slabs, stacked two high, for seats, and a single slab for their card table.

The Olympic Stadium Construction Company was nowhere to

be seen. A few inquiries led us down a driveway; around a group of low, trailerlike buildings; through an invisible gap between a trailer and a wall; and through a round gateway into a parking lot. There was a new, perfectly ordinary office building: the construction company headquarters.

Inside, through the glass doors, a pleasant young receptionist told JiaJing that there were no tours to be had. A row of shiny dark-red hard hats, apparently waiting for visitors, lined the counter in front of her. But they were not for walk-ins. We retreated to the inner gate and tried one last approach: If we kept going forward, could we get across to the aquatics center? The guards pointed in the opposite direction, back out of the compound. Then take a left and go all the way around the perimeter to the opposite side.

We turned back to the exit and—figuring the perimeter would get us there in either direction—took a right instead, trudging south along the fence, then east along the Fourth Ring. We passed a golf driving range and a decrepit hotel. On the edge of the ring road, the sidewalk dwindled to a narrow margin of paving blocks, just outside the guardrail.

Losing the sidewalk was no great sacrifice. Beijing sidewalks were not trustworthy, the way American sidewalks were. They were perpetually being laid and relaid, so there were dusty, ankle-twisting gaps and stacks of paving blocks along them. The blocks themselves often turned slick when it rained, China being unburdened by tort law and personal-injury suits. People used the space on the sidewalks for bicycle-repair workshops and free parking; Beijing drivers, especially the drivers of Communist Party officials' black Audi A8s, thought nothing of driving up over a curb. Everyone spat on the sidewalk, slopped out tea leaves and dirty wash water onto it. Power lines drooped perilously low, and in the alley by our apartment, someone had strung a clothesline at precisely eyeball height. When

I told Christina once that I'd come within three inches of walking into it at dusk, all she said was, "Well, why were you on the sidewalk?"

So when the sidewalk dwindled away, we kept going. In the United States, strolling beside a major expressway, we might have been stopped by the police on general principles. But the automobile's conquest of China was still incomplete, and nobody looked twice at pedestrians by the highway. There weren't many other walkers, but there were enough; some of them were coming the other way, on the same narrow track, and we had to side-foot it down the embankment so they could pass.

As we rounded the final corner of the fence, the sidewalk was gone entirely and we were walking in ruts on grass. But then, across a grassless patch of field, a new stretch of sidewalk began—a broad, level sidewalk, worthy of downtown, neatly laid and unmarred by commercial activity or saliva. We followed it, and the eternal blue fence, north, till we got to the gate outside the swimming center. Now the polygonal forms were dimly visible behind the scaffolding box, here and there. Two guards were at their post: an older man with a stern expression and a weather-darkened face, and a skinny youth, his uniform visibly too big for him. The old one had a hard hat, the young one a cap. JiaJing tried again: Could we go in and have a look? The older one turned voluble: Without hard hats there was no way we could go in, but he could tell us about it. The underground construction was all done already; the aboveground work was nearly finished. We could always come back with hard hats. The building wasn't going anywhere, and neither was he. Perhaps JiaJing could give him her phone number? We moved on.

Another gate—this time outside the future communications center for the Olympics—another guard. This one was more brusque: We could not come in, he told JiaJing, and it was a bad idea to stand there talking to him. There were cameras, he said. He nodded significantly in my direction, at the obvious intruder.

Our self-guided tour was over; 2008 was almost in view, but still fenced off, out of reach. We walked on, sticking with the sidewalk, keeping the wall to our right. JiaJing filled in the details of what the guards had said to her. As we kept going, a second construction fence appeared on our left. There were workers around us, in hard hats, looking up in curiosity. The sidewalk had mucky puddles on it.

And suddenly, there was no sidewalk ahead. It ended abruptly in a pit, with earth-moving machines working down inside. Beside us, two more men in hard hats were shoveling some sort of dry concrete or gravel onto the vibrating drum of a sifting machine. The sidewalk was a contingent sidewalk—the plan of a sidewalk, being made real. We had crossed over into the future.

II.

雾　FOG

4.

当局 Authorities

The spirit of change was not unlimited. In selecting Beijing to host the Olympics, the International Olympic Committee (IOC) had given its approval to the capital of a one-party police state, a place where capitalism and prosperity showed no signs of ushering in liberal democracy behind them.

It was easy enough to be alarmed and appalled by this, in a city that was supposed to be an emblem of the future. An American visitor arriving in the People's Republic would be rewarded, at first, by the spectacle of uniformed men at every turn: gray uniforms, pale-blue uniforms, navy-blue uniforms, olive-drab ones, green, black, blue-tinged camouflage. Upon inspection, though, more often than not a dark greatcoat would be missing a button or two, and a pair of white basketball shoes would be poking out of the bottom. The majority of the uniforms belonged to people employed as rent-a-cop guards, if not parking attendants. After that letdown, it would sink in that the same is true in the United States, but we don't even notice all the uniforms.

Living with the genuine machinery of the security state was more like living with a sore tooth: easy enough to ignore for weeks or even months on end, until it flared up—until someone decided to make a visa application more difficult, or closed a previously open event to the public, or censored the incoming news—at which point it would become impossible to think about anything else. And as with a sore tooth, you could never be sure what might trigger it. The workings of the system were opaque, even bafflingly so. It was never clear whether or not anyone was paying attention to anything I did or to any stories I wrote.

I was not, after all, a foreign correspondent. I had friends who were, in Beijing. They had drivers and clerks, and they had government agents who shadowed them. Sometimes they would be detained by provincial police, or firmly invited to the Foreign Ministry so officials could complain about their coverage. They carried spare SIM cards in their cell phones, so they could switch to an untapped line in a pinch.

It was possible, or even probable, that our own phone was tapped—not for my sake, but because my wife was working for an international nonprofit. When she arrived in 2004, China had not come up with an official procedure for recognizing foreign nonprofits and permitting them to operate, but certain allowances were made. Her office, in one of the "diplomatic compounds" where all foreigners had once been required to live, was almost certainly bugged, by definition.

Closer to the Olympics, when I would call the Foreign Ministry with questions about reporting, the officers seemed to be unaware that I was even in the country; on the other hand, an Olympic media-credentialing staffer would tell me, when I called to check on my application, that a Chinese woman had already inquired about my application that day.

Uncertainty is itself an effective strategy. I lost count of how many chatty English-speaking Chinese people approached me on Tian'anmen Square to ask me how I liked China, how long I had been there, what I did for a living, where I was staying . . . It was true that ordinary Chinese people who'd studied English had a habit of buttonholing foreigners at tourist spots to practice on them, and that these people's idea of conversation consisted of blunt personal inquiries. But it was also true that this always, *always* happened if I showed up on Tian'anmen Square alone. It definitely kept me from spontaneously interviewing English-speaking Chinese strangers.

Nowhere was the feeling of uncertain interference more pervasive than on the Internet. The Great Firewall of China did not exist, formally speaking. Your computer would simply be unable to get a response from certain servers. Maybe those servers happened to be down. Maybe something was wrong with the DSL connection (often enough, something was). Nor did the system block out all of the same sites all of the time. Wikipedia was unavailable, then available, then gone again, then available again. Blogspot came and went. Flickr was there, and then Flickr was gone, and then Flickr came back, with all its layout and links and tags intact, but none of the photographs would load. The BBC was always off. *The New York Times* was almost always on. Philly.com, for some reason beyond all guessing, was absolutely locked out; even working through an ano-nymizer site, I could never read a word about Donovan McNabb.

Eventually, the censorship rules became internal. I wouldn't even try to read news about Taiwan, or Tibet, or the Philadelphia Eagles. If a link had "blog" anywhere in the URL, it was not for me to read.

This developed into a half-conscious, magical belief that information access was, like DVD formats or particular food items, something that just happened to be different from place to place—some parts of the Internet you couldn't get in China, and others you couldn't get in America. To a small extent, this was even true: in New York, it was usually difficult to log on to the website of the Chinese consulate. I presumed this was through the efforts of a particular spiritual movement, mutually antagonistic to the Chinese government, whose name people took pains not to mention aloud even in jest, the way you don't joke about bombs in the airport.

I should say here that there was, in my time in China, one incident in which the security state did make itself manifest—not to me directly, but uncomfortably close. Because of it, I scrapped some reporting plans and then, on reflection, took a thick marker and blacked out the contents of several pages of one of my pocket notebooks.

It would be a good anecdote to tell in this book. It had bearing on another anecdote that is in this book. And that is as close as I'm going to come to telling it, even by analogy or by changing the names or circumstances. Here:

Let that stand for the redacted material. At one point in this book, you have gotten or you will get a less than complete account of something, and (I hope and believe, or I wouldn't be doing even this much) you will never know what it is. This fact can be the parable.

Why did the International Olympic Committee grant the Olympics to a country like this? Before settling on a verdict about the character or performance of the Chinese government—the ways in which it may be reactionary or forward-looking, amorally pragmatic or inhumanely ideological, and so on—it might help to consider that 1.3 billion number again: more people live under the rule of the Chinese Communist Party than under any other government in the world.

So above all, the Chinese system is normal. Or, statistically speaking, modal. America had a habit of seeing the People's Republic of China as a temporary phenomenon. For nearly a quarter-century, the United States viewed the revolution of 1949 as a momentary aberration, something that would go away if we refused to accept it. Even after diplomatic recognition of China, the idea was that sooner or later, our idea of freedom would win out. During the Tian'anmen protests in 1989, Americans still believed that a wave of reform was about to wash away the sandcastles of Communist tyranny all over the globe.

But Tian'anmen happened when the People's Republic was only forty years old. By the time the 2008 Olympics came, the government had lasted another two decades, and was a year away from its sixtieth birthday. China was one-quarter as old as the United States of America, and had four times the population—so as experiments in mass governance went, it made up in scale what it may have lacked in longevity.

By granting Beijing's Olympic bid, was the IOC inviting China to join the ranks of leading nations? Or was it acknowledging the facts that were already there? There would be much argument as the games approached about China's fitness to host them, and whether the Chinese government had honored the environmental and human-rights promises it had made in the bidding. How clean was clean enough? How open was open enough? How free was free enough?

When it came to these questions, China showed a sharp eye for hypocrisy—particularly for the sincere-minded hypocrisy of Western liberalism, in which the bad parts of history are regrettable errors, correctable had people only known better at the time. We Americans didn't really mean to make slave labor the backbone of agriculture, or to plow under the whole virgin prairie, or to send the Pinkertons to machine-gun unruly workers. We certainly couldn't accept that sort of thing in modern times. Or could we?

In the buildup to the Olympics, as activists urged athletes to protest China's various misdeeds, the memory of 1968 was invoked again and again: John Carlos and Tommie Smith raising gloved fists in the Black Power salute from the medal stand in Mexico City. But Carlos and Smith were protesting their own country's policies, not their hosts'. This point becomes more relevant in light of the fact that ten days before those Olympics, the Mexican authorities had sent tanks and troops into the public square to quash pro-democracy protests, slaughtering hundreds of demonstrators. With the peace secured, the Games went on.

Or even closer to home, it was hard to judge China's guilt over Tian'anmen without recalling Michael Korda's account of dinner at Richard Nixon's house, with Chinese officials as the guests of honor, shortly after the bloodshed of June 1989. "We too had so-called student riots, protests, anarchy in the streets of Washington," Nixon told his visitors. Then he lapsed from the first-person plural into a deranged but apt third-person singular, the voice of the objective historian: "When Nixon was President and Leader of the Free World, he found that *firmness paid.*" And he would know; Richard Nixon, at least, remembered Kent State.

Still, it would have been bad manners for China to ignore every democratic norm. Late in 2006, the government announced that it would be easier for foreign journalists to get visas and to travel within the country. It sounded better than being afoul of the law, furtively scribbling notes while worrying about losing my tourist visa. So after a series of bureaucratic false starts, the Olympic organizing committee agreed to invite me to stay on a string of short-term reporter's visas, expiring every ninety days. I could get the first of the visas at the Public Security Bureau.

The Public Security Bureau, or Gong An, was the police department, among other things. Its visa office was a newish building with an open stairwell and polished stone surfaces, on the Second Ring, not far from the apartment. It was a quick cab ride, except that taxis were forbidden to drop off or pick up passengers within a block of the Public Security building.

The visa department was on the second floor, in a space ringed with stations behind counters—like a giant, well-kept bank branch, staffed by uniformed police officers. I had been told to report to Window 19. The officer there asked for my document. Having nothing but my passport, I handed it over. She studied my visa. "This is not a journalist's visa," she said. I explained I was there to change it to a journalist's visa. She asked me to wait while she summoned a case officer to deal with me.

While we waited, the officer at Window 19 said she had another question. What was the difference, she asked, between a "journalist" and a "correspondent"? Well, I said, a correspondent is a journalist, but specifically one who works somewhere other than where his or her employer is based. Satisfied, she turned back to her work.

The case officer arrived. Had I filled out a form? (What form?) Did I have an ID photo? (A what, now?) Photos were taken in the back, he said. And I could get the form at Window 38, across the room.

Window 38, when I got there, was empty. I retreated to Window 19. In the half-minute it had taken to go back and forth, both officers there had vanished, replaced by a different set of people in the same uniforms. Everything else was as before.

I turned around again, to Window 38. To one side was an unattended stack of application forms. I took out a pen and began to fill one out. I was halfway through when the case officer reappeared, now inside Window 38, looking down at me. Did I have a residence registration form? he asked. I did not. Then the local police would have to issue me one, he said, and I would have to come back with it.

Also, he said, you can't fill out the form with that pen. He pointed to the instructions at the top of the form, which said, in English, to use "blue or black ink pen." My pen was black, a medium-point Paper-Mate, the pen I always carried. The ink was black; the plastic casing was black. I held it up. See, I said, it's a black ink pen.

That's not a black ink pen, the officer said.

I handed it over. He took it and made a few test scribbles, black marks on the paper. He handed the pen back dismissively.

This is not a black ink pen, he said. This is a ballpoint.

I was defeated. Back in our neighborhood, I stopped in the corner store by the alley mouth and bought a roller-ball—which did count, in the Chinese hierarchy of pens, as an "ink pen." And I went to the local police station to report myself as an unregistered foreigner.

Did I have a copy of my lease? the neighborhood policeman asked. I did not; the lease was a word-of-mouth extension of one signed by my wife three years earlier. Without the lease, he said, I couldn't register. I was not allowed to turn myself in.

Luckily, we were almost due for a new lease. The landlord worked one up on paper, with my name on it. The neighborhood cops issued me a residence certificate, which I delivered to the visa office. I filled out the form, in black roller-ball, and attached an ID photo, and handed in the papers at a now staffed Window 38. For the next ninety days, I would be a legal journalist. I went out and interviewed people, visited places, attended official press conferences. No one ever asked to see my visa.

5.

福娃 Fuwa

The public face of the Beijing Olympics was five faces. In tribute to populousness or bureaucracy, the organizing committee had come up with a team of five cartoon mascots—a new Olympic record. The Cold War superpowers had gotten by with single mascots, Misha the Bear against Sam the Eagle, in the boycotted and counter-boycotted games of 1980 and 1984. Barcelona had the indolent doodle of Cobi the sheepdog; Atlanta the focus-grouped disaster of Izzy, the shape-shifting blob. Athens had indulged in a pair of fleshy Olympian god-cartoons, Athenà and Phèvos.

But Beijing would have a mascot for each color of the Olympic rings: the blue one was Beibei, the fish; black was Jingjing, the panda; red was Huanhuan, the Olympic flame; yellow was Yingying, the Tibetan antelope; and green was Nini, the swallow. Not that they were exactly animals (except for Jingjing, who was an exception in other ways, too). They were animal-themed, totemic. There was a great deal more to them than met the eye. Their names, taken together in the correct order, made up the phrase *Beijing Huanying Ni*—Beijing Welcomes You.

The mascots had been brought out three months behind schedule, but they made up for lost time through sheer ubiquity. Their images adorned billboards, taxi partitions, phone calling cards, notebooks, cell-phone charms. Sheet-metal versions of them danced on the surface of the pond in a local park, frozen in mid-caper. They had their own animated TV series. The buildings of the future might be scaffolding and dust, but the mascots were ready.

The design of the mascots was credited to an artist named Han Meilin. Han had survived persecution in the Cultural Revolution to become a treasured artist of the Chinese establishment, working in every medium and every scale. Elderly and short, he was a Picasso for the current age, if Picasso's most famous innovation had been an ink-painting technique that produced animals of unparalleled fluffiness. While working on the mascots, he had suffered two heart attacks, the Chinese press reported.

In fact, Han alone had been unable to satisfy the Olympic organizers. A committee of eight artists and designers, convened to help him, concluded that the organizing committee's design suggestions—an assortment that included a tiger, the legendary Monkey King, and an anthropomorphized rattle drum—were unworkable, and a subcommittee of the committee was formed to come up with a new plan.

The subcommittee decided to come up with a different set of mascots, five in number, inspired by the five Olympic colors and the five elements in traditional Chinese cosmology—metal, wood, water, fire, and earth. The artists wanted a dragon, but their supervisors on the Olympic organizing committee vetoed it: the dragon was a sacred mythic animal, and it couldn't be seen on a team with any secular creatures. In addition, the organizers had consulted Chinese experts on Western attitudes, who declared that Westerners did not like dragons and associated them with evil. "We thought it was a pity," said Chen Nan, one of the designers.

Western sensibilities, or Chinese ideas about Western sensibilities, haunted the Olympic planning. Beijing would show it could respect foreign values, no matter how alien and inimical. The more alien and inimical, the more satisfaction was to be had. Westerners would never be comfortable with China's love of the dragon. The dragon had to go.

The panda, conversely, was added by fiat—"because foreign friends were so much in love with the panda," Chen said. Chinese people loved pandas, too, but might find a panda mascot a little trite or generic. Nevertheless, foreigners would expect a panda. A golden-haired monkey was kicked out to make room.

On it went. A phoenix was too sacred, a crane was too skinny, a black-and-white magpie conflicted with the panda's color scheme. Chen suggested a swallow—the *shayan*, technically the sand martin. Yanjing, or Swallow Capital, was one of the ancient names for Beijing, surviving as an Olympic-sponsor beer brand, and in a few other incarnations.

Tibetan antelope conservation had been in the news while the committee was working, Chen said. The fish and the Olympic flame came naturally from the Chinese elements of water and fire. The organizing committee's judges kept suggesting changes. "Some were government officials, some were athletes, some were kids," Chen said. One person told them the characters had too many symbolic features; another decided there wasn't enough symbolism. Someone thought the characters were too reminiscent of Japanese or Korean toys; someone else thought they were too traditionally Chinese-looking. Eventually, the designers decided to attach meaningful symbols to the mascots' heads, as needed, till each one was wearing a headdress of ludicrous size.

Jingjing the panda and Huanhuan the Olympic flame were male characters, and Beibei the fish and Nini the swallow were female. Yingying the antelope had been conceived as a girl, but had been given a sex change when the designers learned that only the male Tibetan antelopes had horns. Beyond his transgender status, Ying-ying was freighted with politics: the Tibetan antelope, according to the official materials about the mascots, was a "symbol of the vast-ness of China's landscape." He was an ethnic palimpsest; the crown of his headgear was based on a roof design from the western region of Xinjiang, minus its traditional Islamic crescent; his ear ornaments were of Tibetan design; his hair was curly, Chen said, because baby antelopes have curly coats, and "people in western areas tend to have curly hair."

Collectively, the mascots were known as the Friendlies, and for all the fine-tuning, people despised them. At least, people professed to despise them. One side effect of China's restrictions on dissent was that people tended to be extravagantly outraged about those things that were safe to criticize. Negative consensus spread rapidly through the Internet, as long as the target was small enough—a Starbucks in the Forbidden City, for instance, or a set of aggressively cute, big-headed Olympic mascots.

None of the complaints seemed to depress the sales of the mas-cots, or the proliferation of homemade or counterfeit versions. Still, the complaining people won one victory, over the name. "Friendlies," they said, was an embarrassment to China. First of all, it was English, not Chinese. Second, it was not a real word in English. And third, it resembled, in English, the phrase "friend lies," or the word "friendless."

To hold all parts of this critique in mind at once, one had to simultaneously disdain the use of English, cling to a punctilious standard of English usage, and propound a wholly imaginary set of principles of English wordplay. No native speaker of English would see "Friend Lies" in "Friendlies," unless suffering from an Oliver Sacks–grade cognitive abnormality. But the distaste for English and the oversolicitious English grammar standards were not, for the Chinese, unrelated; the worst sticklers were people who in their hearts believed that the English language was absurd and incomprehensible. A related attitude could be seen in certain Chinese-run Western restaurants, where salad would arrive as a heap of intact, full-sized lettuce leaves: salad was inherently inedible, so why try to make it possible for people to eat it?

So after less than a year, "Friendlies" was stricken from the official mascot materials and merchandise packaging and replaced with "Fuwa," meaning "Lucky Babies," which is what they had been called in Chinese characters all along. People hawking bootleg ones at tourist sites, where the mascots had become as commonplace as postcard books and fake Rolexes, continued to call them "Olympic babies."

Trailing along behind the five Fuwa was a sixth mascot: an anthropomorphic figure with an oversized bovine head tilted at an angle that made it look quizzical or melancholy. It was principally pink and white, but with one green arm, one yellow leg, one yellow ear, and a mismatched pair of green and blue horns. The harlequin treatment I took for a cartoonist's decorative whimsy, till I saw it was accompanied by the logo for the 2008 Beijing Paralympics, which would follow the Olympics. This was Fu Niu Lele, the Lucky Cow, and I realized with a combination of dismay and delight that her color scheme was intentional and significant. Lele was not put together like the normal mascots. She was different.

The Dongzhimen interchange, our nearest interchange, was going to be an important place in the new, international Beijing. The east side of the Second Ring was becoming a solid canyon of office blocks, like Madison Avenue in Midtown Manhattan; an additional building or three would appear every few months, filling in the set. All four corners of the Dongzhimen interchange held a new building, the rising frame of one, or a construction pit.

The biggest project was on the northeast corner, where the long-distance bus depot met the subway station. By the Olympics, the buses and the two subway lines were to be joined by an express rail line to the airport, making a comprehensive transit hub in one gargantuan station complex. Behind the construction walls, in the expanse where the new building would go, no less than eleven cranes were working at once, so many it was hard to get a clear count.

Creation and entropy were collapsing into one another. A chunk of the Third Ring Road fell into a sinkhole where the No. 10 subway line was being dug, paralyzing traffic. Part of the planned No. 4 line caved in a few months later, shortly followed by a second collapse on the No. 10, which killed two workers. Their surnames, according to a report in the Chinese press, were Xiong and Wang.

Twenty-six months before the Games, the city's vice mayor, the official in charge of Olympic construction, was removed from office and charged with "corruption and degeneration." The crime was vague; there were reports of a house full of mistresses. The building and unbuilding continued.

To keep traffic moving at all, Beijing law barred trucks from the streets by day. When the streets cleared out after dinner, the trucks would roll in, like a stage crew changing the set—moving trucks, cargo trucks, dump trucks clearing construction dirt. We rode one night past a procession of trucks bearing trees for planting: not only saplings but several larger ones, and one fully grown mature tree, taking up a whole truck bed by itself.

Reconstruction extended beyond buildings and parkland to the city's taxi fleet, the cabs an ever-changing Old Beijing all to themselves. Recent history could be dated by the evolution of the taxi fleet: I had arrived not long after the elimination of the *mianbao che*, bread-loaf cars, cheap and dirty microvans. Now the era of the next cheapest and dirtiest taxis, the tiny Xiali sedans, was ending, and a new fleet of Hyundais, Volkswagens, and Citroëns spread out, in gold-and-green or gold-and-blue or gold-and-wine livery. The city's three-tiered fare system was unified at the highest price, which was still as cheap as mass transit in America.

The low fares—and matching low wages—made the taxis the meeting ground for two kinds of new arrivals: the international visitors looking for a ride, and the internal migrants looking for a job. This was a point of concern for the Olympic organizers, the fact that grubby, garlicky rustics would be the city's first line of contact with foreigners. And it gave the cabbies an audience, as much as the language line would allow, for their own inquiries and disquisitions about this new city and the new world they were suddenly navigating.

The expat population was growing. More foreign faces appeared in our apartment building, from Europe and the Americas, drawn by cheap sublets near the diplomatic compounds. In the corner store, where the butcher chopped ribs on a piece of log, extra-virgin olive oil showed up on a shelf.

Even so, it was not easy to be a Chinese homemaker. There was, for instance, the problem of simmering. The apartment kitchen had a two-burner cooktop, with double rings of gas designed for pounding flames against the bottom of a wok. On the lowest setting, the inner ring still flared like a small, insistent blowtorch, scorching unattended tomato sauce. To make macaroni and cheese, we first had to buy an oven—meaning a countertop model, essentially a double-sized toaster oven. The macaroni got a nice brown crust on it, but oddly, the oven was never good at making toast.

Beijing was rife with things that looked normal but would fail in ways in which a twenty-first-century American consumer would never imagine things would fail. Thick plastic coat hangers, visually identical to American coat hangers, would snap at the neck under the strain of hanging up a coat. Fur-trimmed gloves would shed profusely; water bottles would crumple and spray their contents when you tried to unscrew their caps. The kitchen-sink drainpipe, one piece of plastic plumbing stuck loosely into another, would disconnect itself. A strip of brown cellophane would bob to the surface of a cup of tea, untangling itself from the tea leaves. A cotton swab would have a sharp end sticking out of it.

Under these conditions, Ikea began to seem less a mildly totalizing convenience than a gesture of cross-cultural engagement, a material Esperanto of universally agreeable goods. Amid aisles thronging with Chinese couples—radiant with the combined glow of upward mobility and joint householding—I could find a pepper grinder, a bread knife, or the same Turkish-made shower curtain that hung in our New York apartment. To hide the cheap circular fluorescent lights in the living room, Christina rigged up a pair of "Oriental"-looking white paper lanterns, courtesy of the Swedes. The final touch was an eight-foot-long oval dining table, another item we had ended up acquiring a copy of on both continents. The last stretch of the table delivery, from my wife's office to the apartment, had been handled by a man named Wang Jiashui, who kept a cargo tricycle parked inside the gate of Yard No. 26. Wang was in his late thirties, neatly dressed, with wavy hair and light eyes. He had migrated to Beijing from Henan Province, where his wife and three children still lived. His main job was collecting scrap, which he would sort and stack next to the compound's guardhouse: cartons, bottles, unopened cases of obsolete software.

I considered myself a hero for having single-handedly wrestled the matching table into a Volkswagen Golf (it stretched from the front windshield all the way out the tied-down rear hatch), driven it along the Long Island Expressway, and dragged it into and out of an elevator. Meanwhile, in Beijing, Wang Jiashui—solidly built, but by no means brawny—had pedaled a fully assembled version more than a quarter mile, then somehow carried it up four flights of stairs.

The bulk of the housework was handled by the part-time cleaning lady—an *ayi* in Chinese, a term that literally means "aunt" and can cover any and all sorts of domestic work: cleaning, cooking, shopping, child care. Our original ayi was a round-faced young woman who had come with the apartment; her husband, it seemed, had done the renovation work for the landlord. She had an obsessive floor-cleaning technique that involved at least three passes over the tiles, but she was less interested in anything more than an inch off the ground. Eventually, for unclear reasons, she started skipping work, and the landlady replaced her with a taller, ruddy woman who insisted on starting the workday before six a.m.

And so this is how one ends up living abroad and complaining about the help. You know that you are doing it (But really, five-thirty in the morning! Clattering dishes!), and then someone else recalls coming home early to find her own ayi in the shower—and not removing the hair from the drain when she was done, even. What can you do?

The Year of the Pig would begin in February. At the Carrefour supermarket, by the north side of the Third Ring, the entrance ramp was lined with pig merchandise and decorations in the red of the festival season till it resembled an inflamed esophagus. There were to be no pigs on CCTV, however. In a gesture of intranational (rather than international) hypersensitivity, the state broadcaster was banning on-air pig imagery, so as not to offend the sensibilities of China's Muslim minority.

This was, according to most reports, a super-propitious year in the traditional animal zodiac, a Year of the Golden Pig. Actually, by the six-decade cycle of five elements and twelve animals, it was supposed to be a Fire Pig year; the Golden Pig had come up in 1971, in the middle of the Cultural Revolution. But people liked the idea of a Golden Pig. It sounded fat and prosperous.

Chinese culture was proving oddly malleable. The thing about Chinese people is that they are always telling you what the thing about Chinese people is. For a long time, I made the mistake of trying to pay attention to the specific things themselves. The Chinese will tell you that Chinese people are less formal than Westerners, and they will tell you that Chinese people are more formal than Westerners. Chinese people are outspoken, and Chinese people are reserved. They are very blunt, and they are very indirect. They are too curious and not curious enough. Chinese people are naturally thrifty (or cheap); they are inherently generous (or wasteful). The outlook of the Chinese is inflexible, and it is adaptable.

Once you get going, it's hard to stop. The thing about Chinese people is that they insist on bundling up against the slightest threat of cold. The thing about Chinese people is that they wear replica basketball uniforms without player names or numbers on them. The thing about Chinese people is that they love watermelon and fried chicken. The thing about Chinese people is that they never take the manufacturer's sticker or plastic label off anything they buy, ever— microwaves, security doors, rice cookers, DVD players, bathroom sinks—even when the paper starts to wear away or the edges of the plastic film peel up on their own.

Americans tend to get their backs up if anyone (particularly a foreigner) tries to make any sort of sweeping claim about our national habits. I more or less reflexively inserted "tend to" in the preceding sentence, as a bit of protective chaff, to soften the generalization. We will consent to be called "freedom-loving" or "entrepreneurial," but more concrete collective observations—that we watch a lot of television, say, or that we are getting kind of heavyset, or that we shoot guns at each other more often than people of most other nationalities do—are an insult to our sense of dignity as free individuals.

But the Chinese are eager to hear what foreigners think about them, as a nation and a people, to the point of helpfully suggesting essentialist pigeonholes the observer might want to put them into. One prevailing explanation for the countries' different attitudes is that America has always had a dynamic culture, while China is more tradition-bound. This is a terrible explanation. A thirty-year-old Chinese citizen has seen more disruption and change than a sixty-year-old American has; a sixty-year-old Chinese citizen has seen more than a two-hundred-year-old American would have. It was routine business for the government to rewrite the entire holiday calendar, or outlaw a whole category of motor vehicles, or ban and un-ban particular enterprises or classes of merchandise or kinds of information.

So what was one more spasm of change? Out behind the

apartment, where a dead-end street crossed an arm of the Liangma River, construction walls had appeared, with heavy machinery working behind them. When I peered through the fence one afternoon, I saw that there wasn't a building going in; what was under construction was the river itself, in its man-made banks. A cement truck was parked at the bottom of the riverbed, waiting to pour new pavement.

In the demolition zone at Xingfucun, where the graffiti had been before, the remaining buildings had been leveled, the trees cut down and carted off in autumn. All that was left by winter was a wide, bare lot, strewn with rubble and patrolled by magpies. The lone structure in the space was a small open shack, furnished with a filthy tan armchair and wooden dining chair gone pigeon-toed in its old age. In places, the floors and foundations of the vanished houses still showed on the ground. Between two poles that were left standing, fish had been strung up to dry. For some reason I couldn't imagine, deep deposits of broken eggshells filled the hollows in the dirt, along with broken bricks and burnt-out fuel cakes of pressed coal. Two men on the west side of the lot were tending a motorized pump, the only sign of any work going on at all. A smartly dressed woman passed through, walking a fluffy dog. The dog was grimy.

On February 11, the city sent out a text message to everyone's cell phone, declaring that "line-up day" had arrived. This was part of the Olympic effort to reform public manners, one day each month when Beijingers were supposed to practice forming orderly lines at entrances, ticket windows, public-transit stops, and everywhere else an outsider might be appalled or endangered by the city's usual jostling, swarming free-for-all. The date chosen was the 11th because the two 1's represented the principle that even if only two people were waiting for something, one should line up behind the other.

At the Dongzhimen transit hub, as the 966 bus pulled up on the avenue, waiting passengers crowded the entrance, refusing to yield to the people getting off. A motorized tricycle cab weaved aggressively through the pedestrians. Where the 623 bus stopped, more would-be passengers formed themselves into a solid wall, again blocking the doors. The same happened for the 916. Down inside the subway station, people were sacked out in the pedestrian tunnel, lying on thick beds of dirty blankets and rags. At the ticket window, things were less crowded, but the rule was clear: even if only two people were trying to buy tickets, one would be shouldering in while the other was still finishing up. Habit was stronger than etiquette, or numerology.

6.

天气 Weather

Rain was falling on the alley. This was unexpected for a morning in late March. There'd been no rain in the forecast, and spring was a dry season in Beijing—the third of three dry seasons, coming after the dry fall and the dry winter. Beijingers watched the weather in spring not for showers but for seasonal dust storms, sweeping down from Central Asia.

But the Beijing Meteorological Bureau, the local branch of the Chinese Meteorological Association, was doing more to the skies than watching them. At 3:30 a.m. on March 29, as clouds gathered, workers for the bureau's Weather Modification Office had begun to burn chemical flares in specially built outdoor stoves at nineteen stations in seven counties or districts around the municipal area. Till nine a.m., they kept sending the silver-iodide smoke up into the clouds, where particles of it could mingle with tiny droplets of water—leading, in theory, to the formation of ice particles, which would melt into heavier drops, which would fall as rain.

The burners were what the Weather Modification Office relied on in the slow months, from October through April, when clouds are low and precipitation is rare. On May 1, the office would mobilize twenty-one emplacements of antiaircraft guns and twenty-six rocket launchers, firing silver-iodide munitions. A small squadron of planes, flown from a military airfield, would deliver silver iodide or dry ice from above.

Outside the apartment window was soft gray light and the sound of tires on wet pavement. The rain continued, off and on, for two days. According to the Beijing Meteorological Bureau, it added up to three millimeters.

The existence of the Weather Modification Office was not a secret. The Meteorological Law of the People's Republic of China directed "governments at or above the county level" to "enhance their leadership over weather modification" and "carry out work in this field." In all, there were thirty-one provincial or municipal weather-modification offices in China. Under the ongoing Eleventh Five-Year Plan, as in the Tenth before it, China had increased its spending on local weather-manipulation projects and courted other countries hoping to affect their own weather.

Weather modification, as science, had a vexed and winding history, but China's position was straightforward: it was the world's number-one nation in the field. Weather-modification feats were a recurring theme in the official media—human-assisted sleet in north Shaanxi Province (between 5 and 13 millimeters of it), or artificial snowfall in Tibet (2.2 millimeters). And the Beijing Office of Technology had reported that it was at work on a special chemical "shell" that would guarantee clear skies over the Bird's Nest for the Olympic ceremonies.

The English-language version of the Olympic story did not make it clear whether "shell" meant a protective dome or a piece of ammunition for artillery. Like most of the individual reports, it only served to give the operations of the weather modifiers a science-folklore quality, creating a background mystery of daily life. Residents, foreign and local, harbored pet theories about the signs that the government might have been tampering with a particular day's weather: unusually fat raindrops might be the giveaway, or rain from clear skies, or oddly well-timed breaks of sunshine.

That the government should do something about the weather didn't seem unreasonable. The weather could stand to be interfered with. Conditions in Beijing are fickle and harsh, with a naturally inhospitable climate overlaid with Industrial Revolution pollution. The city proper, on its inland spur of the Huabei coastal plain, is dead flat, wrapped in a deep bowl formed by overlapping mountain ranges—the Taihang to the west and the Yan to the north and northwest.

By the turn of the twenty-first century, the natural clash between frigid, dry mountain air and the humidity of the plains had acquired a man-made dimension: Beijing, trying to improve its air quality in the 1990s, had moved much of its heavy industry out of town, to the surrounding Hebei Province and the port city of Tianjin. Even the venerable Shougang Iron Works on the west side of town, a mascot of China's industrial might, was being uprooted piece by piece and rebuilt more than a hundred miles away, in the city of Tangshan.

But when the wind blew off the ocean, from the south and east, the factory-choked air of Hebei and Tianjin carried up the coastal plain, till the mountains funneled it to a halt over the capital. When southern air predominated, the returning smokestack pollution thickened for days on end, mingling with the emissions from the millions of car tailpipes, sinking the city into its characteristic gloom.

If weather is what you see and feel when you go outside, then the majority of Beijing's weather was man-made, with or without the Weather Modification Office. Filth was the city's affliction—worse than the Siberian winter winds, summer monsoon heat, or creeping drought. It was not unusual to check the international forecast on the *New York Times* website, supplied by AccuWeather, and to be told that where other cities' weather might be "partly cloudy" or "overcast," Beijing's was "smoky."

The official Chinese term for the haze was *mai*, which meant "haze" in Mandarin. The use of the term *mai* had been introduced in February 2006; before that, the longstanding policy had been to refer to it as *wu*, meaning "fog," which was how regular citizens still referred to it.

When the haze was light enough, the official designation for the weather was "blue sky." The city's Environmental Protection Bureau kept an annual tally of "blue-sky days," with ever higher quotas to meet. In 2006, the target had been 238 days, and the city officially logged 241. For 2007, the target was 245.

It was the blue-sky system that had first drawn my attention to the daily fluctuations in weather and pollution. The badness of haze depended on how you looked at it: a sky that seemed blue with the sun at your back might be a mess of gray-white glare if you faced the light. A brown haze on all sides might still show a patch of blue at the zenith. My notes on the conditions grew more and more baroque: "deep murk, purplish in the evening" . . . "hints of some unidentified color: pink? orange?" . . . "gloomy and filthy."

The official standard was more prosaic, though not without its own artistry. By definition, "blue sky" meant that a particular day's air quality readings fell into one of the two cleanest classes on the five-level pollution scale. (At level five, residents were told to stay indoors and avoid any exertion.) The air-quality readings themselves ranged from 0, the cleanest, to a dirt-saturated 500, with the cutoff for "blue sky" at 100. But though the process was supposed to be automated, certain anomalies showed up in the numbers. Dozens of days registered scores at or below the 100-point mark, while a year went by without a single day scoring a 101.

Could the authorities do anything about the actual amount of pollution? In October 2006, Beijing had hosted a pan-African summit, another formal display of China's engagement with the world. The weeks before the summit were a rush beautification job: floating red lanterns and photo-mural billboards of African wildlife lined the airport expressway and other arteries; new sod and saplings filled the median strips. In the places the diplomats would go, they would see a suddenly clean and prettified city, at least at ground level. Then, shortly before the summit began, the sky turned a gorgeous autumnal blue—a Hudson Valley sky, not a Huabei Plain one. It was another mystery for the weather folklorists.

Now we were into another erratic spring, mild and smoggy spells alternating with slashing, dusty winds. Two days after the unexpected rain, there came what looked like a beautiful day. The skies were clear, with a strong west wind. According to the forecasts, Beijing's true spring was imminent: hundreds of miles inland, the dust had taken to the air and was on the move. News photos showed cities in Inner Mongolia tinted amber by flying sand. I'd seen that same color in 2006—orange sky, dull-gray sun—at the tail end of a May storm that dumped hundreds of thousands of tons. Afterward, the dust lay in sheets and drifts on the ground, like a good dusting of snow, only without the snow.

This time, though, the sky outside stayed blue. By afternoon, online reports from three state-approved news agencies offered three different accounts of the storm's progress: the dust is coming soon; the dust is coming tomorrow; the dust has already been here for hours. To settle the question, I walked east by the Liangma River. On an ordinary windy day, Beijing's ambient sand and construction-site dirt would go airborne, leaving silt in one's eyelid folds and making chewing gum go gritty in the mouth. Though a few people were wearing dust masks, the air was, if anything, unusually clean. A black Suzuki drove by, spotless and gleaming. Where was the dust?

To help unravel the mysteries of the government-controlled weather, I enlisted a Chinese friend named Zhang Xiaoguang, who went by the English name of Mack. Mack was well over six feet tall and lanky, with unusually prominent eyes, and his excellent English was matched by a gift for mimicking Chinese regional dialects and accents. He was an improviser by nature; he had arrived in Beijing in the nineties, after skipping out on his assigned provincial college, leaving his official education and employment file behind. Now he was a freelance corporate trainer, but also ran art galleries off and on, while doing his own calligraphy and photography.

In his spare time, Mack found it entertaining to work with report-ers as an interpreter and fixer. He'd heard through Chinese-language media that there was a weather-gun emplacement in Gujiang Village, an hour or so north of the urban center. We set off for there on a mild day in May, with a few thin clouds overhead and minor pollu-tion at ground level. Roses bloomed along the expressway out of the city, and the mountains showed green and softly jagged through the haze as we approached. Leaving the highway, our hired car passed factories for Yadu brand humidifiers and Deer brand thermos liners. The roads got smaller. Donkeys stood by the roadside.

Rural life is not necessarily isolated life. The village proper was a dense clump of buildings in orange brick or fieldstone, with narrow lanes between them. A building boom was under way—Gujiang is popular with rusticating tourists—and stacks of bricks and brush pressed close to the roadway. The main street cut an S through the middle of town and made a hasty exit between a pair of upright stone discs, monumental versions of the *jiang*, or general, pieces from Chinese chess, in honor of the town's name.

The gun compound was a brick enclosure on the opposite side of town from the chess pieces, reached by a hairpin turn onto a narrow unpaved lane. From the dirt road, a smooth concrete driveway led to an unmarked red metal double gate. The gate was slightly ajar, and through the gap we could see a grassy courtyard with the gun in the middle of it, its double barrels covered by olive canvas. There was a building off to the right, and a cluster of weather instruments to the left.

Across the road, beyond a ditch, orchards of peach, apricot, and persimmon trees led toward the mountains. Two farmers came over to chat. One of them, a tiny man in a camouflage jacket, plucked a toon tree's new leaves, a seasonal vegetable, and offered them as a snack. The gun, he told us, could shoot 8,000 meters, or about five miles. The report was loud—louder, one of them told Mack, than the most deafening Spring Festival firecracker. "We all suffer from this," he said.

We stopped for lunch at a roadside restaurant, where we ate more toon leaves, cooked with tofu, and pancakes stuffed with donkey meat. Officially, we were still in the city of Beijing; a regular municipal squad car was parked outside. The clouds thickened briefly, promisingly, then thinned out again.

The Gujiang firing site had been in the news a year before when Wang Furong, one of the villagers, sued the weather bureau and the local government, claiming that the noise from the gun had caused the foxes on her fur farm to have spontaneous abortions or to die of fright. The sound, Wang told us as we sat in her living room, was "like the wall next to you just collapsed." The nearest wall, at the moment, had hand-drawn cartoon characters on it. A pair of taxidermically prepared white fox furs, with heads and hind legs attached, hung by the door.

The courts ruled against Wang's suit; the government provided her with what she called "very minor" compensation for her loss. The foxes were ruined as breeding stock, she said, so she had to get rid of them. She had switched to raising raccoon dogs, mask-faced wild canines, for fur instead. "They are slightly braver," she said, and they delivered their pups before the firing season. We wended our way to her farmyard. The firing station was some two hundred meters away. Litters of baby raccoon dogs peered out of their pens. A cat shared an enclosure with one batch, acting as wet nurse. Across the aisle, two foxes remained, alone in their cages.

While Beijing was occupied with Olympic planning, Jilin Province, in the far northeast, was preparing a different celebration for August 2008: a ceremony and conference to mark fifty years of weather modification by the People's Republic of China. *"Ren ding sheng tian,"* went an old aphorism embraced by Mao—man must defeat the heavens. The program was first proposed by weather bureau chief Tu Changwang in 1956, during a meeting called by Mao to discuss agricultural strategies. The Chairman gave it his blessing—"Man-made rain is very important. I hope that meteorological professionals put more effort into it"—and in the late summer of 1958, the first rain-seeding flights took place in Jilin and Gansu provinces.

Did any of it work? Modern weather modification was born a decade before the Chinese flights, with field experiments in cloud seeding by the General Electric Laboratory. The notion of manipulating the weather has a mid-century futuro-quaintness about it, at least as to current American sensibilities—the kind of Man Over Nature thing that people believed in back when bright students still went into engineering, now the province for flimflam men or movie supervillains. In its U.S. heyday, though, influencing the weather was a respectable scientific project. It was at least as plausible as sending a man to the moon.

The original principle, established by the GE experiments, was sound: seeding can cause ice to form in cold clouds or droplets to condense in warm ones. Yet cloud physics turned out to be considerably harder than rocket science. The moon is an object of known size, moving predictably through space at a distance of about 240,000 miles. To put a man on the moon, you put people on rockets and shoot them closer and closer to that target. When the astronauts get there, they bring back rocks.

A cloud seeder, by contrast, is never shooting at the same target twice. Not only is today's cloud unlike yesterday's, it is unlike the cloud it was five minutes ago. Its top is unlike its bottom, and the two may be changing places. Liquid water in it may be colder than neighboring ice. Rain is falling inside it that may never reach the ground. Even if more rain does make it to earth, rain gauges might not measure it accurately enough. Progress in weather modification, the National Academy of Sciences wrote in a 2003 report, "is not possible without a concerted and sustained effort at understanding basic processes in the atmosphere."

Wringing water from the heavens is one thing. Wringing a statistically significant, double-blind placebo-controlled study from the heavens is another. Six decades after weather modification's enthusiastic beginnings, American scientists grant it only a few firmish operational conclusions. Over mountainous areas, in the winter, seeding seems to be able to moderately increase snowfall. Insurance companies paid fewer hail-damage claims over the years in counties where private anti-hail contractors were at work. Recent studies suggest that seeding clouds in the tropics with salt seems to produce more rain—but later and farther away than the available theories can explain.

In their own studies, the Chinese concluded that their cloud seeding increased rainfall by 10 to 25 percent. China had seeded clouds not only to offset drought and fill reservoirs, but even to fight forest fires. Had the weather modifiers brought on rain to quell the dust storm? First, had there been a dust storm at all? Mack arranged for us to visit Li Xin, an air-quality official with the Beijing Environmental Bureau, who confirmed that the air had been dust-free. Storms often replenish their dust supply as they advance, but this time the rainfall had tamped down the local soil. "So," Li said, "no dust storm."

One of the easiest mistakes to make about Chinese bureaucracy, however, is to assume that because it is so pervasive its arms are in any way coordinated. Li, in charge of air quality, had not known that the Weather Modification Office had been trying to induce rain. Zhang Qiang, the weather-modification chief, meanwhile, said that her modifiers had simply been hoping to increase rainfall. If government cloud-seeding had stopped the dust storm, it had happened without any government agency trying to do it.

The blue skies during the Africa summit had been something beyond even the most hopeful capabilities of the Meteorological Bureau. The credit instead belonged to the traffic authorities: to prevent congestion, the city had banned most government vehicles from the roads, cutting traffic by 20 or 30 percent. An obliging west wind had swept away the traces of the old gridlock.

Beijing's weather planning, like its urban planning, seemed to demand that the subject be shrunk down to size. Just inside the doorway of the Beijing Meteorological Bureau's rainmaking command center was a scale model of Beijing Municipality, in tans and greens, with white tags marking bureau facilities. Mack and I had wandered away from a press briefing in bureau headquarters, a drab compound beside the Jingmi Canal on the west side of town, and spotted the model from the hallway. Most of the white tags were scattered around the high ground of the mountain bowl, in the rural districts.

A row of past and present cloud-seeding rockets stood on the floor beside the model, the tallest of them more than a yard high: silver, olive, multicolored. A 37-millimeter silver-iodide antiaircraft shell completed the set. The olive rocket, the RYI-6300, was the current-day model. Like the rest of the Beijing bureau's armaments, the RYI-6300 was produced at State-Owned Factory No. 556 in Wuhai City, Inner Mongolia, a former military plant that now made weather-modification gear and industrial blasting fuses.

A bank of ten computer screens ran along one side of the room. Only two of them were on, one showing a radar readout, another offering graphs of clouds' temperature and water content. A voice coming through speakers delivered a forecast: overcast again tomorrow, lasting possibly till the day after.

The opposite wall was taken up by windows that could have been called panoramic, had they faced out on something other than a Beijing afternoon. The murky light might have passed, to the untrained eye, for a sign that a shower was imminent, but the weather modifiers were unstirred. It was not going to rain, with or without intervention. The Fragrant Hills, less than five miles away, were invisible from the bureau. The city looked as if someone had shaken out a city-sized sack of instant concrete over it.

For the Olympics, the Weather Modification Office was not trying to encourage rain but rather to make it stop. The countdown to August 8, 2008, would lead right into Beijing's brief but emphatic wet season; on average, more than half the annual precipitation on the city falls in July and August. The original design of the Bird's Nest had included a retractable roof, but it was lost in a cost-cutting revision along the way. So the weather administration was all that was standing between the Olympics and an untimely downpour.

At a press conference about weather and the Olympics in late April 2007, Beijing bureau deputy chief engineer Wang Yubin announced that historical data suggested the natural chance of rain for the opening and closing ceremonies would be about 50 percent. Reporters had been cleared out of half of the front row to make room for the representatives of various weather administrations: the Beijing Meteorological Bureau, the Academy of Meteorological Sciences, the Research Institute of Urban Meteorology, the Central Meteorological Observatory.

They were there to discuss the Beijing Olympic Meteorological Services Center, a new, temporary weather authority that would blanket the city with real-time mini-forecasts, covering individual sports arenas. One of the first slides in the presentation was a labyrinthine organizational flowchart, followed shortly by a Venn diagram of responsibilities. But unavoidably, the talk of institutional coordination and upgraded Doppler radar turned to the subject of the guns. Wang assured the press that the bureau was "drafting the implementation plan for the artificial rain mitigation." But its rain-stopping powers, he added, were not absolute. "We find that our measure is quite effective if it deals with rainfall in a limited area," Wang said. If there is widespread or heavy rain, he said, "at present we cannot reduce this rainfall to the minimum, to be frank."

The press and the public have a limited understanding of weather modification, Zhang Qiang told us later. A scientist by training, with a friendly but cautious manner, she spoke in Mandarin, through Mack's translation. Her department, she said, constantly received complaints from couples on the city's outskirts who were about to get married. " 'Please do not send clouds,' " Zhang Qiang said, " 'because we have only one wedding ceremony.' "

"Our objective is not to change the nature of the weather," she said. "Rather, when we are suffering from hail, we are looking for methods that can reduce the damage. When we need more rain, we are looking for possibilities to increase rain."

The office, she said, had sixteen full-time employees directing the activities of several dozen part-time modifiers, mostly local farmers, who fired the artillery. If a day was rainy at all, she said, the bureau was probably intervening with the weather to increase the rainfall. "Normally, if conditions permit, yes, we would modify," she said.

Beijing's plan to fight rain during the Olympics was a variant of the usual plan to make more rain, and was related to the technique for stopping hail. All depended on the supply of particles in the air to serve as nuclei for rain formation. In a brewing hailstorm, Zhang Qiang said, we should think of the available droplets of supercooled water as *mantou*—steamed bread rolls—and the supply of ice-precipitating nuclei as monks. "If you give 1,000 *mantou* to 100 monks, each of them is going to burst to death," Zhang said. (*Mantou* are notoriously filling.) In hail-formation terms, the overloaded monks would come crashing out of the clouds as dangerously large hailstones.

The silver-iodide shells delivered more monks to the scene. "So in the end," Zhang said, "each monk gets two or three *mantou*." The resulting ice pellets should be small enough to melt on their way down, arriving as raindrops.

The metaphor left out a few things—hail also requires powerful thermal updrafts, to serve as a buffet line, so the monks can keep on overeating—but it captured the basic strategy. Thus, if you divide up the *mantou* even more, eventually no one gets enough to eat, and the droplets stay in the cloud.

In his office at the Academy of Meteorological Sciences, Yao Zhanyu, a professor and weather-modification expert, explained the strategy for protecting the National Stadium. China had occasionally tried rain-prevention ventures before, Yao said—at the Tian'anmen Square celebrations of the fiftieth year of the People's Republic in 1999, for instance, and at the tenth National Games in Nanjing in 2005. But the traditional leading practitioner of anti-rain seeding was the former Soviet Union. "This will drive weather modification in China another step forward," Yao said.

Yao, a compact and muscular man with thin-rimmed glasses, pointed to a floor tile to represent the Olympic grounds. "We have already set up three front lines," he said. He traced three semicircles, one inside the next, to his left, where the mountains would be. The majority of summer storms, Yao said, come from the northwest, the west, or the southwest; the defensive perimeter was better located to handle the first two directions.

Starting at Line No. 3, the outermost line, the modifiers would seed approaching storms to encourage rainfall, in the hopes that they would rain themselves out. By Line No. 1, the goal would be

BEIJING WELCOMES YOU   83

instead to overseed the surviving clouds, to suppress rain entirely. So rain seeding and anti-rain seeding "are not two strategies that are contradictory to each other," Yao said. "We have to use them both."

Not all overseeding and rain suppression was deliberate. The concentration of nuclei in the air, with and without seeding, is one of the great outstanding questions of weather-modification science. The silver-iodide monks were beside the point if the steamed buns had already been nibbled to bits, and the skies over China are rich with aerosol particles from dust and pollution. Atmospheric scientists know that even under the relatively cleaner conditions of American cities, rainfall patterns track the days of the week, as car and industrial pollution declines on the weekends and builds up again through the workweek to Friday. In a paper published in *Science* in 2007, Yao and a team of researchers concluded that in the mountains near Xi'an, heavy pollution was suppressing rainfall by 30 to 50 percent. Dirty air wasn't only smothering Beijing; it was helping turn it into desert.

Thunder was rumbling at the Xinzhuang Village firing station when Mack and I arrived on an afternoon in June. This time, the Meteorological Bureau had consented to let us visit the countryside. In a city taxicab, a Volkswagen Jetta, we headed in more or less the same direction as before. The day was stifling and overcast. It had rained earlier in the week—Beijing's whole network of modifiers had been at work, the Weather Modification Office said, as had neighboring provincial sites—and the humidity hadn't gone anywhere since. A flag along the way flapped listlessly toward the northeast: more wind from the plains.

Xinzhuang, near the tomb complex of the Ming emperors, was more orchard territory: trees by the roadside with whitewashed trunks, more brush piles, more donkeys. Boxes of ripe cherries for sale lined the way.

The station was on a ridgetop, 1,400 feet above sea level, in the middle of a fifty-acre orchard run by a farmer named Jing Baoguo. The taxi climbed a dirt track, past low trees with green peaches on them, laboring up the last rise and through the gate. Inside was a rectangular courtyard paved in concrete blocks, surrounding an irrigation reservoir. There was an island platform in the middle of the reservoir, under a striped canopy, with catwalks leading to and from it. Along the far side of the enclosure was a grape arbor; tomato plants grew on the near side, flanking weather instruments.

The artillery stood off to the right: two antiaircraft guns, their barrels poking out over the fence top, and a pair of blocky rocket launchers mounted on single-axle trailers. Nearer up the row, in front of a large shed, was a silver-iodide burner, model RGY-1, a gleaming barrel-shaped contraption resembling a barbecue smoker, with three wheels, a conical nose, and a long chimney. Around the side of the shed was a doghouse, white with blue trim. A medium-sized black dog rested inside.

Jing, a wavy-haired man in earth-tone slacks and a pullover, had leased the orchard six years ago. After he'd suffered hail damage to his trees in his first year, the Beijing Meteorological Bureau approached him about taking up modification. The Xinzhuang site was one of four emplacements the bureau had added since 2001, with farmers supplying the property, local government funding construction, and the bureau supplying the guns and other equipment. The modifiers were paid fifty yuan, or about six dollars, for every shell their crews fired.

Heavy clouds were blowing overhead, and a sprinkle of rain began to fall. An assistant, wearing a round straw hat, ducked into the shed and began bringing out rockets, one by one, and loading them into the nearest launcher. He slid each one home, lining up the tailfins with slits in the firing tubes. The launcher had spaces for a half-dozen rockets at once. When it was loaded, he ran a cable out to it from the shed. The far end was plugged into the trigger module, a cream-colored box on the floor just inside the doorway.

Jing joined him, and the two men swung the launcher around and cranked it skyward. Orders for modification begin with an advisory from the Beijing bureau to its district sub-bureaus, alerting them to a suitable weather system. The district offices mobilize the local stations and direct them to fire. Via cell phone, the station got the final orders: no firing today. Air-traffic controllers, the ultimate authority, had vetoed the operation. "Lots of airplanes circle this area," Jing said.

We retreated to the platform in the middle of the irrigation tank, where Jing had put out apricots and cherries. Rain fell on the canopy, and Jing poured hot mineral water from a thermos. He had originally been skeptical of modification, he said, but at least in the case of hail prevention, "it definitely works." He indicated one of the apricots, which were medium-smallish. "Before the guns were installed, the hail was as big as this," he said.

Jing said he had prospered since going into agriculture. He sells his fruit by word of mouth. "I love to make friends," he said, "and every year I have a lot of customers."

"Last year, my peaches grew to one kilo," Jing said. He corrected himself: 0.95 kilos. The pears, he said, had reached 1.1 kilo.

The thundershower passed. The rocket launcher was still pointing upward as we left. Between air traffic and the southerly origins of the storm, the bureau informed us, none of the other weather-modification stations had been able to fire, either. As we returned to the expressway, though, drops began sprinkling the windshield, then pelting it. Before long, we were in a downpour again, and we rode home through the unassisted rain.

III.

好运 GOOD LUCK

7.

出生 Birth

A motorized cargo tricycle putt-putted up the alley, carrying a load of tall, swaying potted plants. Black smoke trailed behind the moving green thicket. Step forward, step back. It was springtime; the men of Beijing had begun rolling up their shirts to bare their bellies—their hot-weather custom. The official Xinhua News Agency reported that 10,000 bags for spitting into had been distributed over the weeklong Labor Day holiday at the beginning of May, and fifty-six people had been fined for spitting in the street.

A new sticker in the front seat of taxicabs advised the drivers to brush their teeth regularly, change clothes, open the window and let air circulate, avoid smelly food, and not live in the car. Video screens appeared on the back of taxi headrests, and an animation clip showed humble cartoon animals being invested with an aura of superhero magic—Billy Batson as Tibetan antelope: Shazam!—and reborn as the Fuwa.

The reality of the city was noticeably rattling the Olympic plans: the No. 5 subway, the first of the new lines, had been due to open in July, but now it was going to miss the mark and open in the fall. Tunneling through Beijing's underside was not as simple as making an office tower spring up on schedule. The timetable for the other subway lines said only that they would be done by July 2008; the No. 10 had caved in again, killing six laborers. A news report said ten people had been arrested in that incident, after the construction company delayed calling for rescue and confiscated cell phones from its other workers. The opening of the Bird's Nest, slated for year's end, had been pushed back to March 2008.

I followed the changes with a mix of attention and detachment. My wife and I had no illusions about belonging in Beijing. The old city was becoming a new city, but we were passing through. Christina had come over to start up an office, and the more that the starting up turned into the running of it, the less specifically she was obligated to stay. The professional problems of China—how to organize an enterprise, how to work with officials—had answers, and she basically had figured out what they were. Meanwhile I was waiting on the Olympics, off in the middle future, but with a clear end date. We had an apartment in New York still, in the midst of a perpetually uncompleted renovation job.

Then, at the end of a Christmas trip home in the last days of 2006, I had woken up one morning to the sound of vomiting from the still-unimproved New York bathroom. Christina had been suffering from what seemed to be her worst case of jet lag ever, groggy and ceaselessly catnapping. And she had been ravenously hungry. Suddenly, those dots of information connected themselves. By August 2008—in fact, the doctor estimated, by August 2007—there were going to be three of us in Beijing.

The delivery would be in New York, we had decided. Beijing was not much different from New York for a normal birth, if you were an expat with decent health coverage, but why take chances? At thirty-three weeks, in late June, we'd fly back and settle in for two months of American life while we waited for the baby. We would just have to miss the one-year Olympic countdown in Beijing.

We had enrolled in a birthing class at a hospital catering to expats, tuning out the lessons that were specific to China: laughing gas as anesthetic, advice on dealing with Chinese staff midwives. I was not ready for Chinese midwives. Thanks to language school— two hours a day now, with friendly teachers in rooms like interrogation cells—the daily hum of Mandarin around me had begun to crackle into and out of intelligibility, like a far-off AM broadcast. New York was the way to go.

The plan seemed even better once our Beijing landlord informed us, via the ayi, that we'd be losing the apartment. The collective housing for bank employees was being decollectivized, as part of privatizing the bank. In preparing to transfer ownership, the bank had discovered that our unit was smaller than what our landlord, a branch president, was entitled to get. So we would have to rent his new, larger apartment—another fourth-floor walkup, a long block away down Outer Dongzhimen Avenue, a dark and chilly space in a building even less charming than ours. The landlord would redecorate it, and he would take care of moving our stuff while we were away.

I bought some boxes at the post office and began packing things. We wouldn't need sweaters before then. I filled a carton with bootleg DVDs—there was nowhere to rent DVDs legally in Beijing, and most foreign titles weren't cleared by the censors for import anyway, so everyone ended up with a stash of countless pirated movies, most bought on impulse at a dollar a pop. The intellectual-property breakdown had led to the creation of products that didn't even exist on the legal market: looking for *The Big Lebowski*, I ended up with a box containing every movie directed or produced by the Coen brothers, for something like ten dollars.

Olympic tickets were going on sale to Chinese residents in an online lottery. For this, we qualified as residents. The lottery system was an elaborate one. You could put in for as many as eight different batches of event tickets, and for each batch, you could pick multiple fallback options. The best tickets for track-and-field were more than $100 each, while tickets to watch runners stagger into the Bird's Nest at the end of the marathon were free. People debated strategy—request too many events and you could be stuck buying thousands of dollars' worth of tickets; request too few, and you could be shut out. By the time the lottery closed in June, it had received applications for more than 5 million tickets. We requested track-and-field tickets, two batches. If we got ours, the Olympic organizing committee would notify us in late August.

In the evenings, Christina and I went out walking, around the neighborhood and beyond. It was exercise. Till April, Christina had been enrolled in ballet class, but then the biddies who tended the door had turned her away for being pregnant, before she could even talk to the teacher. The thing about Chinese people is that they have strict rules about pre- and postnatal behavior. Pregnant expats in Beijing, with all the wrong habits, faced a dressing-down for even taking their delicate bellies outside to run errands. Dancing ballet at five months was unimaginably reckless.

So we strolled down the alley and out, this way or that. It was a way also to get a last look at the city of the moment, to see what we might be missing during a summer away. The construction fence was coming down by the Liangma River, the water flowing again in

its repaved and refilled bed. The footpath beside it, formerly an institutional mottled pink, was patterned with black and yellow blocks.

Down by North Workers' Stadium Road, the old socialist coli-
seum and its neighboring Workers' Gymnasium were closed off and
scaffolded, to be rehabbed into Olympics-worthy venues. Along the
south side of the street was a strip of parkland with freshly installed
benches and flower beds and planters, and with a set of outdoor
exercise equipment. This was a marker of the New Beijing, wherever
renovation or demolition created a narrow open space: all-weather
workout machines, in primary colors, a full fitness center mechanically simplified to basic pedals, levers, weights, and wheels.

In America, this sort of project would have been an almost certain boondoggle and a failure, an empty gesture at including average
citizens in the athletic spirit. But Beijingers still believed in public
space. Wherever the fitness machines went up, even squeezed in by
the highway, people found them and got going—stair-stepping or
ski-sliding, leg-lifting or chest-expanding, hanging from the pull-up
ladders. If there was exercise equipment, why not exercise?

By June, the weather was baking hot, even after dark. On the
backstreets, the sidewalks were taken over by ramshackle tables and
chairs from tiny restaurants. Throngs of people were out eating,
drinking beer, and smoking under stark white lightbulbs.

About two weeks before our flight to America, we followed the
Liangma all the way out to the Third Ring, then doubled back toward
home on Xinyuan South Road. Ahead of us a truck appeared, driving slowly. It had a tank on the back, and riding on top was a crew
of workers wearing orange vests and round straw hats. They were
spraying down the treetops, using twin hoses the size of firehoses.

For a moment, I had the innocent thought that they were spray-
washing the dust from the leaves. Then we smelled a synthetic-sweet
vapor: the truck was pumping out gallons and gallons of pesticide.

We hailed a cab and shut ourselves inside for the last few blocks home. The spray dripped from the trees and lay in puddles on the pavement. So much for walking.

This was not the place to be having a baby. From the bootleg Coen brothers set, we watched *Raising Arizona*, and laughed out loud. America was a good place for babies; the presumption of baby-safety was so strong that an infant could go through kidnapping and armed robbery and come out okay.

Two days later, we were at the expat hospital. Christina was having bad cramps, and there was bleeding. A doctor from New Zealand, with cropped silver hair and an old-fashioned, fatherly air, delivered a verdict: bed rest, at home, for weeks. Flying to New York was out; we would be stuck in Beijing till the baby came.

Then something made him reconsider even that. It might be better, he said, to start the bed rest there in the hospital. While they processed the admission papers, Christina lay down in an empty room. As we waited, we started tracking the cramps as they came and went, the way we'd studied in birthing class. Just to see. What we saw was that they were coming about two minutes apart.

You could tell the difference between false labor and real premature labor, the doctor advised us, by whether a baby came out at the end or not. Those anxious, inconvenient weeks of bed rest were now what we might get if we were lucky. The admission was to the maternity ward.

The room was tasteful and up-to-date. No sooner were we in it than a man in dark slacks and a dress shirt was in the room with us, seeking insurance authorization. China's medical system asked for all payment up front; the expat hospital sold birth packages in advance, for people planning to have their babies there. We had not planned any such thing. We gave him the insurance card, and he withdrew.

I took a cab home to pack an overnight bag, the overnight bag that the parents-to-be in birthing-instruction stories always keep packed, as a talisman of readiness. I had been going to pack a good one as soon as we got to New York. Now I couldn't figure out what I would need to put into it. On my way back down the alley, I passed a bamboo-slatted pram or shopping cart, in which a naked baby boy stood up, in a muscleman pose.

The contractions did not subside. Afternoon plunged on into night; tape spooled out of a fetal monitor. As the baby squirmed, the heartbeat reading drifted in and out. They had given a steroid shot, to try to finish up the fetal lungs in a hurry. It would take twenty-four hours for the shot to work. The lungs were the key.

At a café up the block, over a sandwich, I used my fading laptop battery to Google what I could about premature birth. That part of the Internet was unblocked. The message seemed to be that birth at thirty-four weeks was not much to worry about, while birth at twenty-eight weeks was a lot to worry about. This was thirty-one weeks, right in the middle. Nobody said anything about thirty-one weeks.

Coming out of the café, I walked right up to another pesticide truck preparing to hose down the trees. Jaywalking was not a good idea in Beijing traffic, but I jaywalked to get away. As the hose started up behind me, the pump failed with a bang.

What had started was not going to stop. The perspective of the father-to-be on these things is too impoverished to dwell on: fetal monitor, watch dial, music rigged up to play on the computer. The overnight nurses and the doctor were speaking in a Chinese far beyond the reach of *Intermediate Chinese Dialogues, Book One*. The baby was breech and was making no move to settle into delivery position. Fetal monitor, watch dial. Despite being roughly the same geographic size as the United States, China observes a single national time zone, and on the eastern end, where Beijing is, dawn breaks before five a.m. in the summer. We were into a second day.

At thirty-three hours, things had gone as far as they could go. This was how it was going to be. The neonatologist—the neonatologist was out of town. Another doctor, a Westerner, looking rattled, said that he was almost a neonatologist, all but the certification, really. Now the operating room was tied up. Someone else had been getting a C-section. Well, how fast could they get cleaned up in there? We needed the operating room, badly, now. The nurses, speaking Chinese, were preparing my wife. I was in and out of the hallway. Why was it—

At this point, a drab woman buttonholed me. She was from billing. Our insurance plan was set up to reimburse us after payment, meaning we would have to pay directly, up front, meaning now. The C-section would be—she named a figure. And then the neonatal intensive care—another figure. The figures reeled around my head, as I tried to convert the currency and compare it with the dollar limit on our credit card. Sounds of agony were coming from behind me. The woman stood there, impatient. It seemed to me, as I did the math, that we could probably cover the birth and one day in intensive care. Intensive care. Clarity settled over me. I was not going to talk about this now, I said. One of my wife's colleagues—a doctor previously with Médecins sans Frontières, who had come to the hospital to keep an eye on things—steered the billing woman away with promises of secured cash payment.

Except for the not-quite-neonatologist, the team of doctors in the operating room was all Chinese. They spoke Chinese behind their masks as they cut. I stayed behind the protective sheet, by my wife's head. They were cutting. Then—then they came up with something in their hands, something purple and gray and limp, and as they hurried it across the room, I recalled that the very first moments were not supposed to mean anything, and I willed the image not to sink in: not purple, not gray, not limp; these would not be the facts until I allowed them to be the facts. The birthing instructions had said so.

He yelled.

The sound carried across the operating room, loud and full. Time did not need me to hold it back; time slipped loose and trickled away, out of sight again, underneath the mechanisms of the world. The baby yelled. He was pulling air into his lungs and pushing it out, strongly, on his own. The doctors had machines to make you breathe, but not to make you yell. Only you could do that.

It was 5:15 p.m. on June 9 in Beijing, China. Later, when it was time to fill out the birth certificate, I would learn that I was the only person in the operating room who had remembered to look at the clock. They brought him to us, with a too-big knit hat drooping low over his eyes. He looked at us quizzically, not without alertness. He weighed 1,685 grams, or 3 pounds, 11 ounces. The not-quite-neonatologist offered the conversion from metric.

His name, we decided after a few days with the blank birth certificate, would be Mack. We had all sorts of reasons we liked the name, reasons that seemed to be singular and personal. The other American babies from our birthing class, when they arrived, would be named Mookie and Duke, so possibly there were larger forces at work. That left the middle name, his Chinese name. There was a generational protocol for coming up with the names, a complicated set of traditional rules. We called his grandparents to ask them what the name should be. Zhong-Sheng, they said. It had nothing to do with the system. It meant "Born in China."

———

The breathing was not completely solved. Every once in a while, he would stop, and someone would have to tickle him a little to get him to restart. This was quite normal, they said, but it put us at a disadvantage in arguing with the doctors. In the United States, the goal is to get premature babies into their parents' arms as much as possible, which has been clinically found to help them thrive. In China, a preemie goes into a plastic box, under close medical supervision, until it hits certain targets of growth.

At least that's what happens to a preemie who gets medical care at all. "I think you love your baby too much," an English-speaking intensive-care nurse said, smiling. She meant it nicely. But she also had mused to Christina, by way of chitchat, that Mack was very lucky we were wealthy enough to put him in a hospital, unlike babies where she had come from.

He was the only baby in the neonatal intensive-care unit. We settled into a routine of commuting to and from the hospital, dividing the days into shifts. In the next room, full-term babies were constantly being examined and vaccinated as they arrived—awkward, blocky, improbably pink caricatures of humanity. By comparison, ours looked more like a person: slim, long-limbed, with a neatly shaped head, thick hair, and huge, serious eyes. To be honest, he was sort of liver-colored, when he wasn't turning yellow from jaundice, and his ribs were showing, and one had to mentally subtract the heart-monitor leads and the blood-oxygen-sensor lead and the feeding tube that was always in one nostril or another, but one miracle of parenthood was how easy it was to edit all of that out.

Outside, as we came and went, Beijing went on. It was still hot. Horse carts of watermelons, in from the country, were parked by the roadsides. The massage girls at the beauty parlors across from the hospital hung out by the storefront, calling and waving to pedestrians. The vacant lot by the apartment had grown into a full-blown meadow. People were still driving badly; time after time, the trip to or from the hospital was prolonged by the local custom, enshrined in law, of preserving every accident where it had happened. Cars with no visible damage would sit askew in the middle of the roadway, gently touching, while their drivers stood around, talking on cell phones and traffic backed up for a mile.

The renovations on the new apartment had never begun. Some of the bank employees were unhappy with their compensation in the privatization plan, and the whole process was tied up indefinitely. We would renew the lease and stay put. After three weeks, Mack had put on enough weight to get out of intensive care and into a recovery room.

Not long before Mack was discharged, he received some visitors: two relatives from Henan Province, on his grandmother's side, from a branch that had never left the mainland. Christina had been to visit them once before, early in her time in China. Now they were up in the capital, bringing with them a rectangular zippered bag as big as an old steam radiator, made of clothlike plastic bearing images of Mickey and Minnie Mouse—or, as the text on the bag had it, Mikey and Mimi. Inside was an infant's trousseau: one quilted winter outfit after another, handmade sets of jackets and padded pants, some accompanied by little matching coverlets. Some of the fabric was in traditional patterns and some was in black-and-orange shark-themed print like surfer-wear from the mall. The trousers, even the thickest ones, were open at the crotch, so a child wearing them could squat down and relieve itself in the street. This was the usual Chinese practice. For warm weather, they had included little aprons, designed to protect the baby's belly from drafts while the rest of the baby ran bare and free. And there were packages of store-bought socks. Ours was the first male baby born to Christina's generation, and we could not risk his getting cold.

Then it was time to bring him home. I put a new Ikea crib by the window, laid sheets on the mattress, and set a stuffed Fu Niu Lele, the mismatched Paralympic cow, in the corner. The cab that took me back to the hospital had to brake hard to avoid a rear-end collision, then spent the rest of the drive honking and flashing its lights. Friends moving back to the United States had left us a hand-me-down rear-facing infant safety seat. As I struggled to fit it into the back of a Hyundai cab (forgetting to properly level it) the hospital staff wondered aloud, in Chinese, why we didn't just hold the baby.

8.

许可 Permit

In late June, the Olympic press center telephoned: Would I be interested in getting a driver's license? It was, as far as I could remember, the first time since I'd become a certified journalist that the media department had offered me something—an interview, a tour, a visa extension—without my asking. Till that moment, I hadn't planned on getting a license. Beijing's driver's exam involved a grueling and pointless written test; the expat tales about it dealt with either brutal cram sessions or well-placed bribes. Since cars were expensive and taxis were cheap, it didn't seem worth the bother.

But Beijing was working to make life easier for foreign journalists. I could drop in anytime that week, bring in my American license, and fill out a form. Maybe I did want a license. I pictured myself taking a rental car for a spin out the Liangma Bridge Road, to the neon-bedecked drive-in theater I kept seeing out my taxi windows. I told the press center I would sign up, then let a few days go by.

The press center called again and repeated the invitation: easy license, no hassle, come by this week. They also called to say that there would be a press conference—Sunday, nine a.m.—to announce the opening of a new one-stop service center for the media. If I applied before then, I could pick up my license at the service center that morning. I would be coming to the press conference, right?

Slowly, it dawned on me that there might be a reason behind their solicitousness. I told them I probably couldn't drop off my application till Saturday afternoon. Would that be okay? The office would be open, they said.

The press center had left its first home, in a shabby hotel off to the north, for a space in a gleaming municipal office tower by Cha-oyangmen Bridge, site of the Sun-Facing Gate in the old city wall, two interchanges south of Dongzhimen. It was more New Beijing architecture, with a wavelike glass roof and a full-height atrium, and a matching wavelike building was going up behind it. I arrived late, in heavy rain, to find four staffers from the Olympics and the Public Security Bureau (the Gong An) waiting. They took my New York license and gave me the application form. There was a space for the duration of the license—that, they explained, would be the same as the expiration period of my short-term visa. When I got my next ninety-day visa I would need to sign up for a new license to go with it.

Also, it needed a photo—did I have a photo? I had some spare ID photos left over from the Public Security Bureau's visa office. The Public Security Bureau officer in charge of the driver's license examined the pictures. They were the wrong size, she said.

There was a moment of mutual dismay. The one-stop media service center did not have a photo department. But! A market in the neighborhood could take the photos for me. Out the door, across

Chaoyangmen Bridge, on the left. One of them wrote the size and background-color specifications out in Chinese for me.

Had I been considering only my own interests at the moment, I would have hailed a cab and gone home. But there were greater historical issues at stake. I was the Western media; China was trying to do me a favor. I set off through the downpour. The market was a ten-minute hike away. With soggy feet, I tramped up and down the escalators, looking for the photo department. I found it in the grocery section—a tripod, rate sheet, and foam-board backdrop set up by the checkout-line exits. I hunted up a clerk, sat for the pictures, collected them, and sloshed back.

The whole building was dim and empty by the time I got back, except for the guard at the door and the team in the one-stop center. As I handed the photos over, I tested my hunch. How many other journalists would be picking up their licenses the next day?

"You are the very first one," the lead media-center staffer said. "So don't be late!"

The next day's program began in the press-conference hall on the top floor, under the swooping glass roof. A banner at the front read: "Launch of One-Stop Service for Media During the Beijing Olympic Games and the Preparatory Period." A snippet of "Greatest Love of All" played, then went away. There were more than a hundred people in the audience. About half were from the press, mostly Chinese. The rest represented the agencies, bureaus, and companies taking part in the service center—twenty-nine organizations in all, including the Public Security Bureau; the State Administration of Radio, Film, and Television; the Bank of China; the State Administration of Foreign Exchange; the People's Liberation Army.

Even by the standards of press conferences, Chinese press conferences tended to be dry affairs. A series of officials took the microphone and hailed the service center as a "brand-new innovation" and an "unprecedented approach." Invoking the new press-access rules, one declared the center "a solid step forward to implement these regulations and show that we really honor our promise to the media." China, another said, will "bear in mind the principle of treating the media kindly." With a flourish, the final speaker declared that "one-stop service for the media . . . now starts!" The crowd was invited, offhandedly, to stop by the fifth floor on the way out and see the center at work.

Whatever was in store for me was about to happen. Rather than waiting for the elevator, I took the stairs. As I hit the fifth floor, my cell phone was ringing: an Olympics official, checking to make sure I was there. Staffers intercepted me in the crowded hallway and guided me toward the room where I'd done the paperwork the day before. I went in like a man being escorted into his surprise fiftieth-birthday party.

At the far end, next to the driver's-license station, a mass of photographers and television camera crews was waiting. Someone had put flower arrangements on the table. Behind the flowers was a smiling Public Security Bureau officer, a tiny woman in uniform. My completed application form was presented with a flourish and with remarks to me in Mandarin, untranslated. Camera flashes went off. The Gong An officer held up an ID card with my picture on it, in loose plastic, then gave it a ceremonial pass through a laminator, to the rattle of shutters going off. She handed it to me, still warm.

Officials closed in, shaking my hand, with cameras popping all the while. The card had a made-up Chinese name for me—"Tuo Ma Si" in characters—and an expiration date twenty-seven days in the future. It also said, in the fine print, that if the police stopped me, I would need to show them an official Chinese translation of my American license. So, technically speaking, the license alone did not allow me to drive. Could I get the translation at the one-stop service center? I could not.

The photographers asked to see my license, and began holding it up in the foreground as they kept snapping away. A man on the far side of the table began asking questions: How long had I been in Beijing? What sites had I seen? Had I eaten Beijing duck? When my answers flagged, he confided, sotto voce, that he was just trying to keep me talking and smiling for the cameras. This is kind of alarming, I told him, grinning. Yes, isn't it? he smiled back. A photographer hollered something. She says, the man said, if you smile bigger, you'll be on the front page.

Interview time. Going in, I had resolved not to be a stooge. My talking points would be strictly truthful: that I was glad to see this new emphasis on coordination and convenience, and that I hoped they would follow it up by making it easier to get a long-term visa. As far as I could tell, I repeated the message to everyone I saw. I did an interview for Beijing Television, then one for China Central Television.

The English translation of the official Beijing Olympic news story about the event described me as the "most elated" of the journalists at the event. "I am extremely happy," the story quoted me as saying. "I know that traffic management in Beijing is very strict. I'd never have imagined that I'd get my driver's license so quickly. Now I can drive by myself, which will make interviewing a lot more convenient."

The last bit struck me as especially implausible. But who needed to know what I'd said? I was a representative of progress. And I was a picturesque one. Owing to a previous bad experience with the language barrier and thinning shears, I had not had a haircut since leaving New York. People began to stop me and tell me they'd seen me on TV or on the front page of the *Beijing Evening News*—a teacher at my Chinese school, a nurse in the pediatric ward, the man who sold phone cards outside the corner store. A sports newspaper invited me to write an essay about my observations of Beijing, for one yuan a word. Another TV station, Phoenix Television, asked if I would sit for a follow-up interview. I agreed. By text message, they sent an additional request: Could I drive my car to the interview?

   With regret, I told them I did not yet have a car. I went to the interview by taxi.

9.

准备 Get Ready

It was August 8, 2007, or 8/8/07, two-thirds of the way to numerological completeness. An opening celebration for the countdown day, a pre-celebration of the pre-celebration of next year's celebration, was happening at the Millennium Monument, a blocklong concrete creation that commemorated the last indispensable abstract moment in time. It was off to the west, beyond the imperial Altar of the Moon and just south of the nine-hundred-year-old scenic ground of Deep Jade Pool Park. The early sky was blue, the haze light but certain. There had been an ominous downpour the day before, and my shoes were still damp. Police lined the Second Ring at intervals for the occasion; a municipal police officer by the roadside hawked a gob. Twelve months of civilization lessons to go.

Troupes of performers were doing their routines at the lower end of a long, narrow plaza, which rose in tiers toward a sort of mast or sundial at the north side. Whatever the structure had signified about the turn of the millennium, it was now strung all over with pennants like the ones on used-car lots. Grandstands below the sundial needle were full of people in identical neon-lime T-shirts. Gold confetti shot into the air; there were lion costumes, and banners with Fuwa, and inflatable Fuwa with substandard renderings of their facial features. A white-clad tai chi troupe finished doing its slow-motion exercises on the plaza and filed out—up close, they were mostly female, mostly middle-aged or beyond. They fanned themselves with the red fans they had used in their performance. Dragonflies hovered, and the heat and glare intensified.

Out behind the monument was a display of Olympic statuary, part of an ongoing sculpture contest. An earlier installment had been on the Wangfujing shopping street the year before, with 200 scale models of proposed monumental works. The artists were mostly from China or C-list European nations, and their entries had made up a survey of the kitsch potential of twentieth-century art— from lifelike kitsch bronzes to kitsch Cubo-Futurism, kitsch abstraction, and finally, with a proposed monumental line of color-painted, O-mouthed synchronized swimmers, kitsch kitsch. A sculptor from Tianjin had created a slit-eyed, Vandyke-bearded Chinese man and a thick-lipped African Sambo playing hacky sack together; one from Slovakia had made a grotesque spherelike starburst by fusing together two or three dozen stiff human figures by their heads, so that their legs and bodies radiated outward.

Now some of the model works had been blown up to full size: one of the Qin emperor's terra-cotta warriors using a terra-cotta army horse as a pommel horse, a red plastic or fiberglass sprinter with a silver prosthetic leg and an expression of anguish. I stood in the shade of the monument as the performers streamed offstage and up into Deep Jade Pool Park. A dirty man with blue clothes and crusty eyes stepped on my foot, then circled in close, touched my shoulder, and said something unintelligible to me. It sounded like "Cheney." Behind his back, he was clutching a grubby wad of cord.

The countdown itself was in the evening. At the fancy new Olympic press headquarters, the center atrium was filled all the way to the top with scaffolding—the swooping glass roof had failed under the weight of the rain. For the working press, there were bottles of water and bags of McDonald's food; staffers marked people's neck credentials with a pen to keep track of who had already gotten theirs.

The press was delivered to Tian'anmen Square by motor coach. Imprisonment by motor coach is part of what certifies a major event as major—part of the ritual certification and quarantine of the media. We (there was no sense thinking of oneself in the first person singular) stepped out into a narrow chute, between two of the rows and rows of tightly packed buses at the south end of the square.

It would have been possible to fit many, many motor coaches into Tian'anmen Square. The space is, beyond its various historical resonances, the great open public space in the city, like Central Park in New York, if Central Park were totally flat, treeless, paved over, and crawling with undercover police. People go strolling there on normal days, and fly kites. When Beijing had won the Olympic bid, a million people had reportedly filled the square for spontaneous celebration. Tonight's production was invitation-only and tightly limited. Around us, disembarking from their own motor coaches, were teams of people in colored T-shirts: lime green again, yellow, black, royal blue, red. The shirts read *"Weixiao Beijing,"* meaning "Smile, Beijing." Inside the security perimeter were K 9 cops in black fatigue pants, real U.S.A.-style jump-out uniforms. Their effect was diminished by the fact that the dogs came in a sundry assortment of breeds.

At Mao's mausoleum, renovations were unfinished. The National

Museum on the east side of the square, likewise in mid-renovation, had been draped with a scrim that vaguely resembled an intact building façade. The press was on risers facing the stage and Tian'anmen—the gate itself—beyond, with its endlessly photographed portrait of Mao gazing back. The colored T-shirts filled rows of chairs around the stage. It all seemed tiny and constrained against the immensity of the square; the crowd was no bigger than was necessary to fill up a TV program. That was how Beijingers were going to experience the countdown, not as a street party but as a telecast. The security perimeter was less a show of police force than an aggressive act of entertainment production: a protest banner would have interfered with the stagecraft. I wondered what would happen if someone were to unfurl an Iraq protest banner in the middle of the Super Bowl halftime show.

An introduction was read over loudspeakers, repeatedly, in a last-minute rehearsal. Video of fireworks ran backward and forward on big screens. The real production began with singing at ten minutes after seven, by performers in tuxedos and ball gowns. Then came a Paralympic music video starring Andy Lau, the superstar actor and singer from Hong Kong, equally popular on the mainland. In the video, he was a runner who lost a leg in a car crash. He threw out his running trophies and drank heavily, then (with the help of Adidas running gear) rehabbed himself, went running on the Great Wall on his prosthesis, and became an elite amputee runner. On the stage, the real-life, two-legged Andy Lau sang, or seemed to sing, along with the video. I had always thought he looked tall in the movies, but Hong Kong, like Hollywood, inflates its leading men, and he was a wee elfin figure compared with his backup dancers. "Everyone is number one," he sang. Then came Chinese ethnic-minority musicians onstage, followed by a children's choir.

The sun went down, and the lights came up on the Gate of

Heavenly Peace—white lightbulbs tracing its outlines and the unreal glory rays of spotlights radiating out from it, solid-looking in the smog. The volunteer cheerers waved placards and purplish pinwheels as the show headed into a big number, the new theme song of the Olympic preparations, "We Are Ready." More and more singers appeared on stage, revealed one by one, all in matching white polo shirts. There were dozens of them; the whole Chinese-language pop-music community had mobilized for the effort. I was still bad at identifying Chinese stars, but I recognized the androgynous winner of the national Super Girl TV singing competition in the mix. Pigeons were released, and balloons. Men in white uniforms with black caps and black boots marched in, carrying a stream of flags of Olympic nations, military parade troops for One World. Jackie Chan, looking tiny, appeared onstage with a little girl toting a red lantern. The countdown was in Chinese, and it ended at eight o'clock sharp. This was a point of confusion: there had been conflicting word about whether the official Olympic start time would be 8:00 p.m. or the even more auspicious 8:08. A ripple of consternation went through the international media, where people had prewritten the 8:08 figure into their coverage. Fireworks went off, and more dancers filled the stage, including teams in traditional lion-dancing costumes.

A few pigeons were still lingering around the square. The dance-tacular went on and on. On camera, the floor on the edge of the stage was twinkly underfoot, an effect not clearly visible from the press section. There were drummers, and the rhythm of the whole frenetic scene was not unlike the rhythm of "We Will Rock You." At 8:08— there, the magic minute—it all subsided, and a podium rolled out for a reading of ceremonial paperwork. We were into the performative part of the Olympic experience, but we were still in China, where every important moment must be bureaucratically solemnized.

The flags of nations and their black-booted bearers filled the stage. The Olympic anthem played, and the flags of the Olympics, the People's Republic, and the Beijing organizing committee were presented. The minister of sports spoke. The president of the organizing committee spoke. "Principle of being frugal" . . . "final and most crucial stage" . . . "winning honor for our nation" . . . "respect and understanding."

Three times, speakers brought up the subject of China's "century-old dream" of hosting the Olympics. This had surfaced recently in Olympic coverage, and it would be a recurring theme through the next twelve months. It referred not to any national goals expressed by the crumbling Qing dynasty in 1908, but to an apparently obscure article published in a newspaper in Tianjin that year—unearthed, it seemed, through a heroic bit of applied research.

The speakers kept going, invoking former president Jiang Zemin's "moderately prosperous society" and the points of his political philosophy, the "Three Represents." International Olympic Committee president Jacques Rogge then handed out formal invitations, one by one, to presidents of national Olympic committees in attendance. The Greek Olympic Committee president went first. Then the Canadian Olympic Committee. The British Olympic Committee. The Russian. The Americans were absent. Finally, China's own Olympic committee received an envelope, inviting it to come to Beijing. Then the required official speech act: "The invitation ceremony now concludes. Please enjoy the performance."

A video of a gleaming and clear Beijing played as a multitude of dancers and drummers reappeared. A bright-red piano with the Olympic logo on it was moved into position, then the whole platform with the piano rolled from west to east, a seated orchestra trailing along behind the piano. At the piano, in a red tailcoat with gold buttons and gold lapels, was the Chinese virtuoso Lang Lang.

Behind the risers, there was a stirring so sharp it seemed as if security had been breached after all. The press whipped around to look, and there was the towering form of Yao Ming, being hustled around the stands by a CCTV crew. A spontaneous cheer broke out as the crowd caught sight of him moving through the darkness off-stage. The wide-necked superstar Liu Huan, with his signature gray ponytail, was singing a duet with someone, with lavender-lit dancers all around, and nobody cared. The flags of nations streamed back onstage; the singing was operatic. Uniformed soldiers appeared on the media riser—coming up for a better look. Yao emerged onstage, in the thick of the national flags, carrying a big Olympic flag of his own. Fireworks went off again, and more fireworks, indigo and green and magenta. The music, subdued, kept playing, even after a final volley, and the flags kept waving, even as the crowd began to filter out. One thing about Chinese people is that they head for the exits. They may be the heading-for-the-exits-est nation on earth.

There were almost no empty cabs on the road, after the motor-coach ride back to the press center, and the empty ones wouldn't stop. After something like half an hour of trying, I took the subway home. The next morning, a taxi driver told me that the drivers had all stayed home to watch the countdown on television.

The police knocked on the door around ten in the morning, on August 20, right after the ayi had left for the day. There were two of them, a man and a woman, in uniform. How many people live here? they asked. Could they see my passport? Might they come in and inspect everyone's papers?

"No" didn't seem to be a workable answer. They were very polite, which may come easily without the Fourth Amendment in the way. They didn't need to explain or justify their presence; the state was everywhere, and now the state was inside the apartment. They came in with their shoes on, despite Chinese custom and the freshly cleaned floors, and sat down at the dining table to study the family's documents. I was barefoot. My wife and baby were asleep in the bedroom.

I rummaged for the passports and certificates. For once, all the household's paperwork was in order. We had recently extricated Mack from a bureaucratic Kafka-loop: the local police station wouldn't issue him a residence-registration certificate without a visa, and the main Public Security office wouldn't issue him a visa without a residence-registration certificate. In the end, as usual, the local cops yielded to reason before the main office would.

Still, it was one thing to have a problem with the security-bureaucracy paperwork, and another to have the undercoordinated security apparatus suddenly coordinate itself into the dining room. What if the police had showed up one of the many times my foreigner registration had lapsed? What if we had missed something this time?

The officers copied the information from our papers onto their own papers, with unnerving slowness. I asked if they were local, and they said they were from immigration. So we were not a neighborhood matter, but part of a bigger national concern. When they finished, they asked if I knew any other foreigners in the building, gesturing up and down toward the other apartments. Not having been introduced to any of them, I said truthfully that I did not.

One by one, the first set of sports facilities was being finished on schedule, or mostly finished, and so each one was to host a test sporting event, of variable wattage: the women's soccer World Cup, the world junior wrestling championships, a low-ranking ITF tennis tournament. The whole series of warm-ups, stretching from the summer of 2007 into the spring of 2008, was called "Haoyun Beijing" in Chinese, a play on *Aoyun*, or "Olympics." In English it translated to "Good Luck, Beijing," a phrase that could be said with several different inflections.

For the beginning of the Good Luck games, the city was cutting back again on traffic—not just government cars this time, but private cars as well. Odd- and even-numbered license plates would stay home on alternating days. It had been announced as a two-week exercise, but by the time August came, it had been cut down to four days, two of them on the weekend. Citizens and businesses were only willing to rehearse their Olympic privations so much.

The first event was beach volleyball—a fourth-tier pro tournament, the lower tier of the lower-tier international pro league—in Chaoyang Park, by the east side of the Fourth Ring. The park was so big that I had never quite understood where its edges were, partly because it kept expanding over demolition zones. The arena was itself a transient phenomenon, built of struts and sheets of gray-painted steel, designed to be dismantled once the Olympics were done. The sand, after a lengthy sand-evaluation process, had been brought in from the celebrated tourist beaches of Hainan Island in the south.

On the Saturday of the semifinals, the traffic restrictions had just gone into effect, and the air was grayish. Turnout was light, but the arena was ringed and threaded through with volunteer staff. The only truly full section of seats was occupied by people in matching T-shirts, like the audience brought in for the countdown ceremony. Down on the court were Chinese cheerleaders, dancing to "Who Let the Dogs Out?" The cheer squad was a special touch that had been announced for the Good Luck games. They were Chinese Basketball Association dancers, someone said. Male dancers joined them, along with a pair of inflatable-costumed Fuwa—Huanhuan the flame and

Nini the swallow. The other three mascots were missing. After a Brazilian team rallied to defeat a team from Thailand, the cheerleaders threw collapsible souvenir cups and flying discs to the crowd. The mood was sweet and backyardy.

I had come to Chaoyang Park with a Chinese-American friend, an intellectual-property lawyer and volleyball fanatic. Intellectual-property protection is labor-intensive work in China, because the law is inclined to treat small tweaks to a stolen design (the body of one car, say, with the grille of another) as enough to establish a wholly new product. Near us in the stands was a female photographer wearing a pair of what had the unmistakable look of New Balance sneakers, with a few key differences: the N on the sides was backward, and the sole had been quadrupled or sextupled in height, so that the original orthopedic struts and bulges had become a too-trendy-for-walking platform. I snapped a photo of them, and my camera informed me that the file was corrupted. The memory card, which I had haggled for in a tourist shop, had quit working. It was labeled as San Disk brand, but I suddenly had doubts.

Now a Chinese team was playing a Swiss one. The crowd gave the Chinese players the universal national sports cheer: *"Jia you!"* meaning, literally, "Add gas!" With the Swiss trailing 10–8 in the first set, the public-address announcer gave them a *"Jia you!"* too. China won, but Switzerland stretched things to three sets.

Attendance was better for the tournament finals the next day, though the haze was thicker. After the Games, the Olympic organizing committee would report that the traffic restrictions had reduced particulate matter 10 to 15 percent. The cheerleaders wore violently fluorescent-orange bikinis and rainbow Afro wigs. Then came yellow-gold top hats, like the ones the NBA dancers wear, to go with outfits of red bandanna tops and gray bottoms. Beibei the fish and Yingying the antelope now showed up, almost completing the set of Fuwa.

The Chinese played Brazil for the championship. Brazil picked on the weaker of the Chinese players for an easy win in the first set, but China got out ahead in the second set and stayed in front, all the way to set point. The public address announcer was hoarse; the audience yelled *"Jia you!"* on its own, caught up in the action. Then, although trailing 20–17, Brazil came back to wrap up the match.

The crowd thinned, but not with the usual Beijing rapidity. There was still a bit of spectacle to be had. The cheerleaders remained on the court, in pink skirts, dancing with the Fuwa. As volunteers prepared a podium for the medal ceremony, a second cheer squad appeared, in silver bikini tops and red boy-shorts, waving red fans. This was how there had been so many different costume changes. An inflatable Jingjing the panda also arrived, the final Fuwa. Only half of the split cheerleading squad seemed to have an actual dance routine at any time. The team in silver and red kicked the sand desultorily while the pink skirts danced a number; then the silver-and-red squad jumped into motion to dance to "The Twist"—the remake with the Fat Boys joining Chubby Checker.

Volunteers surrounded the court for the medal ceremony, arms swaying to a recording of "We Are Ready." Outside the arena was a sand volleyball court for the public. People were eagerly taking possession of their piece of the Olympics, squeezing into the court to play a game of more or less fourteen on sixteen, while children dug in the few open spots of sand.

The grounds around the Chaoyang volleyball site, according to an official Xinhua News Agency report, were one of the sites where Olympic organizers had planted a collection of 2 million flowers, specially bred to bloom out of season and survive in the August weather. I wandered south, along the flower beds. Chrysanthemums, marigolds, petunias, and Chinese roses held themselves up in the haze and glare. On the way out of the park, a crew was installing

Fuwa signage. They were debating which one was named what. Wasn't the antelope Nini?

The heart of the Olympic Green was still under construction and off limits, so the first round of Good Luck games was marginal, in terms of the sports involved and the locations. The baseball tournament was out in the western neighborhood of Wukesong, on the inner edge of the far side of the Fourth Ring. Baseball was a curiosity in China; the national team would be granted an Olympic berth as the host country, but it had no hopes of winning a medal, and there was no point in trying to get better, since the Olympics were dropping baseball after 2008.

But even a lame-duck sport needed to try out its venues. In the smaller of the two ballparks, I watched a French baseball team put on an implausible exhibition of how not to run the bases against the Czech Republic, somehow turning eleven hits into only one run, while the Czechs scored six on nine hits. For entertainment, there were two people in inflatable Jingjing suits, another case of mascot mismanagement. The Fuwa seemed to have Beijingers' natural aversion to systematic lining-up.

The crowd numbered no more than 250 people, and many of them kept binoculars trained on the next field over, where Japan had built a 2–1 lead against China in a sold-out game. The listed capacity of the larger park was 12,000, but it was hard to tell if it held that many yet: in our own field, the grandstand only extended from one on-deck circle to the other; a gravel bed ringed the rest of the field, marking where the rest of the ballpark would go. Over the left-field fence were at least fourteen cranes, slowly vanishing in the polluted dusk along with the green monolithic bulk of the unfinished basketball arena.

Archery was in the middle of things, by comparison with the distant baseball fields—in a cluster of venues between the main Olympic Green to the south and the unfinished Olympic Forest to the north. The drive took me past the Bird's Nest, where people were standing on the highway guardrail to film the construction. The archery stadium was another temporary steel job, like the volleyball arena, this one shaped like a not-quite-folded fan. And as with the baseball field, the venue was ready only in the narrow sense that it was possible to hold a sporting event in it. Big stretches of the stands were missing seats, and out beyond the archery targets were mounds of dirt and sections of uninstalled sewer pipe.

In the archery semifinals, South Korea was facing a team called "Chinese Taipei," which was competing under a neutral Olympic-committee flag. One common prediction in the Western press as 2008 approached was that the People's Republic might take the occasion to threaten or invade Taiwan. From inside Beijing, though, the One China problem seemed to be anything but a casus belli. The governments were constitutionally antagonistic, and reciprocally so: even as the mainland counted Taiwan as a renegade province, Taiwan counted the mainland as thirty-some renegade provinces. But no one was in a hurry to settle the irreconcilable claims. The mainland press used scare quotes in all its political coverage of Taiwan—the "legislature" did this, the "president" said that—but in most other respects, where Americans might have expected to see the cross-straits equivalent of Freedom Fries, Taiwan's existence and influence were freely and frankly identified as such. The new Beijing was full of Taiwanese restaurants and Taiwanese luxury malls, with a Taiwan Hotel downtown and a complex in the works called Taiwan Center. Taiwanese pop stars sang alongside mainland and Hong Kong ones on "We Are Ready."

Between South Korea and Taiwan, certainly, the archery crowd was pulling for Taiwan. Korea had a slim lead, but maintained it with pitiless precision, matching every bull's-eye and near-bull's-eye the Taiwanese could muster. By one point, Korea sent Taipei into the consolation round against the United States. As soon as the bronze-medal match was over, the whole row of Chinese spectators in front of me cleared out, not waiting around to see the Koreans shoot for gold against Malaysia.

Next, the Good Luck games moved to the wrestling gym on the campus of the Beijing Agricultural University. In the name of fiscal responsibility, several of the planned venues had been switched from the Olympic Green to university sites, so they could be used as campus gyms after the Games.

Zhang Xiaoguang—since we'd had the baby, he'd been known as Big Mack to us—came along to see the wrestling. In his undocumented days, he had once lived in an unheated room on the Agricultural University campus, with an uncle who worked there. We had visited the Agricultural University months before, when the gym was still under construction. Workers were crawling on the roof, and a construction fence along the front proclaimed the future "Olympic Rassling Site."

Now it was completed, with an elaborate entrance walkway of gravel under glass, from which a squeegee-and-mop crew was busily cleaning water from an earlier rain shower. Inside, the ceiling was studded with at least thirty hanging security cameras, and the wrestling was going on in three rings at once. After each championship match, the finalists were brought back for a medal ceremony, escorted through a double door by tall, maidenly attendants while a fog machine went off.

An Iranian wrestler overwhelmed an American at 84 kilograms, to the crowd's warm approval. Other contestants hailed from

Germany, Kazakhstan, Ukraine, Armenia, Kazakhstan, Kazakhstan. Something resembling the world, at least enough of the world to fill a gym, had arrived in Beijing. Another American, by the name of Bubba Jenkins, took on a Turkish opponent named Okay Köksal for the gold and won. In victory, he bounced on his toes and did a high-stepping dance, then kissed his hand and pointed to the rafters, and wrapped it up by doing a flying leap off the platform. America! It implicated or embraced the sportsgoing crowd in its self-centeredness: I love myself, because I love a winner!

The Weather Modification Office was not practicing rainstorm suppression during the Good Luck rehearsals. One evening in August, we took the baby out to a restaurant a few blocks away, under clear skies, in a Little Angel–brand stroller that Big Mack had given him. We got out of dinner as the summer rains erupted, sheets of water pouring from the sky. Till that moment, we had insisted on using the safety seat, which Beijingers saw as incomprehensible American folly. I had learned how to ask for a rear seat belt to hook around it—*"Houmian you meiyou anquandai?"*—and had kept using it, looking for the one cab in four (if not five, or ten) that would have belts. Now, in the dark and in the rain, there was only one cab to be seen, and we didn't have the seat anyway. We got in with the baby loose and rolled slowly home, through a foot of floodwater. Full-grown poplars had toppled along Outer Dongzhimen Avenue; waves rolled across the intersections, and pedestrians waded by. There were limits to how safe Beijing would let you be.

Chinese folk belief said that children born premature at seven months were better—tougher, stronger, smarter—than the ones born at eight months. No one had an explanation; possibly, in the traditional past, sickly eight-month preemies might have grown up sickly, while only the hardiest seven-monthers survived at all. This, along with our success in having a male baby, was one of the few points of Chinese tradition that went in our favor. Little Mack had expressed his own will to survive by packing on fat till he resembled a bright-eyed, stubby link of sausage, but strangers still exclaimed "So small!" or "Too small!" at the sight of him. A baby that young belonged at home, confined with his mother, and with the air-conditioning turned off. Store clerks would lunge to shut off the air when we carried him in.

By early September, he was old enough to fly to the United States. Our last night before leaving, we hauled the car seat out to a fancy French restaurant in a Taiwanese mall by the Central Business District, a pink-and-silver shrine to wealth and cosmopolitanism. The baby slept through the meal, in his seat, while stylish people came and went from a promotional cocktail party outside the restaurant. At the end of the meal, he woke up hungry. The mall was forward-looking enough to have a nursing lounge and changing room on the top floor, so mother and child went off to it.

While they were away, as the rest of our dinner group wandered the complex, the clerks began drifting toward the front of their shops or departments, standing silently by the walkways. Finally, one of us asked what was going on. A clerk explained that it was closing time and they were waiting for the last customers to leave, but the staff was under orders not to clear anyone out. So they waited, hovering. The moment we got the baby and headed for the elevators, the lights dimmed and the clerks hastily broke formation, hustling us into the elevator with them en masse. Public time was over; we were behind the shiny backdrop now, backstage. Here was a bit of the human infrastructure that made it possible. On the first floor, we were steered toward a back exit and into a Pamplona of shopgirls, almost all of them already out of uniform and quick-changed into civilian clothes—running to grab their time cards, hit the exit, and get on a row of waiting buses. They hurried by on all sides, flowing around us. In the middle of the stampede, one walked slowly, with a cigarette.

IV.

欢迎 WELCOME

10.

内 Inside

There was dust in the October sunbeams, and dust outside in an otherwise clear blue morning. We had flown back to Beijing on Air China the night before, into the old burning smell, off a plane reeking of someone's feet. The new terminal wasn't due to open for three months, and at the old terminal we found no jetway—only a steep flight of steps to carry the baby down, then a long tarmac bus ride. Near the end of the ride, the bus passed a row of empty jetways, then an Aeroflot jumbo jet pulling away from a gate. Why Aeroflot got better access than a state-owned airline was a mystery.

New York and America had been the same as ever, our extra months away measured only by a dead car battery and a stack of unforwarded mail. In Flushing, Queens, in the Chinese-immigrant-heavy section where our apartment was, one streetside art vendor had propped a framed picture of the Fuwa against a parking meter, amid his other merchandise. Beyond that, though, the rush to 2008 was as remote and abstract as the Boxer Rebellion.

But in Beijing, absence had sharpened the details. An old man in a cloth cap and jacket was walking up the alley, carrying a tea-kettle. He pinched one nostril and blew the contents of the other one onto the ground. The line at the corner bank, where the phone bill needed to be paid, stretched into the vestibule. Cabbage sizzled in a wok by the alley. In front of the corner market, the pavement was all torn out. A sign said the construction work would last from October 8 to December 31. At a little alleyside table, men were eating big bowls of brown noodles and drinking big green bottles of beer, at eleven-thirty in the morning.

The wind blew, and by afternoon it was clear enough to see the mountains all the way across town to the west. I tried to keep an eye out for the mountains when I could. It was easy to forget they were there, for days or weeks, in the usual pollution. From the windows of Chinese language school, five stories up in a hotel-complex sky-bridge, I had worked out an alternative set of landmarks, doubling as a pollution gauge: on days that were only moderately dirty, I could make out the shape of the Ikea out by the Fourth Ring; when it was less dirty still, I could tell that the Ikea was blue and I could see the towers of the Wangjing neighborhood behind it. Only on the rarest, most excellent of days would the mountains to the north make an appearance. (The bad days? On bad days, the buildings across the street would fade out and haze would be visible in the school's hall-way, like cigarette smoke.)

The mountains were still showing on the way to the Good Luck Beijing tennis tournament later in the week—at least, until the cab turned north. Tennis was somewhere up by archery, out beyond the Olympic Green. There was a brownish blur in the distance, in the direction of the Green, getting thicker as we drew near. By the time we hit the edge of the Olympic site, we were driving in a dust storm. Beijing's soil is naturally fine and silty, and the construction zone was wide open to the north wind. Tan clouds boiled up all around, indifferent to the dust-suppression netting. We skirted the perimeter, heading north. Sheets of dust seethed past the monumental thatching of the Bird's Nest and the now installed polymer-bubble walls of the Water Cube as we went by.

Signs pointed the way past archery. The worst of the dust was behind us, on the Green. We drove along the edge of the Olympic Forest, with its rows of braced and staked trees, and through a stretch of brand-new unmarked roadway, weaving around jutting manhole covers. A little farther south the signs led to a gateway. Beyond was an expanse of asphalt, the usual Good Luck entrance trappings— white canopy, metal detectors—and then the tennis stadium: a clean-lined thing of concrete facets, flaring from bottom to top, somewhere between an inverted pyramid and a Spielberg UFO touching down. Officially, it may have been a stylized flower.

An attendant stopped me short of the security check. This was the staff entrance, he explained. The spectator entrance was on the opposite side—on the west, across the wind-whipped expanse of the complex.

Or not across the wind-whipped complex. A trio of guards blocked the path. I should go back to the road and walk around the outside, they indicated. That was really inconvenient, I told them, in Mandarin. This was an expression that had come up early in Chinese class. Too inconvenient, I added. Extraordinarily inconvenient!

Extraordinarily inconvenient, the guard agreed. Nevertheless. The road I was supposed to be walking not only led south, away from the tennis center, but it curved off to the east. I grabbed a taxi, one of two that seemed to be waiting for nothing in particular.

According to the taxi meter, it was a two-mile trip. The spectator entrance was only slightly less desolate than the staff one. It was an hour into the tennis, on the next-to-last day of the tournament, featuring the men's doubles final and the men's singles semis. The top seeds in the tournament had world rankings in the 200s. I was nearly alone on the broad walkway, passing pair after pair of empty side courts on the long approach to the flower-UFO.

I peeked in on the singles matches, then walked over to the main stadium for the doubles final. Only one of the stadium gates was open. Wind roared in my ears as I circled around to it. Three other would-be spectators waited on the terrace for a changeover. The wind wailed. The dust was invisible, but the lens cap on my camera made a grinding noise when I took it on or off.

The doubles final was already in the second set when the gate opened. China led Taiwan, 7–6, 3–2. My ticket was fourth row, courtside, the best I'd been able to buy. All the seats down there were empty. There were fewer than a hundred people in the whole stadium; some sections were still waiting for seats to be installed. Before I made it to the seat, the Chinese pair closed out and started packing their things. The public-address system thanked us for coming. In the Olympic spirit, it delivered the message in Mandarin, French, and English.

By the gate, there was a notice in Chinese and English, instructing spectators in how to "keep a safe, cheerful, and orderly atmosphere." The list of inappropriate deeds included "Smoking in non-smoking areas"; "Crossing the guardrail"; "Distribution in the venue of unauthorized printed materials or items for advertising, demonstrating, or fund-raising purposes"; and "Besieging the referees, athletes, or other staffs; Gambling; Affray after Drinking Alcohol."

The Olympic organizing committee had convened a dinner for foreign journalists at a roasted-duck restaurant just south of the Olympic Green. The rest of the guests were short-term visitors, scout troops of the international media invasion to come: a white-haired French sportswriter in sandals, an aristocratic Argentine-American who ran some sort of publishing concern, a volleyball player (Belgian, I thought he said) turned Olympic sports columnist, a Russian TV crew of two slouchy young men in jeans shepherded by a manager with her hair in a glossy bun. It was a full, revolving-table banquet: duck liver, fish head, lotus root, and Great Wall wine for toasting. The media center's sub-boss, Li Zhanjun, bustled around the room. He had black-dyed hair, mandatory for aging male officials, and was round and jolly and amused by the idea of seating male foreign journalists next to young female interpreters.

Beside me was Wang Hui, the director of media operations. Wang would be the spokesperson for the Beijing Olympics through the end of the Games, presiding over press briefings and calling on reporters for questions. She was in her fifties, formal but friendly, the polite face of engagement between the old, suspicious China and the equally suspicious global press.

If Wang's eyes, through the year ahead, didn't always smile along with her mouth—and in her job, no one's eyes could have—they never made an obvious lie of the smile, either. At press conferences, when she would refer to China's "friends in the media," she was able to make it sound at least like an aspiration, rather than a sour irony. Her appearance was put together, without ever being lacquered or brittle; in a moment of crisis, she might seem weary, but her equilibrium never wobbled. I was glad I had worn a sport coat.

As a parting gift, we were presented with little Fuwa pins, a set of all five Olympic mascots in a box. There certainly were a lot of mascots, I observed. "Too many," Wang said, smiling. What hostile apparatchik would chitchat with such frankness? I asked the staffer on my left if she had a favorite Fuwa. The red one, she said. Why? "I like fire."

Everybody liked fire. In the gift shop at Olympic headquarters tower, on the northwest side of the Fourth Ring, Huanhuan was the teapot in a souvenir gift shop, while his fellow mascots only rated teacups. They could have done worse. There were more than a hundred shelves of merchandise in the shop, only two of which—tucked behind a display case—offered Fu Niu Lele products for the Paralympics.

The blessing of the media center included an invitation for the foreign guests, me included, to at last see the Olympic Green proper. On the way there, morning rain and drizzle had given way to honey-colored sunlight, filtered by the smog. I was developing a helpless fondness for the dirty-afternoon glow, diffuse and shadowless. Along the Second Ring, apartment towers were getting a touchup—a thin surface of new concrete, covered with bright paint, to cover their accumulated blotches and scabs. The resurfaced ones did look better, at least at the moment. The light was kind to them.

The tour began at the Olympic Exhibition Center, not far from the Bird's Nest, on East Pole Star Road—about where JiaJing and I had tried to get onto the site. Today, media-center staff guided the tour group through a maze of corrugated, aqua-colored metal fencing to the Exhibition Center's front door. The Russians stepped through a gap in the fence with their camera to shoot an unobstructed view of the stadium. The latticework was complete now, and a translucent membrane was being installed in the gaps in the upper reaches. At dinner, the ex–volleyball player had declared it the most beautiful stadium ever built.

I would want to visit the Colosseum before signing off on that, but the Bird's Nest was more impressive, at every stage of construction, than any sports facility I'd ever seen in the United States. It was inherently huge—the capacity was to be 91,000—and the intricacy of the design emphasized the hugeness: the overall bulk dwarfed the longest ribs, the long ribs dwarfed the medium ones, the medium ones dwarfed the shorter sections, and those smallest segments still loomed over the tiny, laboring backhoes and itty-bitty people on the ground. Even against the bare expanse of the building site, it was impossible to lose the sense of scale.

Inside the Exhibition Center—which had, perhaps in tribute to the dust, a shoe buffer beside the reception desk—humans could salve their diminished sense of self by contemplating a meticulous, glowing model replica of the Bird's Nest. That was followed by a model of the Water Cube, then individual models of the National Indoor Stadium, the basketball arena, the table tennis gym, the wrestling gym . . .

In the center of the hall, a layout showed the venues in place on the Olympic grounds, connected by model roads, model lawns, and model trees. I picked out East Pole Star Road. Where the Exhibition Center would have been, there was a clump of trees. A staffer confirmed what the model said. Within months, the building around us would be demolished.

The bus moved on, to the interior of the construction site. Out on the Fourth Ring, people were snapping pictures of the Bird's Nest, as usual. We drove into the compound, down construction-site roads, around and behind the National Indoor Stadium. Through another gateway or two, we reached a parking lot and a raised observation platform for visitors.

Behind the platform was a half-installed stone plaza, planted with skinny trees. Ahead, the Bird's Nest was to the left, the Water Cube to the right. Farther around to the right were the dark-gray Indoor Stadium and the darker-gray, microchip-inspired Digital Beijing information center—which, taken together, had been much less ominous as models.

Before now, the bubble-covered surface of the Water Cube had always looked like a mildly quirky graphic design. From the platform, for the first time, the strangeness of the building had depth to it. The curve of each individual bubble showed.

The Russians went looking for a worker to talk to. Just outside the platform parking lot, a small forklift was offloading paving stones from a container trailer. The driver took a break and told the TV crew, through a media-center interpreter, that he was glad to be working on the Olympic project. How did he get to work? they asked. He took a bus. The forklift zipped up into the truck, brought out another load of stones—for the camera, and also to unload some stones. Up and back. Pallets of stones were all over the place. Our guides were eager to find us facts, whatever we could think to ask about. The stones were from Zhejiang Province, someone said. The trees between the stones were gingkos, brought in from Suzhou.

The smog and the lateness reduced the sun to a dim circle behind the Water Cube. Within a week, the viewing platform would be dismantled to make way for more construction. We got on the bus and went north, past the Olympic Village—closed to the tour by the developer, despite the Russians' best efforts—to the tennis, archery, and field hockey venues. Field hockey was another of the lightweight-steel temporary complexes, designed for a five-year lifespan. Our guide said he did not know the plan after that.

I went down inside the building and onto the field, through the player entrance. The field was covered in International Hockey

Federation-approved artificial turf. I walked out onto the ground where Olympic medals would be contested. Stray tufts of colored fake grass had migrated from the sideline onto the green playing field, and there were puddles from the rain. A cloud of flying insects flitted all around me—gnats or midges, I thought for a moment.

They weren't gnats. They were mosquitoes—Beijing's durable, urban, hard-biting mosquitoes. The cloud trailed me off the field. Tennis and archery, I'd already seen. I waved good-bye to the tour group and hurried off toward the main road. The mosquitoes paced me like a wing of fighter planes escorting a blundering jetliner through restricted airspace, all the way out.

11.

进步 Progress

Change and urban improvement had finally reached even the backwater of Outer Dongzhimen Side Street. One day in the middle of October, I heard the rattling of chainsaws, and looked across the street to see a crew taking down the trees on the overgrown vacant lot—full, mature trees, the last trace of whatever neighborhood had been there before. The logs were piled high and trucked out.

The worry this raised was counterbalanced by a thrill: we were about to be part of something bygone. The price of progress is well recorded, but the dividend of progress is nostalgia. Beijing, devouring itself, was a great city for souvenirs. Weekends at the Panjiayuan flea market, you could buy posters of the old revolution, cheap. And old Mao buttons and statues, but also apolitical detritus: old cameras, old eyeglasses, old housewares, collected and speculated into curios of someone's idea of the past. (I liked old trays of Chinese printers' type, myself.)

East and south of the Drum Tower, on a very handsome and important alley, there was a T-shirt shop called Plastered that specialized in a sort of anticipatory retro. There were shirts with red ovals reading "1.20," the discontinued rate sticker from the discontinued low-end Xiali taxicabs. In the old days (last year?), I had ridden in Xiali cabs. I went looking for shirts with the iconic blue-and-white image of Beijing's Line 2 subway ticket—which a few weeks before had become the former subway ticket, replaced by a four-color design, though still on paper. They were out of stock in my size. It seemed to me that they were giving too much space to a new line of Olympic-inspired sports-themed shirts, and I caught myself brooding that the shop wasn't as good as it used to be, before.

The nice alley with the T-shirt shop was called Nanluogu Xiang, in a neighborhood of hutongs that had been not demolished but renovated. "Preserved" is not quite the word. The low courtyard houses lining the way were now coffee shops and boutiques, their crumbling gray bricks replaced with clean-edged new ones. The paving underfoot was flat and true; the alley had become a raceway for bicycles, electric bicycles, and hutong-tour tricycle rickshaws.

Outer Dongzhimen Side Street had been evolving at its own pace, by its own logic. The bicycle shop had disappeared at some point. The poultry-slaughtering stall, under threat of avian flu, replaced its wire pens with tubs of water and started slaughtering carp instead. Then it became a restaurant selling food on skewers—part of an alley-wide fad for skewers. At the peak, at least eight stalls were offering either grilled skewers, known as *chuan'r*, or stewed ones, called *mala tang*, served with beer at scavenged-looking alleyside tables.

But now the alley was in professional hands. The repaving project in front of the corner store was spreading up the street: a crew set to work breaking up the pavement in front of the shops, leveling the dirt margins, and laying curbstones. Then, with mallets and string, they started installing the pavement blocks for a sidewalk. Or two sidewalks, one on each side, as if Outer Dongzhimen Side Street were a real thoroughfare. They were the standard-issue new municipal sidewalk, made of dark-gray blocks, with a row of larger, textured yellow ones down the middle to guide the disabled.

The crew worked in sections, here and there, squeezing the sidewalk as well as they could. The cargo tricycles and mounds of stuff by the alley wall were cleared aside to make way for the new surface. Then they were moved right back. At dusk, a *chuan'r* vendor set up his charcoal burner on the freshly laid pavement, posting a menu on the wall behind.

Finally, with the other obstacles overcome, the sidewalk reached the back end of the defunct minibus turned fruit stand that marked the end of the retail strip. Crates of fruit were piled against it, as high as the windows. I had been waiting to see what would give: Was progress a resistible force, after all? Or was the bus, against appearances, a movable object?

The next morning, the bus was hunkered down a few yards up the alley from its usual hunkering spot. So there was the answer. One answer, anyway. By afternoon, the bus had resumed its old position. The sidewalk was under its wheels. If you had just arrived, you would never know it had budged.

Christmas was coming, and the Chinese were perfectly willing to observe it. The secular, commercial Christmas, ritually denounced by would-be Puritans in the United States every year, had established itself in Beijing. Who doesn't welcome an occasion to decorate a shopping mall? In the new mall where the Japanese supermarket used to be, the checkers wore headbands with stuffed antlers on them. The big Manchurian restaurant nearby displayed a stuffed and mounted young deer, red bow between its little antlers, harnessed with tinsel to a cart full of wrapped gifts.

Chinese people were open-minded about festivities, because the official calendar of celebrations was endlessly being revised. In November, the news reported a government plan to celebrate three pre-revolutionary traditional festivals—Tomb-Sweeping Day, the Mid-Autumn Festival, and the Dragon Boat Festival—as legal holidays in 2008, while chopping the weeklong Labor Day break to one day.

At the Liangma Flower Market, in a riot of low-end ornaments and tinsel, Santa decorations were accompanied by a Golliwog blackface doll swinging on a swing. I bought a few batches of colored balls and ornaments, a string of white lights, and some sort of short-needled evergreen—a spruce or fir—a bit taller than waist-high. The vendor agreed to trade the plastic pot for a blue ceramic one and deliver it later. It arrived repotted at a crooked angle, still in its original hard clayey soil, its needles filling the apartment with the smell of cigarette smoke from the delivery van. Along with the Christmas decorations, I hung from its branches a set of charms depicting the five Fuwa, meant to be dangled from cell phones.

The Olympics were eight months away. The Yuyang Hotel, a high-rise just east of Hujiauyuan, was being gutted so it could be renovated before then. A skin of ice, or possibly scum that looked like ice, was on the Liangma River. Heavy olive quilts were going up over the doorways of the markets to keep out the cold. Tall green-fabric wind breaks went up on frames on the north side of the city's trees; green slipcovers went over the roadside hedges. My heel began to crack open from the dryness.

On the road by the bus depot, west of our apartment, construction fencing was up and demolition workers were well along with the *chai*-ing. Along the Third Ring, a crew with a cherry-picker was hanging ornament balls and tinsel on tall evergreens in planters; the trees had arrived by the truckload, roots in balls, a week before. Farther down, toward the Central Business District, a low-rise building was being demolished, leaving a scabby line along the face of the newer tower behind it, where the roof of the other building had touched it. The narrow alley between the two buildings was being peeled open.

The two halves of the CCTV building—each one a thick, leaning tower—had reached their full height and then spread sideways, cantilevering toward each other. Up in the sky, orange sparks rained into space as workers closed the loop, one thin joint at a time. Glass skin was rising up the building's legs.

A ridged metal façade was creeping up the new skyscraper across the way—the China World Trade Center Tower Three, its prodigious shaft facing the vertical opening of the CCTV building over the Third Ring in a colossal Freudian standoff. It was going to be 1,000 feet tall, the tallest building in Beijing, and in the architectural furor, hardly anyone paid any attention to it at all.

In the lobby of some friends' new apartment building, where a Christmas party was being held to recruit buyers, we ran into a hired Mao impersonator, part of the entertainment. The impersonator had blackened hair and a high hairline and otherwise looked nothing at all like Mao. He posed with us for a picture, unsmiling, in front of a Christmas tree.

New, empty flowerpots lined the streets leading north to the Olympic Green. According to plan, there would be 30 million of them by the Olympics, and with flowers. It was December 1, a day the city government had announced on posters as a cockroach-elimination day; people had been calling in to the radio to share their methods of killing roaches.

The Good Luck games, working their way up from the more obscure events and venues, had finally reached the main Olympic Green, with gymnastics in the National Indoor Stadium. For this, a sport China was good at, in a major Olympic arena, the public was coming out. The security checkpoints were overwhelmed; the crowd backed up on the south side of the building. It was long past sundown, and there were no lights on the surrounding grounds yet. The footing was lumpy dirt, covered with netting that had been weighted down with chunks of concrete and broken paving blocks. Christina and I had left Mack at home with the ayi and come with another couple. Volunteers steered our part of the crowd around to the east entrance, where the backup was even worse. Wire fences held the crowd back. Volunteers in headsets yelled conflicting instructions.

As the six-o'clock start time approached, after a long spell of no movement at all, something suddenly gave way. The crowd crushed forward; people went yelling and stumbling over the uneven ground, kicking up billows of dirt in the dark. It was verging on a stampede, bodies on bodies, with no way to stop moving or change direction. Then, as the mass surged into the glow of the building lights, the frenzy subsided. The volunteers herded men and women into separate security lines. Calm was restored.

Inside, operations were still at less than Olympic levels of readiness. The concession stand was offering popcorn, cooked one bag at a time in a single microwave, as customers piled up to wait. The bathrooms were furnished with Chinese-style squat toilets. Spectators had been equipped with inflatable thundersticks, sponsored by Crocs. Crocs was heavily invested in Good Luck Beijing.

Our seats were up on the end, in a section that was empty when we arrived. As we settled in, an army of boys and young men showed up—all of them slightly built, most of them wearing baggy jackets. Some of the jackets had a Chinese flag on them and the logo of Li Ning sportswear, the company started by the Chinese gold-medal gymnast of that name. One of the boys, finding himself in the wrong row, nonchalantly vaulted himself over the seatbacks. Somehow, the tickets I had bought at the box office were in the midst of the national gymnastics program. "Only 180 degrees," one youth said, watching someone do a superficially impressive half-spin below. "Boring."

The gymnasts were effusive, piping up with *"Jia you!"* cheers for the Chinese, but also applauding an American's "I Love Rock 'n' Roll" floor routine. The American was named Chellsie Memmel, and she ended up with the bronze. A gymnast named Jiang Yuyuan had won the women's all-around the previous morning—I had jotted in my notebook that she looked about eight years old—but tonight, in front of the adoring crowd, she powered herself out of bounds on the tumbling floor. China's Cheng Fei won the floor gold, and took gold in the vault as well. Two nights later, she would win the balance beam, as China came away with one-third of all the available gymnastics medals.

A teenager next to us broke down his predictions for the men's pommel horse. Lu Bo of China would do well, he said. He was in a position to know, because he was Lu Bo's roommate. But a different Lu, Lu Bin, would get first place for sure. Lu Bin won the pommel horse. Lu Bo was fifth.

The pollution rolled in, thicker and thicker, the daylight getting weaker even as it got shorter. Beijingers were burning coal against the chill. I came down with a racking cough and fever, and an expat clinic took a chest X-ray and sent me off with something like two weeks' worth of hydrocodone. They were thorough about medication in the expat places. Little Mack came down with a wheezing cough of his own, and the doctor prescribed two steroids and a broncho-dilator. None of those were of much use for an infant, according to drug studies online. Two weeks after the cough subsided, he started coughing again.

On Christmas Eve, utter filth hung in the air. English-language radio instruction in our cab explained the concept of knock-knock jokes—"Mary who?" "Merry Christmas"—and then discussed the question of whether or not there were pawnshops in the West. The cabbie offered a "Thank you" and "Merry Christmas" in English at the end of the ride.

The official blue-sky count for the year was at 244 days, one short of the target of 245, but it had been stuck there since the middle of the month, as the days got darker and dirtier. The sun on Christmas morning was a dull tangerine. The gray carried on to Boxing Day, and the next day was grayer still. On Outer Dongzhimen Street, the Agricultural Exhibition Center—three long blocks away—was invisible; the landscape of the Third Ring was a blur. The official pollution reading was 500, the top of the scale, apocalypse.

There would be no sun the next morning at all: the morning of the 28th was lightless, with snow falling unseen through the clotted air, wetting the pavement. Then, at last, the wind came: pushing debris up the alley, tossing a traffic cone around in front of the English school, and throwing grit in my face. Eventually, the sun emerged. It would take another day of wind to bring the pollution down to the legal blue-sky threshold, but the wind obliged. The 30th was spectacular, the mountains in view. The 31st brought the blue-sky count to 246. The last year before the Olympics was done, and the air quality had exceeded expectations.

12.

晴空 Clear Sky

C utting Wind Combs Bones," the weather headline on the
back page of the *Beijing News* said, in Chinese. "New Year
Enters Sternly." Cranes were lit against the evening sky,
and the stars were out. This was 2008.

To mark the occasion, we'd hung a new poster over the couch. It
was a photo of a sixteen-story Beijing apartment tower, green and
white, its geometry irregularly dotted and checkered with the markings of actual life: varied models of air conditioners, mismatched
windows, laundry up and drying. We chose it because it seemed to
epitomize the shabby-but-not-squalid Beijing, the unimproved city
that we'd arrived into.

Half attentively, I studied the background, trying to place the
general area in the city of millions. The towers behind it were hope-
lessly generic. In the lower right was a gas station with no distinctive
features. I knew an apartment tower next to a gas station. No.

Something clicked. I knew this apartment tower next to this gas station. It was on Xinyuan South Road, just east of where it meets Xindong Road, a short offset block from the eastern mouth of Outer Dongzhimen Side Street. I could walk there. I had walked there. This was the route home from Chinese school. This was the way we went to go to the tailor. The trees were the trees the pesticide crew had been hosing down. The Platonic image of Beijing was where we lived.

Two days later, I went looking for it. The weather was merciful; light reverberated through clear air. The afternoon sun made plain buildings' surfaces bright and sharp, and glowed through the glassed-in balconies on their corners. A crew of workers with shovels was out on the frozen Liangma River; the sunlight fell on the bare, drooping branches of the willows on the bank. Firemen were out jogging. A man slept in the bed of his cargo tricycle on the bridge. Four people rode by on a single motor scooter. I found the building, the easternmost of a set of three, almost as it was on the poster. The green and white of the façade had been intensified with new paint; the towers had already gotten their Olympic facelift.

The other kind of Olympic treatment was still spreading down the opposite side of the neighborhood. The east side of the street leading away from it was all a rubble field now; the west side was painted with *chai* characters, marking it for destruction, but it was still standing. Farther west was even more expansive rubble, in front of the string of apartment complexes called Moma.

Moma was a still-evolving monument to the compressed time-table of Beijing architecture: its first towers in the vulgar mode of early Chinese prosperity, with curving mint-tinted windows; then, later, politely modernist dark-gray ones; then a more flashy modernism, with copper highlights. Finally, under construction in the newest position, would come a state-of-the-art, green-technology-equipped cluster of buildings called the Linked Hybrid, a must-see destination for the architectural critics who were descending on the city in advance of the Olympics. The buildings would have flat, cutout-looking faces, and their unifying gimmick would be a series of sky-bridges connecting them all—not an unusual feature of Beijing buildings, but evidently exciting to the rest of the world, or at least the architecture writers of the rest of the world.

Trees were still standing in the wreckage. Chinese slogans had been stenciled repeatedly on the metal fences: "Remaking the environment benefits the people," "Safe demolition and relocation depends on everyone," "The Olympics connects you, me, and him." Opposite Moma, there was a closed restaurant, with a sign in English identifying it as "Top Chef Snacks & take-away." On the north side of the stripped interior, a 2007 calendar was still hanging, with a picture on it of Nini, the green Fuwa, advertising beer. Plates were stacked on the floor, and a paper Chinese flag was taped to the inside of the glass door, flying from a little plastic stick.

The Kirov Ballet was performing at the new National Grand Theater, or the National Center for the Performing Arts, or the National Opera Hall—the facility had just opened in December, after long construction delays, and no one had settled on what to call the building or its sub-parts in English. Mostly people were calling it the Egg: a titanium-paneled dome, 150 feet high, off Tian'anmen Square beside the Great Hall of the People.

Literally, the Mandarin nickname was "The Boiled Egg," which was not quite right. It was shaped more like the contents of a fresh, raw egg, with the wide, bulging dome as the yolk and a broad moat as the puddle of egg white.

Still, the point was, the Egg was one of the first pieces of Beijing's international trophy architecture to have actually been completed, and Chinese people were unimpressed. The project had been one more target for the Internet mobs; its French architect, Paul Andreu, had designed the new terminal at Charles de Gaulle Airport, which collapsed in 2004, in the middle of the Egg's construction. Not only was the design alien, unattractive, and (thanks to the moat and the underground entrance) reckless about feng shui, it was dangerous.

After more slowdowns and cost overruns, no one seemed worried anymore that the dome would cave in. That still left the aesthetic question. One line of criticism was that the Egg was insensitive to its surrounding context—a reasonable-sounding thing to say about an immense, shiny dome, until you looked next door and saw the brooding rectangular mass of the Great Hall of the People. The edge of Tian'anmen Square was no place for welcoming, human-scaled architecture.

But if its size did seem appropriate, that still didn't mean the big architectural idea of the Egg was a particularly good idea, or an interesting one. The Egg was conceptually and actually hollow: three separate theater buildings with a cover plopped over them, like dishes on a hospital lunch tray.

The sunken entrance was on the north side. The trees outside were festooned with strings of lights, with electrical cords roping them all together. The face of the entrance was a dark red, with gold characters on it—a commonplace treatment, and a sign of things to come. The passageway under the water had dark sludge on the glass ceiling, ambient Beijing dust that had already settled as silt to the bottom of the moat.

Once inside, there was no sign of the stark simplicity of the outer dome. The decorating of the Egg was scrambled. Here, around the concourses of the opera hall, were bronze-toned screens resembling roll-down storefront security gates; over there were stairways of white marble wrapped around white-marble elevator shafts, bright and sarcophageal, like phone booths for the dead. There were dim burgundy-colored passageways—dim, dim, dim—the lighting feeble, energy-conscious, and erratically colored. Far overhead, the inner surface of the dome was paneled in wooden slats. The symbols marking the bathrooms were so elongated and stylized as to be unrecognizable. The interior of the theater was in medium-brown wood with red web-weave seats, the balcony facings covered with fields of cutout dots lit from within.

Our row of the balcony was already occupied. The usher checked the tickets, pointed the way to the full seats, and left us to sort it out.

Down in the orchestra seats, a woman was wearing leather pants and a dowdy striped sweater. The pants were baggy, their cut and fit at odds with the whole idea of leather pants. This was in keeping with the Egg itself. We were in the sleekest and newest theater in the capital, with a crowd that could afford expensive tickets, and there was no sense that anyone agreed on what dressing up might entail. It was not like an American crowd, where clashing dress standards marked clashing ideas about fashion and formality. Rather, there was not even a language for taste. Prosperity and consumerism had come up all at once, with no historical context for style. How could you have seventies or eighties retro where the seventies and eighties hadn't happened?

Entire aesthetic categories failed to translate. The idea, for instance, of bourgeois people wearing work clothes as a class-status antisignifier, of hipsters in work boots and utility pants, was inexpressibly alien. Even workingmen didn't wear work clothes. Waist-deep in a pit, a pick-wielding laborer might wear slacks and a sweater and a floppy knit hat with earflaps.

And so, confronted with a plain metal dome, people couldn't help but suspect that a fancy foreign architect might be trying to put one over on them. The hodgepodge of materials inside was meant by the builders to be reassuring: Look at all the different kinds of stone and wood and metal we spent our money on. Rumor had it that something similar was in the works for the CCTV building—that having agreed to the crazy-angled loop of a structure, the career bureaucrats of the national television authority were planning to fill it with the things they understood, so that they would float high above the New Beijing in offices trimmed with heavy marble and dark, thickly ornamented wood.

Getting rid of the Christmas tree was a challenge. Things did not have the courtesy to disappear once you tried to dispose of them, the way they would in America. Instead, they entered a chain of review, as other people tried to extract value from them—not far-off strangers at scrap yards and recycling stations, but people right around you.

First came the ayi. To help care for the baby, we had hired a new ayi, full-time, an enterprising young woman named Chen Yanqun from rural Sichuan Province, who divided her time among child care, cleaning, and cooking lunch. She herself was one of eleven children, and she would tell Christina anecdotes about her upbringing: when she was six years old, say, an older sister had given her a real pair of pants; till then, all her clothes had been pieced together out of dishrags. So the ayi would always double-check: Had we meant to throw this or that away?

Then Wang Jiashui, the cargo-tricycle man by the gate, would review the leavings. Beyond his scrap-collecting work, or as an outgrowth of it, Wang acted as an unofficial ombudsman for the apartment compound. As the gatehouse guards got younger and more incompetent over time, he took it upon himself to announce when packages had arrived, or to explain when the water service might come back on. Meanwhile, he would gather and bundle anything that might make saleable cargo. After that would come the actual garbage collectors, in orange coveralls, who would go through what remained in the bins, separating the still somehow recyclable from the tiny remaining fraction of actually worthless refuse.

The tree was an embarrassment. We had bought it only a month before, and it had been delivered, and now we were done with it? Chen Yanqun was flummoxed. Admittedly, it was dropping needles and failing to thrive in its clayey old soil, but still, it was a whole tree, and in a pot. She referred the problem to Wang Jiashui, and he told her to have us put the tree on the landing. I dragged it out to the stairwell, scattering needles in my wake. There were needles on top of the door latch box when I came back in. The next morning, the tree was gone.

Olympic tourists would be upon the city in eight months. By then, Big Mack planned to be in the hotel business. Big Mack was perpetually starting something or other, in tribute to the city's expanding possibilities; over time, I had gotten used to being asked for advice about what might be a good name for a cell-phone media company, or for a women's-wear brand. Now, with friends, he had secured a lease on a courtyard house, down a side lane in Xisi in Xicheng District, the western part of the ancient city center. The idea was to renovate it into a boutique hotel for foreigners.

Amid the beige haze of a cold morning, the neighborhood's distinguishing feature, the seven-hundred-year-old White Pagoda Temple, poked above the buildings out across the main avenue. Xicheng was less of a destination than its eastern counterpart, Dongcheng; its oldness not quite as layered with self-awareness. In the alley itself, there wasn't much to see. No coffee shops or crafts dealers had put out windows here yet. Any people who were out were on their own business. This was Old Beijing at its most drab and introverted: the plain gray walls, gray pavement underfoot, all its centuries of life and history somewhere behind a surface as monotonous as a cinder-block basement. It called for imagination.

Down the alley was a recessed set of double doors, painted red with gold trim and shaded by an ornate polychrome overhang. I had been preparing for decay, heritage sadly left to crumble. Instead, Mack opened the doors onto a tidy entrance court, like an open-air hallway, framed by painted latticework. Straight ahead, in a sort of viewing niche, were two pillar-shaped decorative stones, one tall and one squat. Along the left wall, under ruffled, multicolored eaves, were two doorways, dark red, trimmed in mint green and gold. Above the nearer doorway was a panel with a rustic landscape on it, trees by the water with little boats in the middle distance.

The house was an *er jin*, Mack said, a compound with two main courtyards. It had not been occupied lately, but the owner had gotten it painted in the elaborate, old-fashioned mode. The front courtyard was surrounded by a colonnade, its open crossbeams covered with interlocking designs: gold over blue, green twining with teal, teal under gold. Pink-on-pink blossoms adorned the blocks atop the supporting pillars; green-and-red latticework filled in the sides. And that was before the eye made it down to the fan-shaped blind windows, with pictures painted on their backs, or the rails and lattices at knee level, or the gateways framed by big golden characters.

Some part of the renovation would mean paring back the Chinese version of antique style into something more simple. What did I think of the paint job as it was? Mack wanted to know. In other words: What would I, as a foreign visitor, prefer a traditional Chinese courtyard to look like? A less minty shade of green would be good, I allowed. Or maybe it might be a good idea to knock out the green entirely, to replace one-third of the dominant mint-gold-red scheme with something more subdued, like black. Or bare wood. Bare wood with red and gold would look old-fashioned for sure.

At the very front of the courtyard was the largest of the buildings, with a steeply pitched roof. Inside, it had shabby flooring and a dropped ceiling, with a gold-highlighted molding and compact fluorescent bulbs poking out of can lights. Mack planned to tear out the whole thing up to the rafters, opening up a space that might even be high enough for a loft. They could put a kitchen in at one end and serve coffee.

The guest rooms would be on the second courtyard, in the rear. From the doorway of the front building, you could look straight down the main axis of the house, across the first courtyard, through a connecting doorway, across the rear court, and into the doorway of the rearmost building. Against the back wall was a tall potted plant, scruffy but green.

An old, thick jujube tree grew up out of the rear court, and a few dates were still scattered on the paving stones. The rooms around it would all need work: a ruinous kitchen had to go; the floors stepped up and down irregularly; a wall would have to be recentered. At the very rear were the bathrooms—narrow afterthoughts, tacked on outside the back door a few centuries after the rest of the house had been laid out. To contemplate the awkwardness of them was to feel the weight of history. The toilets were the squatting kind, and each bathroom was barely even wide enough for that. A sloping glass roof offered dirty sunlight through bamboo leaves, and the promise of frigid winter mornings—and, at the moment, a glass-bottomed view of a neighborhood cat strolling overhead. A narrow bathtub could fit, maybe, sideways, but you'd have to step on the toilet seat to get into it. Indoor plumbing was not traditional. Later, when a work crew dug up the courtyard, they would discover that there were no real drainpipes leading away from the toilets, only skinny water pipes.

The bathroom, I advised Big Mack, was where the Western traveler would prefer that all signs of the archaic and unfamiliar be suppressed. The fixtures need not be luxury brands, but they would have to be reassuring and sturdy. Not the rattling Chinese-made modern toilets in our own apartment. Out in the courtyard were more of the marks of the everyday. Below the picturesque tiled roofline, cables sagged haphazardly, slung from one building to the next. A jumble of air-conditioning units and rusting electrical boxes stood out in the open. The hardware would need to go.

The goal was a combination of clean ancient and clean modern, with art involved. Mack wanted some sort of large artwork in the front court, to set the tone—a tall contemporary vase, maybe, or a sculpture. We could see where it would go, by the colonnade, where foreign visitors would stroll by it with their morning coffee. Eventually, he would settle on the idea of an outsized lantern: the hotel would be the Lantern Courtyard. The big front building would visually counterbalance it. From where we were standing, its roof rose so steeply that it blocked out the low dusty haze. A pigeon flew past against the part of the sky that we could see, which was blue.

V.

烟花 FIREWORKS

13.

春节 New Year

In the late middle of January, a whitish tent appeared by the Liangma River, near the Pizza Hut. A banner on it announced *yan hua*—"smoke flowers," or fireworks. Checking the banner against the dictionary on my smartphone, I transposed the words and called up an entry for *hua yan guan*, meaning "girlie opium den." The dictionary was always coming up with surprisingly particular phrases ("to remain poor and clean at retirement [of officials]," "obstruction from middle-level cadres"), but the revolution had not reversed itself quite that much. Two days later, another tent appeared, farther east along the river. Another Spring Festival, or Chinese New Year, was nigh.

Spring Festival was something of a misnomer. The river was frozen and covered with a thin coat of dirty snow. A vicious wind pulled smoke across the alley.

This was the peak season for alcohol and tobacco sales. Beijingers marked the New Year by expressing their gratitude and friendship toward their bosses, business contacts, and government officials— premium liquor and expensive cigarettes being the acknowledged signs of appreciation. Right after the holiday, there would be a thriving resale market, as the officials unloaded the surplus tribute they couldn't consume. A friend had told a story, too well sourced to be apocryphal, of someone who'd bought a secondhand carton of cigarettes after one Chinese New Year and opened it to find it stuffed with hundred-yuan bills—a bribe that had gone unnoticed in the annual bounty.

In the liquor trade, China's traditional past trickled into the boomtime future, by way of the industrial present. A club that specialized in Chinese culture tours had arranged a visit for foreigners to the Niulanshan Distillery. Niulanshan had been in business since 1952, and it specialized in the clear liquor called *erguotou*, a sorghum-based, twice-distilled version of *baijiu*, white liquor, the standard Chinese drink—a national constant, like scotch in Scotland, slivovitz in the Czech Republic, or ouzo in Greece. Patriotic alcoholic drinks are usually acquired tastes; their being tough to swallow adds to the national mystique. But the flavor of *baijiu* might have been the single most insurmountable thing to the foreign palate in all of China. Flavor profiles varied, but a bottle I'd bought at the airport was typical: it began with a nose-filling, cloying floral aroma like that of fabric softener, then washed through the mouth like smoky kerosene, leaving in its trail the stinging, acrid taste of the vomit after a vodka binge.

The plant employed 1,500 people, working eight-hour days, with two days off each month. With the holidays coming, there were shifts round the clock. Workers in bright-blue coveralls carried burlap packages of liquor bottles or shoveled steaming piles of mash around the floor. The liquor came in two varieties, light fragrance and heavy fragrance. The light was fermented for thirty days, in neat ceramic-lined tanks set in the floor. The heavy went for forty-five days in pits lined with mud. At a tasting in an unheated room, I tried to compare the two, but the little cups got jumbled and I was loath to keep nipping until I tasted the difference.

Five bottling lines were going at once, in parallel. Newly filled bottles would come off a filling machine, and a woman would set a loose cap on top of each one, by hand. Nearly all the line workers were women, with white bonnets over their hair. Another woman would pick up each bottle, stick the top into a cap-tightening machine, and return it to the conveyor. The next would check the volume against an illuminated panel as it traveled by. Then someone would pick up the bottle, wipe it dry with cardboard, put it back. Pick up the bottle, stick on a label, put it back. The nearer lines were handling little green flask-shaped bottles, with gold-on-red labels; farther back, the bottles were tall and colorless. Pick up the bottle, put it in a foam-netting sleeve, put it back, and then on out through a hole in the wall, to where crews of men were loading them into cartons. There were something like a hundred people in this one bottling section, hands moving nonstop, none of them doing anything that couldn't have been done by machinery.

The Water Cube, pearly white in the sun, was ready for the press, or ready enough. The ethylene-tetrafluoroethylene membrane bubble wall bulged out against a blue sky and high cirrus clouds. Dark streaks of dirt ran down the faces of the bubbles.

Inside, there was a blissful swimming-pool warmth to the air. The interior surfaces were clean and white, with attractive circle patterns on them. Television camera crews clustered by the railing overlooking the main swimming pool, trying to secure the best access they could get. Gradually, it dawned on them that the press was free to roam one whole side of the hall, with unprecedented ease of movement. A reporter for the Xinhua News Agency interviewed me about what I thought of the building. Afterward, I asked him what he thought. He said he thought the interior of the building looked ordinary.

That seemed a bit jaded. The struts of the bubble framework made dramatic patterns overhead; the spectator seats were either blue or white, the frequency of each color shifting from all blue in the bottom rows through a pixelated middle to all white at the top. The press handout said that the project had been financed by donations from overseas Chinese, at a total cost of 830 million yuan, or about $110 million; later the declared figure would end up above the 1 billion yuan mark. It was something to look at while officials, down on the pool deck, delivered lengthy remarks in untranslated Mandarin. The fittings on the springboards were ivory; the panels on the diving towers were mottled greenish-white. The cold blue-tinted interior light was unkind to the differences in the whites. There was a presentation of a big gold-toned key, not the least bit bubble-themed, with a red tassel hanging off it. The dignitaries stooped to ceremonially touch the pool water.

Then the officials were turned loose in the stands for chaotic interview scrums. The press—the usual Olympics-beat foreign and local reporters, now joined by lead-news correspondents—closed in around the head of construction, Yi Zhun. How many people were killed in construction? Was it true ten people had died building the Bird's Nest? That was a "rumor," Yi said. How many bubbles were there in the building's exterior? More than 3,000. You could see brown dirt streaks through the roof from below; the press had noticed the dirt; the dirt was a story. How much of a challenge was it to clean this? Why were the Australian architects not at the ceremony? "I don't know. They should be here." What about the reported deaths? "I personally think it must be rumor."

Another scrum, with another official, more on the dirt. "It will be totally clean. . . . To clean the whole façade will take a week." When was the last time it was cleaned? "About three weeks ago." Who gets the design credit? What are the safety standards? Why are there cracks on the diving boards? What about feng shui? Feng shui was "sort of" considered, but they had not consulted a feng shui expert. An answer that would neither satisfy nor dissatisfy anyone.

Away from Beijing, by the end of January, China was a disaster zone. Blizzards had struck the center and south of the country, killing dozens, causing fuel shortages and blackouts, and shutting down the national transportation system while more than 100 million people were trying to travel for the Chinese New Year's holiday. The vaccines for Mack's scheduled immunizations were stuck in transit from Hong Kong; television was full of images of rescuers from the People's Liberation Army digging through the snowdrifts. Olympic meteorological officials assured alarmed reporters that "we have very little probability of extreme weather conditions during the Games."

The capital, however, was sunny and almost tranquil—but for the early arrival of New Year's fireworks. At odd hours of the day or night, there would be a whiz, squeal, and bang, accompanied by delighted screams of children. A power shovel had appeared on the vacant lot across from our apartment, and a team of laborers set to work with some sort of drilling machine, a tall metal screw that sent brown water gushing from the ground.

Five days before the New Year, I visited the headquarters of

Chinese Central Television, still across town from the looping CCTV building. Every year, CCTV broadcasts a live show, the Spring Festival Gala, a variety program that puts the ratings boasts of the Oscars and the Super Bowl in humbling perspective: every year, more or less everyone with a television in China watches the CCTV Gala—meaning, by the most conservative estimates, more than twice as many people as have ever watched an American TV broadcast. It certifies new stars and affirms old ones; its comedy sketches launch national catchphrases—including the original appearance of the slogan *"Beijing Huanying Ni,"* in a bit in which migrant workers were welcomed to the capital in ever more formal terms.

"The Gala usually is four hours and twenty minutes long," Chen Linchun, that year's director, said in Chinese. Pan Deng, a part-time researcher I'd hired who happened to work for CCTV's international station, helped with translation. There would be roughly two and a half hours of comedy, Chen said, an hour for song and dance, and about another hour for interactive programs with the audience. There were no commercial breaks; instead, advertisers would pay millions of dollars for passing mentions by the hosts and placements in sketches.

This would be CCTV's twenty-seventh Gala, and Chen's first turn as the lead director. According to plan, it would be the final edition to be broadcast from the old CCTV campus; the 2009 show would move into the brand-new CCTV building. "I think I will definitely miss this place," Chen said.

The Gala was the definition of mass entertainment. "The Gala cannot be done in a Westernized way," Chen said. "It must have a strong Chinese flavor. It is a Chinese tradition that a whole family stay together and wait for the New Year to come." So the whole thing had to be rigorously structured. The comedy bits, Chen said, were scripted to follow a pace modeled on that of "the famous American comedian Charlie Chaplin": "We require our comedy programs, which are usually twelve minutes long, to have the same number of laughing points as his movies."

The pop group S.H.E. and Taiwanese singer Jay Chou would be performing, Chen said, as would veterans with more than twenty Galas to their credit: comedian Zhao Benshan and folksinger Peng Liyun, the wife of Politburo member Xi Jinping. (A month later, Xi would be named vice president of China.) The budget was a relatively low 20 million yuan, or about $3 million—since the cost of paying performers was minimal. "This is the program with the highest audience rating in China," Chen said. "If you don't get a chance to perform in the Spring Gala, then you will be forgotten by everyone in several years."

The Gala would go through a full dress rehearsal, which would be taped. The night of the live broadcast, the tape would be kept running, so that in the event of an on-air gaffe or other disruption, the producers could switch seamlessly to the canned version. There would be no way to tell the difference between the live event and the taped one.

The Gala stage was set up in the largest studio, a round auditorium covering more that 10,000 square feet. The circular hallway around it was serving as one large dressing room; child performers wandered around and dancers applied their makeup. Some of the dancers, from the military's performing-arts program, were half changed between warm-up wear and their People's Liberation Army uniforms.

A half-moon-shaped platform alternately rose above and sank below the stage. Little white starry lights shone against dark backgrounds off toward the wings. Rain effects and fountains came on and off. There were ten pillars covered with LED screens, with swirling patterns on them. A test pattern played on a video screen on the back wall, then gave way to images of tumbling flowers, followed by the character for "spring."

An Olympic torch—the curving silver official Beijing 2008 torch design—was being tested onstage. On cue, it shot sparks, and one of the codirectors caught the sparks on a sheaf of paper. The paper began to burn, which was not supposed to happen. This was a cold pyrotechnic effect. The director stomped it out, the torch underwent adjustment, and they tried again. The fire stayed where it was supposed to be.

New Year's Eve would be February 6. The Year of the Pig would give way to the Year of the Rat, the beginning of a new twelve-year cycle. Down at the corner market, two days before that, I stopped at another newly installed fireworks stand. The merchandise was out on a table on the sidewalk, with tall boxed pyrotechnics displays at either end, and littler explosives in the middle. The bigger boxes were priced in the hundreds of yuan. I fought off the clerk's effort to upsell me and picked out a box for 180 yuan, a knee-high block with a single fuse. Then I grabbed some add-ons: little cardboard tanks with missiles on them, extra-long sparklers, brightly wrapped cardboard tubes.

Fireworks had been subject to off-and-on bans in the past, but for 2008 it was open season. By the night of February 5, the alley smelled of gunpowder. A volley of explosions sounded after nine p.m.; then, after midnight, another barrage went off on Outer Dongzhimen Street. I could see colored sparks reflected in the building windows out there. Deeper in the night, the explosions got louder.

By the sixth, the explosions were going on all day. The sound carried inside the windowless bathroom while I took a shower. The shredded red remains of firecrackers lay at the foot of a street sign declaring a no-firecracker zone near the embassies.

After nightfall, there was smoke inside the apartment. We dressed Mack in his Chinese inheritance, one of the thick padded jackets from the Henan relatives, bundled him under a matching quilt in his stroller, and set out for a walk. Skyrockets were flying everywhere, squeaking and trailing brushes of sparks behind the Heaven Beyond Heaven restaurant in the main Hujiayuan compound, down by the alley mouth. The fireworks sellers stood at their table outside the market, heads tilted up, watching the soaring merchandise, with banks of fire extinguishers at the ready. At the China National Offshore Oil Company building, the guards were playing with sparklers. Little bursts of sparks were going off, and pyrotechnics suitable for a municipal Fourth of July show. Eventually, as we rolled Mack through the din and flash and smoke, he fell asleep.

We went down by the riverside to light our own load of fireworks. There was a breeze, and the lighter we had would barely work. We started with the long, droopy sparklers, which threw off the sparks loosely, nothing like the tight, contained sizzle of American sparklers. We moved away from Mack's stroller, to make sure we didn't light the handmade quilt. There was no reason to think that the Henan relatives' trousseau would be fireproof. Up the riverbank, on the roadside by the Pizza Hut, two women were setting paper on fire, in the absence of gunpowder products. I took a burning sparkler and used it to light the fuse of one of the cardboard tubes, gripping the tube by the other end, pointing it away from me.

Years ago, in my middle childhood, my Uncle Ray once visited from California bearing a whole suitcase full of fireworks. (I assume he traveled by plane.) These would have been wholly illegal in Maryland, a sparklers-only state, and my parents were usually inclined to abide by laws in general and safety laws in particular. But probably for our sake, or our Uncle Ray's, the usual rules had gone on jubilee, and we were allowed to stage a one-time-only fireworks display at the head of the driveway: cones that sent up fountains of colored fire, and devilish little numbers that blazed and whirled on the ground, and maybe even a few Roman candles. My favorite was something called a "California sparkler"—a red-white-and-blue cardboard tube you could hold by one end while it sent a plume of sparks out the other. It was not alarming or intimidating; it was simply, and satisfyingly, better than the usual puny variety of sparkler.

I supposed that I had found something like those California sparklers again, in Beijing. Here, though, the fuse burned down into the tube, and no spray of sparks came out. Instead there was a pause, then a muffled boom as the tube bucked a little in my hand. The tube boomed again, and again, and I sluggishly realized I had been looking around for the sparks too close nearby: the tube was an artillery piece, and it was blasting orange-white pyrotechnic rounds way out (boom!) into the darkness . . . across the frozen river (boom!) and . . . over the fence into a luxury expat apartment-tower compound. (Boom!) I swung the tube upright, so it would send the rest of its magazine harmlessly toward the sky.

Alarmed—and worrying about the guards—I turned away from the river, just as my wife set herself on fire. Her sparkler had thrown a spark the wrong way, and flames were burning in the flank of her coat, an old fake-fur one, fire racing upward through the synthetic fibers. She beat at the flames; I reached out to try to tear the coat off her. A stranger, an expat woman who had wandered onto the scene, began yelling "Roll! Roll!"—not good advice, when plastic is burning, but also not helpful for making decisions. There are times when you don't want to think about multiple strategies. Christina stayed with her original plan, beating out the flames with her hands. There was a long ragged burn through the coat, and the fire had burned holes through her pants, stopping shy of the long underwear beneath. A few more seconds—

The baby was still asleep in his stroller. We gathered the unused fireworks and the stinking remains of the coat and retreated to the apartment, through the unfaltering festivities. Rockets kept exploding. In the span of one minute, around nine o'clock, I counted roughly seventy-five booms; the longest pause in the barrage was less than three seconds. It was a typical minute.

What was happening outside was anarchy—actual anarchy, the kind the idealists dream of. People were roaming around individually or forming into little bands to set off explosions however they pleased, and wherever: on the street corners, in their courtyards, out in the middle of the roadways. There was no center or focus or program to it; the whole city was boiling with fire.

On CCTV, the official, centralized Gala was on, in the background. I went from window to TV and back again. Dancers in bare midriffs and round red hats—a sort of ethnic go-go costume—were doing frenetic NBA-dance-squad moves to slow, piping music. Then came more dancers, on treadmills. A woman in a ruffled white dress sang a musical number while floating across a pool of water inside a boat-sized inverted green umbrella, then somehow got out of the umbrella and turned it right-side-up to finish the song.

The fireworks outside kept gathering force. A little before eleven, a full volley of professional-grade ones bloomed high in the air halfway out to the main boulevard. In the Gala, there was a skit about a man who had accidentally locked his ID inside a chest and then was unable to show the locksmith any ID to prove that the chest was his to open. Wang Zhizhi and other athletes came on for a group musical number. A ceremony honored heroes, including a man, left a widower a year into his marriage, who had kept supporting his late wife's parents for thirty years. A pair of comedians playing peasanty old people did a long bit about waiting for the Olympic torch. The dialogue on the TV speakers was drowned out by the rising sound of fireworks outside. In mid-sketch, one of the performers delivered a message to the snowbound south: With the government taking care of things, we'll be fine. The Olympic torch arrived on the scene. The comedian playing the common man held it aloft, and it spat out its sparks, without incident.

Now the fireworks were roaring with no pause at all. In the near distance, the lights in apartment-building stairwells flickered on and off, again and again in random patterns, their sound-sensing switches overwhelmed. A white glow suffused the sky. Jay Chou was singing something about porcelain in front of an image of a traditional blue-and-white vase. Then, as midnight came swooping down, they brought out astronauts from the Shenzhou space program. The barrage was everywhere at once, deafening white noise punctuated by flash bombs. The vacant lot looked as if someone were shining a floodlight on it—a steady brightness, with only the shifting tint betraying the chaos of the source, gleaming on the surviving trees and the worker barracks and the icy puddles.

Right below the window, out of view, the whole alley was lit with a sustained green glow. I put on my coat and shoes, grabbed the second cardboard tube, and went outside to see what was making it. A crowd had gathered in the mouth of the apartment gate, and Outer Dongzhimen Side Street had become a free-fire zone. Multiple boxes of skyrockets, fat coils of firecrackers, little handheld explosives— everything was erupting at once, from curb to curb. The pavement was covered with scorched scraps of paper and cardboard. A policeman in a blue uniform coat was out in the street smoking, stooping down to light flashpots and mortars with his cigarette. People shuffled forward to add their own contributions. An old woman stood with a thick bouquet of the dangerous sparklers, all burning at once. A car crept up the alley, waited for a lull, then got waved through.

I held out my tube, labeled a "dragon tube," for a light, pointing it upward. The fuse burned down, then nothing happened. Just before my doubt reached the point of getting me to do something stupid—Daffy Duck peering down a gun barrel—it went off. And off. And off. Down by the river, in my confusion, I thought the tube had maybe popped off a half-dozen rounds. This time, I counted ten shots, twinkling gold, high up above the rooftop. I added the spent tube to the mountain of used cardboard ordnance by the guard-house, and went back upstairs to bed.

Fireworks kept going off through the next day, and the noise began building again after dark. By nine, it sounded like a thunderstorm. Shortly after that, the skyrockets began again, backed by a steady roll of explosions. Something began booming sharply enough to create a delayed double echo: BOOM!—BUM-BUM! BOOM!—BUM-BUM! Then came a series of loud whams that seemed unlike anything from the day before. The real difference was that there were spaces between the whams. The night before, there had been no pause. The third day, blasts were still setting off car alarms. The explosions would go on for more than two weeks, slowly diminishing, till everyone rallied for the holiday-ending Lantern Festival, one final blast of all-night white noise.

Across town at Wukesong, the basketball arena opened for another of the press sessions. The informational march toward the Olympics was growing in size and pace. Since August, the green exterior of the arena had been painted gold. The outside had been covered with an LED display in the original plans, so that the whole building would be a video screen for people outside, but austerity had eliminated that feature. Now the leading opinion among reporters was that the surface, with its striated vertical panels, looked like it was made of pressed tofu skins.

The theme from *Star Wars* played in the press conference hall, down in the underparts of the building. This time, the presentation focused not on the wonders of the construction, but on the relocation of the people who had lived on the Olympic sites before. Beijing was showing it could address outside criticism. Human-rights activists were putting the number of dislocated people citywide at more than 1 million; the organizing committee, dealing specifically with people whose homes had been on Olympic grounds, said that relocation had involved 6,037 households and a total of 14,901 people. Of those, 10,355 people had been moved from the Olympic Green—low density, for Beijing—and the rest had been moved from other Olympic sites.

As presented, it would have been irresponsible not to relocate people. The city's 1983 master plan, nearly two decades before Beijing was awarded the Games, had identified the Olympic Green as "an important urban function area for culture, sports, exhibitions, and leisure," the press handout explained. As for Wukesong, "this area has always been reserved for sports facilities. To build the Olympic venues here is to materialize the planning." Because the sites were outside the old city center, there was only one historic site involved, the Niangniang Temple, for the sake of which the Water Cube had moved a hundred meters north of its planned location.

A slide show supplied aerial photos of the sites as they had been before, as "relatively much more vacant" areas. The lack of population was not especially evident from the pictures. Then came the question period. How much had been spent on relocation? They had not yet come up with a number for release. Had people needed Beijing residence permits to get compensation? Well, the compensation was for homeowners, so a Beijing residence card was necessary to own a house, so of course everyone involved had been a legal resident of Beijing.

So renters had not been compensated? Er, no, there were compensation rules for renters, too, but they were too complicated to explain. What about the farmers who'd been moved off agricultural land? They had been legally converted from villagers to urban residents, which entitled them to social welfare programs, and they had been trained in other lines of work—vehicle maintenance, cleaning, and such.

To illustrate the generosity of the arrangements, the presenters told a story: for many of the people, the compensation was so generous and the new housing they'd chosen was so affordable, they had money left over to buy cars. People who'd taken jobs as street cleaners were able to drive themselves to work in the morning. Street cleaners with cars! It was a marvel.

Questions of social justice settled, it was time to see the arena: 18,000 seats, 42 skyboxes, and a 22-ton video scoreboard. The interior LED system had been approved by the NBA. A program was running on the wraparound screen, urging the nonexistent crowd to "Make . . . Some . . . Noise." As it cycled through messages, tiny logos for the New Jersey Devils and New Jersey Nets appeared. Presumably some of the software had been remaindered from the Meadowlands. "Count the basket . . . and the foul," the screen said. Then the word "Awesome" appeared, with an A that appeared to be the logo of the Arizona Diamondbacks. The *Star Wars* theme was pumped in at brutal volume. Then the LED filled with an image of a billowing Chinese flag.

14.

反对 Opposition

Six months before it could show off its new image, China's existing image became a problem. On February 12, Steven Spielberg announced he was withdrawing as an artistic consultant to the opening and closing ceremonies, as a protest against Chinese policy.

Spielberg had signed on in 2006 to assist the film director Zhang Yimou, who was overseeing the ceremonies. At the time, it seemed to be a straightforward partnership between industry superstars: Zhang—the maker of *Raise the Red Lantern* and *Not One Less*—was a Spielbergian success in China's movie industry, and he had won decades' worth of artistic awards on the international film-festival circuit. To prepare for the Games, Zhang had announced that he was taking a two-year break from making movies, to ensure that Beijing would put on a world-class spectacle.

Zhang had also skipped two years of filmmaking in the 1990s, involuntarily, when the government suspended him from the industry as punishment for *To Live*, his bleak epic of Mao-era hardship. But those bad feelings were in the past; lately, Zhang had been making lush, heroic costume dramas, about the glories of a unified and strongly ruled China.

Now it was Hollywood that was rejecting Zhang's project, and the rest of the Olympics. "Spielberg said, 'No, I'm not going to go,'" a reporter said, thrusting a Fox News microphone at the British filmmaker Daryl Goodrich. So why, the Fox man demanded, was Goodrich cooperating with the Chinese?

This was the definition of a public-relations crisis: an employee of Rupert Murdoch—who had kicked the BBC off his satellite system to ease his way into the Chinese TV market—badgering someone about cozying up to the Chinese regime.

Goodrich was one of five directors who had made short films about Beijing to mark the Olympic year, and who were now at a press conference to promote them. He managed to get something out about the necessary separation of sports from politics; then, as the Fox reporter pressed for follow-up, Goodrich's producer backed him away from the stage, pleading another interview.

There were not many contexts in which Daryl Goodrich would have been compared to Spielberg. Goodrich, an adman by trade, was still working on his first feature film; his most widely acclaimed work was a short subject that London had used to promote its successful bid for the 2012 Olympics. That had been enough to convince the government-backed Beijing Foreign Cultural Exchanges Center to invite him to participate it its Vision Beijing short-film project.

And that was enough to bring a whiff of the stink bomb that Mia Farrow had set off in Hollywood wafting into the Olympic media center. Farrow's target was Spielberg—or, from her point of view, the target was Darfur. The Sudanese government was causing slaughter and misery there. The Chinese government was trading with the Sudanese government. The Olympics would be in China. Spielberg had signed on as a creative advisor to the opening and closing ceremonies of the Olympics. Ergo, skipping over a few sub-contractor-liability issues and the proceedings of the United Nations Security Council, E.T. was killing people in Darfur.

So, I supposed, was I. Because I had watched three of the Vision Beijing movies and interviewed the organizer, Shirley Zhang, back in December, the Foreign Cultural Exchanges Center had called me up two days before the press conference and asked if I would write about the films for one of its magazines. Somewhere not far up the org chart, this meant taking an assignment from the propaganda office of the Beijing municipal government.

Then again, I had just negotiated a kill fee on a service piece for an American men's magazine, after they'd urged me to write something "more positive" about the fact that all the bookable hotel rooms in Beijing during the Olympics had already been block-reserved by travel companies. I told the Foreign Cultural Exchanges Center to send over a full set for me to preview.

While I waited for the disc to arrive, I wandered over to one of my neighborhood DVD shops. It was carrying copies of *Lost in Beijing*—director Li Yu's tale of exploitation and squalor in the modern metropolis, which had been first censored and then banned outright by the Chinese authorities in January. To demonstrate its commitment to Western intellectual-property-rights norms, Beijing was cracking down on the bootleg DVD trade as the Olympics got closer, leaving most stores with denuded shelves. But the old free-flourishing business survived in scattered shops. So there was *Lost in Beijing*—the unexpurgated version, according to the box. Nearby was something titled *The Bloody History of Communism*.

"Respect for human rights is important wherever you go in the world," Goodrich said at the press conference, when the Spielberg question was raised for the first time. But, Goodrich said, he had been invited to make a movie about sports and children, so that was what he did.

Two of the other four directors were also there fielding the Darfur question. Andrew Lau, the director of Hong Kong's blockbuster *Infernal Affairs* trilogy, said in mixed English and Mandarin that he was "*hen* surprised"—very surprised—at Spielberg's decision. "It's sports . . . it's not political," Lau said. His own short film had been about Chinese food.

"I believe that art should have nothing to do with politics," said Majid Majidi, the Iranian director of *Children of Heaven*. Majidi's Vision Beijing contribution, *Colours Fly*, showed schoolchildren in color-coordinated uniforms dispersing around the city to release balloons, which drifted up to form the Olympic rings in the sky. Owing to environmental regulations, Shirley Zhang had told me, the balloons actually were kept on long tethers, so they could be hauled back down once the camera had filmed them being set free.

The premiere of the films was the next night—Oscar day in America—far south of the city center, in a desolate complex beyond the Fifth Ring Road. The same drive in a different direction would have gotten you out to the imperial retreat of the Summer Palace, in view of the Fragrant Hills. This was southern flatland. Barren fields surrounded unmarked pavement. The red carpeting was thin and industrial; an untended counter in the lobby displayed underwear, the ubiquitous white liquor, cookies, and packaged sausages for sale. There was a buffet with breaded meat and fried rice and broccoli. The directors, now including Patrice Leconte of France, autographed a backdrop that faced the entrance.

The auditorium itself was a television studio with a live orchestra and seating for a few hundred spectators: the premiere was being packaged as a TV spectacular. Each film was preceded by a clip reel of the director's work, then remarks by the directors themselves. Giuseppe Tornatore, the director of *Cinema Paradiso*, sent his regrets in a letter read by the Italian ambassador. Majidi's speech was delivered in Farsi, with no translation into Chinese or English. Subtitles would be added for viewers later.

In the first break between films, a troupe of adolescent acrobats did tumbling routines while tossing and catching wooden spools around the stage, using lengths of cord. The next break brought black-clad dancers with red fans; the one after that brought a male pop singer in a velvet shirt and studded jeans, his backup dancers wearing T-shirts and white sneakers. *"Jintiande Beijing bu yiyang,"* he sang—today's Beijing is not the same. "I love-a Bei-jing!" the chorus concluded.

The last film of the night was Goodrich's. A stern voiceover described the growth of China's Olympic ambitions—the hundred-year dream, again—while serious but winsome young athletes were shown in training. It was the most overtly nationalistic or propagandistic movie in the set, by a considerable margin, a cuddly yet resolute descendant of Leni Riefenstahl's *Olympia*. "We have never faltered in our dream," the narrator declared.

Then came the entertainment finale. A chorus of singers in beaded headgear took the stage. In a language more unidentifiable than Scots, they began to sing "Auld Lang Syne." They were, the announcer would later explain, villagers from a remote part of Yunnan Province, belonging to an obscure ethnic minority—all farmers and all Christians. They had been taught the song by a British missionary in the 1900s, according to the announcer.

The farmers' voices were weathered-sounding, with a pleasant tautness, and the song went through verse after verse. Chinese people love "Auld Lang Syne," all year round, in malls and public gatherings and karaoke parlors. People in the middle section of the audience, the VIP section, began clapping along, in rhythm.

The crooked top of the old Christmas tree had reappeared, through the window of the apartment guardhouse, in among the potted plants the guards kept there. In the lot across the street, two Hitachi excavators had begun digging a gaping square-sided hole, then started on a second pit nearby.

The laws barring trucks from city traffic by day meant that if you needed to move a large amount of dirt, you had to move it overnight. On the lot, they were moving a large amount of dirt. Drawn by the noise one night, I went to the window. An excavator was loading a truck in the darkness. The truck's headlights shone off across the open space, and the rest was invisible but for the taillights. The power shovel swept its own light over the truck as it turned to release a load of dirt; there was a clunk as the weight dropped into the truck bed. Then the light swung over to illuminate the growing pit. The shovel worked swiftly, filling the truck bed from front to back, then scattering and raking the final load.

Another truck arrived and went to the far side of the yard, where the second shovel began scooping up dirt for it. Flaps lifted and retracted, opening the truck bed. The shovel delivered the first load of dirt, and pivoted for the next. It was 10:35 p.m. Clouds of dust floated through the headlight beams, and I could smell dust by the window. In the background, the other shovel was going at the same time, their arms momentarily swinging in synchrony. In six minutes—fourteen scoops—the new truck was full. The flaps came back up, and the truck drove off into the night, with the other truck following it. The nearer shovel raked up the stray dirt that had spilled and cut its lights. For a moment the lot was dark. Then a new empty truck drove through the gate. A minute later, another arrived, with two more behind it. The two diggers swung back into action—and then the lights of a third digger, unseen till now, came on. This time it took only five minutes to make a full truckload. All through the night, the machinery kept chewing away, ton after ton. There were 10,000 construction sites in Beijing—put together, their acreage was one and a half times the size of Manhattan—and this was an ordinary night's work at a single one.

By the time the press saddled up for a tour of the Olympic Village, headcount and crowding and general complication of things had reached a new level: the raggedy outer edges of the actual Olympic storm were blowing ashore. Citizens were playing ping-pong on roadside tables as the motor coaches passed; behind a construction fence, an excavator was knocking over brick buildings.

The Village, the compound where the Olympic athletes would stay, consisted of some four dozen low towers, most of them either six or nine stories. Because the Villages were residential spaces, easier to reuse than 100,000-seat stadia, they traditionally served as a bridge between a city's Olympic planning and its post-Olympic development: college dorms in Atlanta; a fully built suburb in Sydney. Beijing's Village, once the athletes were gone, was to be converted to private luxury apartments. The reception hall had cartoon rat decorations and snowflakes in it, and a red paper-cut work covering a wall. "This paper-cuts is made by an 80-year old lady from a small village in north-west China," a sign explained in English.

Only a few of the buildings were set up for inspection, so the press waited outside to enter in small groups. The Chinese TV crews roamed around, as usual, interviewing foreigners. The foreign reaction to Olympic projects was as important as the projects themselves—how else could China decide whether it was performing at an appropriate international standard? Underfoot, the soft dust of the Beijing soil felt like talcum powder. The guards were kitted out in special new Olympic Village uniforms: black-blue tunic jackets, peaked caps, and high boots, looking uncannily like a unit of Darth Vader's Imperial officers. On the question of security or repression, China lacked even a rudimentary grasp of what American political types call "optics"; foreign photographers crouched down to shoot the looming, dark figures.

The hallways were lit with round fluorescents, the economy kind, and there was a similar fixture over the dining table in a unit opened for press tours. The ceiling cans held compact fluorescents, with an orange tint. The space seemed tight for the six athletes it was supposed to house, or for the apartment-buyers who would come after. The showers were nozzles in curtained-off corners of the bathrooms, with no tub or stall around them.

After seeing the rooms, I went back to the reception center to study the model of the Olympic grounds there. I couldn't tell if it was the same one that had been in the Exhibition Center or not. I checked for the Niangniang Temple by the Water Cube, and saw nothing. I tried to ask a young man in a suit, who was talking to reporters in English, about where the model had come from. After three or four non sequiturs, it occurred to me that he was equipped with only enough English to answer a predetermined set of questions, like a voice-recognition phone tree. Official Beijing was not well prepared to answer questions it didn't expect to be asked.

At the end of February, the organizing committee briefed a full house of domestic and foreign reporters on the city's air-pollution-control measures for 2008. These would be the four-teenth phase of pollution restrictions, dating back to 1998. The goal was to have blue-sky days 70 percent of the time, meaning 256 days, eleven more than 2007's target. Stricter standards for boilers, motor vehicles, and petroleum and chemical plants would take effect before summer; high-emission vehicles would be taken off the roads; 50,000 houses would convert from coal burners to electric heat.

Early March's weather was warm and sunny; it seemed possible that Beijing might not descend into hellishness forevermore. Then all at once the murk came back, inexorably as high tide. We took the baby out to a baby-gear store to buy shoes, under a washed-out sun. When we got back out of the store, in the gathering dirty dark, there were no cabs. The mall was like a warehouse, facing a strip of auto-repair shops. No one was being dropped off there. It grew colder and colder, for fifteen or twenty minutes, with Mack coughing in his car-seat stroller, before we got a taxi home. The filth was like an act of vengeance, the sky over the Third Ring glowing softly with dirt-trapped light, behind the dark bulk of buildings. Carrying the car seat up the apartment stairs, I was short of breath. A cement mixer was working on the vacant lot, under floodlights and the flare of welding torches. The next day was full of harsh glare in a haze-gray sky, a beautiful day ruined by pollution. Ethiopia's Haile Gebrse-lassie, the world record holder in the marathon, announced that he would not be running in the Olympics. The pollution measures were too late. He would not risk breathing the air.

The weather got better again; the news got worse. March 15, the first day of a Major League Baseball exhibition on the Olympic fields, was what people conventionally call a great day for a ballgame. A right-handed pull hitter might have disagreed, feeling the strong breeze coming in from the northwest. Along Chang'an Boulevard, by Tian'anmen Square and the Great Hall of the People, the national flags and accompanying plain red ones stood rippling off their flagpoles, aglow in clear sunlight against the blue sky.

From the other side of the country, in the Tibetan capital of Lhasa, came reports of flag burnings—and other things burning. It was unclear. The Internet was clogged. YouTube was blocked, and its Chinese counterpart, Tudou, had suddenly announced it was shutting down to work on its servers. A *New York Times* account of rioting and death in Lhasa loaded partway, then broke off in mid-sentence: "What actually set off the violence is unclear, as accounts differed between Chinese and Tibetan residents. Monks from the Ramoche Temple, a short"—

But whatever was happening was happening off in Idaho, geographically speaking, remote from the east and the capital. At the Wukesong ball fields, the San Diego Padres were playing the Los Angeles Dodgers—or spring-training travel-squad versions of those teams, anyway. Traffic seized up on the boulevard outside while the American ambassador was throwing out the first pitch: a black Honda and a red Buick had collided in the middle of an intersection. The custom of preserving the accident scene had been formally overturned a few months before by a new traffic regulation that required people to clear the roadway, but the drivers were sticking with their old habits.

Baseball was another idiom that hadn't quite translated into Chinese. In Taiwan, a cousin of Christina's had sneaked out of military duty to join the crowds watching telecasts of Chien-Ming Wang and the New York Yankees, but the mainland took no comparable interest in America's pastime. Earlier in the week, at a promotional event for this China Series, the host was a model wearing a purple jersey with a glittery gold Yankees logo—color-coordinated with a purple Boston Red Sox trucker hat.

The Wukesong ballpark had been expanded since the Good Luck games, with new sections on the gravel beds, held up by a thicket of shiny tubular beams and crosspieces, like scaffolding. Sheet-metal stairways rose through the underside, with no ramps or escalators. As I climbed toward my seat, a man rolled up in a wheelchair to the next set of stairs, tipped himself out, and began pulling himself up the steps with his hands and feet.

The field itself was a lush emerald green—a spray-paint green, it turned out, up close. The Dodgers wore their changeless whites; the perpetually tinkering Padres wore road uniforms in a sort of sand color. It looked like a ballgame, mostly. The Dodgers' jersey numbers—72, 76, 83—betrayed the fact that many of them would be flying home to join the Triple-A Las Vegas 51s. But at shortstop, wearing a big-league number 14, was Chin-Lung Hu of Taiwan, also known, for mainland-competition purposes, as Hu Jinlong of Chinese Taipei.

The Dodgers broke on top with a home run. The Padres tied it; the Dodgers pulled back ahead. Hu struck out, lined into a double play, struck out again. He booted and bobbled ground balls. "I thought that Hu seemed a little nervous," his manager, Joe Torre, would say in his postgame interview.

The game was a sellout, mostly thanks to expats. On the patch of walkway behind the stands that served as a concourse, a vendor squatted on the paving blocks, selling sandwiches and canned drinks. For 240 yuan, the vendors were letting fans carry a whole case of Yanjing beer off to their seats. Try that in the Land of Liberty.

On the other hand, whenever any spectator along the third-base line unfurled a sign, a man in a yellow windbreaker quickly moved in to inspect it. He spent a long time studying one held by a Red Sox fan, taunting Hank Steinbrenner.

Major League Baseball had planned on additional entertainment, but it had been scuttled at the last minute by the Public Security Bureau. So the job of engaging the crowd between innings was divided between a local cheerleading squad—something the Chinese had apparently decided belonged at every Western-style sporting event—and a series of MLB games and quizzes on the center-field video screen.

The video portion was emceed from the field by a local entertainer named Zhu Zhu, a petite young woman with a surprisingly forceful voice and the ability to switch flawlessly from Mandarin to English. The quizzes included the "Pick the Play Game," in which spectators were asked to identify a clip of a routine base hit as "(1) Single; (2) Walk; (3) Double."

For next day's game, the Public Security Bureau relented slightly, allowing an international-school choir and a youth baseball team onto the field to sing the American and Chinese anthems, respectively. Waiting for the second game to begin, Zhu Zhu said that she had just finished recording her first album, which would be called *JUJU*. She wore white-framed Ray-Bans, a Dodgers jersey, and black suede boots. She had played baseball a few times in middle school, she said, but she'd had no idea what the Pick the Play Game terminology had meant.

"If they're going to ask the same questions," Zhu Zhu said, "I know the answer now."

The questions were the same. Torre batted Hu Jinlong in the leadoff spot, and Hu opened the game with a single, moved to second on a bunt, stole third, and tagged up and sprinted home on a medium fly ball to left. "He was the guy I've gotten to know," Torre said, with admiration, in his final press scrum. "He was very special."

While reporters waited for Torre to reappear in the dugout, the cheerleaders posed on the infield for a group photo. They were being marshaled by a woman in her thirties wearing a loose, blousy mini-dress in a vivid print. Her name was Soojin Cho, and her business card identified the squad as the Soojin Dance Team. The American-style Chinese cheerleaders were the work of a South Korean immigrant.

Blocking the Internet was not enough to make the Lhasa problem go away. The next big publicity event was a news conference to announce the plans for the torch relay. Now there was a separate sign-in sheet for the overseas press. The presentation dwelt at length on the procedural integrity of the selection of torchbearers—they had "followed the master plan of the torchbearer selection," they had included representatives of all ethnic groups, etc. The torpor lasted till the third question of the question-and-answer period, when Wang Hui, doing her duty to accommodate the foreign media, called on a *Wall Street Journal* reporter. What about Lhasa, and activists' calls for protests against the relay?

The violence would not affect the torch relay, organizing committee vice president Jiang Xiaoyu said. "The situation in Lhasa and Tibet has basically been stabilized," Jiang said. As for the would-be protesters, such behavior "goes totally against the spirit of the Twenty-ninth Olympic Games torch relay, which is 'Journey of Harmony.'" Going against the harmonious slogan was perhaps exactly the point of the protests; Tibet and Darfur were growing into a campaign to shun China from the polite company of nations, to try to revoke the acceptance implied by Beijing's having won its Olympic bid. But that went unsaid. "Those activities will not win the hearts and minds of people, and therefore are doomed to failure," Jiang said.

What about the calls for a boycott, either of the Games or of the

opening ceremony? "The theme of the opening ceremony is civilization and harmony.... I do believe that the majority of the people
around the world will make the right decision." What about security?
How could the Tibet leg of the relay, including a planned trip up
Mount Everest, be kept secure? "Please be assured that no matter
what happens in Tibet or Xinjiang, those events will never affect the
normal operation of the torch relay."

For the first time, Wang Hui looked weary. On the way out of the
building, I spotted her through a half-open office door, slumped on
a couch.

And what about Tibet, anyway? I should note here that when I
finally collected my freelance pay from the propaganda office, what
had been presented as a flat fee turned out to be a per-word rate, and
my payment was cut in half. People who care about Tibet may take
that as they wish, because my own position on the Tibet issue is that,
considered against the enormousness and enormity of all the other
questions and concerns surrounding the People's Republic of China,
Tibet is not particularly important. Generally speaking, the more
attention people pay China—and this includes people who are
inclined to conclude the worst about it—the less interest they have
in Tibet.

People who do care a lot about Tibet (and are not Tibetan) have
something wrong with their priorities. This goes for the Chinese,
for starters. The passions of ordinary Chinese people run frighten-
ingly hot on the subject of Tibet. There is something wrong with the
Chinese that they care so much about possessing Tibet. And there
is something wrong with the activists who care so much about dis-
possessing China of Tibet.

Neither side's passion has detectably much to do with the actual condition of Tibet. The Uighurs of Xinjiang are at least as unhappy with their role in the People's Republic as the Tibetans are, but no one is holding rock concerts for the Uighurs. Nor are the Chinese flooding YouTube with nationalistic videos asserting their ancient and eternal right to hold Xinjiang.

Tibet is a symbol, and a dull one, a vessel for ideas that people have already settled on. It is a symbol of China's proud history and territorial integrity, and it is a symbol of the universal struggle for human rights and self-determination. That is, it is a symbol of China's totalitarian power and contempt for Western liberalism, and it is a symbol of the West's contempt for China and its envy of Chinese power. Protesting for or against Tibetan independence simply demonstrates that your side is right and the other side is wrong, intractably and antagonistically wrong.

It is odd that the central cause of the world's democracy activists would be the restoration of a god-king—a very nice god-king, an internationally respected god-king, but nevertheless a person whose claim to rulership over other people rests on the authority of invisible and unverifiable supernatural forces. This is probably not a place the authors of the American Revolution would have expected to see their ideology end up.

There is, to be sure, the plain American belief that Tibet should be free because the Communist dictatorship is inherently in the wrong. China's grand, sweeping claims of continuous rulership over Tibet through centuries of history are shaky, at best. But in Taipei, at the Chiang Kai-shek memorial, the displays include the Generalissimo's maps of his own Republic of China—the China that the United States spent hundreds of millions of dollars trying to help Chiang realize. That China, our Free China, stretched across the Taiwan Strait and all the way up to Siberia, enveloping not only the

Tibetans and the Uighurs but the present-day country of Mongolia and an untold number of Central Asian republics.

So neither side has a particularly impressive pedigree. The Chinese do, however, have a point when they compare their absorption of Tibet to the absorption of American Indians. Native Americans make up 1.5 percent of the population of the United States; the 5 million ethnic Tibetans are less than one-half of one percent of China's population.

This is sort of sweet on the part of the Chinese, their overestimation of America's ability to be embarrassed by hypocrisy. Someday, if China blossoms into a mature and secure superpower, it may pay as much attention to the Tibetans as we pay to the Cherokee.

15.

森林 Forest

Spring was coming in, with the help of manpower. There were only four and a half months left to deliver what the organizing committee had designated as a "Green Olympics"—one of the Three Concepts of the Beijing Games, the other two being "High-Tech Olympics" and "People's Olympics." By the roadsides, crews assembled new hedges, sprig by sprig; rolls of sod waited on truck beds. A year before, horticulturalists had injected female poplar trees with growth-suppression drugs to try to prevent the annual clouds of flying catkin fluff, but the poplars, uninhibited, loosed their fluff on the breeze, turning the insides of taxicabs into snow globes. A flock of hoopoes arrived in the neighborhood, with big brown Woody Woodpecker crests—pecking in the courtyard, fluttering through the diplomatic compound, perching on the tower crane on the construction site. The Christmas tree vanished from the gatehouse, then reappeared a few weeks later, even more withered, by the garbage cans.

The biggest area of man-made parkland was the 1,600-acre Olympic Forest, above the Olympic Green, where a half-million newly planted trees surrounded engineered streams and ponds, flowing with recycled wastewater. In honor of the world's press, a Media Forest was being installed down in one corner of the site, among traffic ramps. The organizing committee invited the press to see.

In the middle distance, up a rise, trees in the rest of the Forest were leafing out in pale green. To the south were heavily staked pines. Black netting covered bare ground to the west, and above it rose rounded brick cairns or columns—topped, on closer inspection, with manhole covers: here was some sort of sewer construction, waiting for the ground above it to arrive.

For the occasion, the organizers had brought back some of the citizens who had lived in the area, before it was cleared for the Forest. The relocated people helped the committee staffers shovel dirt around the bases of silver plum trees. The press was urged, awkwardly, to join in the spadework. Most hung back. When the last of the trees had been tipped upright and watered, the former residents got on the press buses for a trip to the neighborhood to which they'd been moved.

My seatmate, representing the Olympic relocatees, was Bao Jingnan, a thin, youngish man with prominent ears, wearing a sweater vest, dress shirt, and olive slacks. The bus arrived at a side street west of the Olympic Green. There was a Century 21 office on the block, and curious real estate agents in their pale blazers stood out on the sidewalk, watching the arrivals.

Bao's new home was a unit on the ground floor of an apartment tower. There were clean tile floors and a large TV on the side of the living room—middle-class comforts. In the bedroom was a large color wedding photograph, in a gold frame, of Bao and his wife, Wang Xuechun. Wang had laid out strawberries, oranges, and roasted seeds and nuts on the coffee table, next to a tea tray. She liked to practice tea ceremonies, Bao said. Bao did the main share of the talking for the two of them. When he was asked to come to the tree planting, he said, no one had warned him that anyone would be coming over, but they kept snacks around the house for guests.

Most of this was translated by Sim Chi Yin, a reporter for Singapore's *Straits Times*, who had also ended up in Bao's apartment. The organizing committee had not arranged for any interpretation. Bao offered us Yuxi brand cigarettes. A team of the Fuwa, handmade from plastic beads, stood atop the TV. A friend had made them. Beijingers had taken to making their own Olympic paraphernalia; by now it was unsurprising to see beadwork Fuwa in a window, or home-welded Olympic rings on a taxi partition. On the enclosed balcony, three pet turtles sat in a glass tank.

Bao brought out pictures from his previous house, the cheap old kind of housing called *pingfang*: a red-brick exterior, a sagging couch, a clutter-strewn courtyard. It had been two kilometers away. One picture showed his old motor scooter. Since the resettlement, he said, he had gotten a car. It was parked outside, a silver Honda sedan.

China's troubles in its west, and with the West, were not subsiding. There had been more riots among ethnic Tibetans, in Tibet and neighboring provinces, and those areas were closed to the foreign press. TV coverage of the kindling of the Olympic flame in Greece was surrounded by footage of Lhasa burning—evidence, for the majority Han Chinese, of Tibetan hatred and violence. The torch, setting off its Journey of Harmony, skulked into Beijing on March 31 like a fugitive, or like a U.S. official dropping in on Iraq: all secrecy, security, and evasive measures. When I tuned in to watch the torch celebration on TV, it was already over. The authorities had switched the ceremony from starting at noon to ending at noon. The flame had fled, heading for Kazakhstan. Protests and scuffles would chase it across Europe and to America.

Meanwhile, the press was being given a chance to meet actual Chinese Olympic athletes. Armed with a Chinese-only briefing sheet, I spent the bus ride north to the old Asian Games compound deciphering the names of the featured sports with my cell phone's dictionary: field hockey, tennis . . . We were not quite entering the heart of the gold-medal machine. Nor would we be mingling with the athletes, exactly—on arrival, we were informed that team managers and coaches were available, but interviewing athletes "will interfere with and disturb the training of the athletes."

The press-conference room was overflowing with reporters, mainly Chinese, penned in by a solid line of cameras. At a table were the athletes who would be permitted to address the media: men's freestyle wrestler Wang Ying, women's heavyweight judoka Tong Wen, women's tennis player Zheng Jie, women's team handball player Liu Ying, and men's field-hockey captain Song Yi. "This is the first time for us to receive the media friends from home and abroad," Cui Dalin, secretary-general of the national Olympic delegation, announced.

There were numbers to be had: 12 teams trained at this center, comprising 430 athletes and coaches; the overall national delegation would have 538 athletes in 226 competitions. Other numbers were for shoveling into sandbags: "A lot of athletes from other countries . . . have shown very good strength in all these events," Cui cautioned. Analysts for NBC, he said, had predicted 42 gold medals

for the United States, and 108 medals altogether ("a very conservative estimation," Cui said). Russia's largest sports newspaper antici-
pated 122 medals for Russia. In swimming and in track and field,
the most medal-rich areas, China was lagging—particularly in track
and field, where there were "still large gaps between Chinese athletes
and those athletes from overseas."

Pity the People's Republic, facing such formidable opponents.
But winning medals, Cui said, was only one goal of the Olympic
program. It was, likewise, important to "promote the exchange and
friendship between people all over the world." Then the officials in
charge of particular sports broke down their own prospects. "The
competition will be very fierce," the weightlifting, wrestling, and
judo official said. The handball, field hockey, and softball official
allowed that those teams were "not of a very high standard on the
international level."

There was no offer of medal quotas or targets. Sharing that sort
of specific information would be indelicate. A reporter from Brazil
asked how many medals was China estimating it would win. "I
myself am curious to see," Cui said. What about the bonus money
for medal winners? In Athens in 2004, it had been 200,000 yuan (or
about $25,000) for gold, 120,000 for silver, and 18,000 for bronze.
The Chinese sports program was not interested in rewarding athletes
who would finish third. With the development of the economy, the
bonuses would be even higher this time around.

How were the athletes prepared for the pressure of competing in
front of their countrymen? All of the teams provided mental training
and stress-reduction courses. Had there been any preference given
to minority athletes in choosing the teams? Ethnic diversity was a
tricky question; the People's Republic made a point of celebrating
the distinctive culture of its dozens of minorities, but more than 90
percent of the population was Han Chinese. So room for minorities

could be hard to come by. The Olympic-qualified athletes represented somewhere between ten and twenty ethnic groups. Xinjiang had multiple boxers and a rider—a woman—competing in dressage. A Tibetan woman had been picked by the rowing team as a coxswain. But there was no preference. "We are upholding the principles of justice and fairness to choose the best athletes for the Olympics."

And what about the individual, human side of the athletic program? A *Wall Street Journal* reporter asked the competitors to tell a little bit about themselves. Liu, the handball player, said that she liked singing and she had a blog. Wang, the wrestler, said his hobbies were reading books, listening to music, and surfing the Internet. Tong—a genial massif of a woman, much larger than the 185-pound, wrestling-scarred Wang—said that when she did not need to train, "I would like to read books, listen to music. . . . Now we are working very hard." Song, the field hockey captain, said he liked shopping, surfing the Internet, and singing karaoke with his teammates.

Had the unrest around the torch relay affected the athletes' preparations? An official filibustered: "Sacred event . . . passion and glory across the globe . . . establishing a harmonious world . . ." The riots were "against the Olympic principles" and "not supported by most people in the world." The news "has not had any impact."

"Our attention has been drawn totally to the Olympics," Liu said, in a sweet voice, "to enjoy every moment of the Olympics."

The press conference broke up; it was time to watch the athletes in training. Outside, it was overcast. Birches grew in bare dirt. The field hockey team scrimmaged against itself. On the tennis courts, Yan Zi, a women's tennis player, was practicing against two men at once. A box of Wilson tennis balls stamped "US OPEN" sat on the sideline.

When Yan took a rest, the cameras and microphones moved in.

The questioning lasted until someone brought up the protests. Then an official stepped in, saying that Yan would catch cold if she kept sitting still in mid-training.

Wrestling practice was taking place in one spacious gym, with judo in a neighboring one, even more spacious, with walls of windows and gauzy white curtains. Young women dressed like flight attendants flanked the doorways connecting the two. In red characters on the walls of both gyms was the message *"Tuanjie pinbo / Wei guo zhengguang"*: Fight together with all your might / Struggle for the glory of the country. As we gazed over the judo athletes, an American reporter told me about the death threats he had been getting since covering the Lhasa violence. Other journalists had been receiving harassing phone calls and e-mails from outraged Chinese citizens, or people saying they were outraged Chinese citizens—there was some skepticism about how much opportunity average Chinese people had to consume foreign media, so that they could be privately outraged by it—but this was something more personal and menacing. He was rattled.

A chilly breeze was picking up, and the women at the doorways suddenly were wearing dark overcoats. In the other gym, wrestlers were working on their core strength: lying prone with their hips on a bolster, they tried to keep their upper bodies suspended straight out in space, while a dumbbell rested on the backs of their necks. Their hands were behind their backs, and a stopwatch lay on the mat for them to contemplate. Whenever one faltered and dropped a hand to the mat for support, a coach would take a can of topical cooling spray and swat the errant arm with it.

A week later, in mid-April, the final venue was open. It was time to see the Bird's Nest: centerpiece of the Olympic construction, icon of the Chinese Century, and site of the 2008 Good Luck Beijing Racewalking Challenge. The early morning was comfortable, with some haze. Not too much, but I wouldn't have wanted to racewalk in it. A thicker pall hung over the north Third Ring. In traffic, out the cab window, a double-decker bus had a UPS ad with the Bird's Nest on it.

The approach to the stadium was full of rubble and loose dirt and paving blocks and sewer pipe. It took a long walk north, away from the stadium proper, to find the gate. A steady file of people trooped north, beside the battered aqua-metal construction walls, wire fencing, temporary buildings. Workers along the way were installing the sidewalk and tree boxes; there were patches of wet concrete.

Across from the security checkpoint was an actual bird nest, a magpie's thick jumble of twigs in a skinny, newly planted tree. The inspection at the gate was more thorough than ever before. I had to demonstrate that my camera and my umbrella worked as a camera and an umbrella, rather than as disguised tools of Tibetan "splittism."

Some of the sprigs in the freshly assembled hedges were ailing, leaving patches of brown. Everyone paused for snapshots on the way south toward the stadium. There were little Bird's Nest–inspired lamps stuck in the ground, their tops round tangles of metal. I reversed direction once more, to reach the north entrance.

Stepping onto the plaza, my feet briefly lost contact with my brain as I tipped my head back to take in the looming, bellying curve. Here was the Nest.

The event was full; people wanted to get inside the Bird's Nest, even if it meant watching racewalking. Two minutes and seventeen seconds of the race had already happened by the time I got to my seat. It was getting hotter, and haze was visible inside, across the open eye of the stadium. The seats were plastic, red ones down low gradually giving way to gray ones at the top, in the same random-pixel manner as at the Water Cube. The logo of the Sinopec oil company, familiar from gas stations, had been molded into each seat back.

Most of the race would take place on a roadway outside. The crowd could go out and watch or follow the race on the stadium screen. Inflatable-suited Fuwa—Beibei, Huanhuan, and Nini—appeared on the track as the racewalkers hit the exit. Jingjing was outside, with the cross-sectional crowd. The universal attraction of the stadium had drawn a variety of Beijingers, and the uncertain temperature meant that none of them could quite settle on what to wear. The result was a sartorial free-for-all. Some young women wore party dresses. I saw a Playboy tracksuit, a woman's green corduroy suit, more than one turtleneck with cap sleeves. People's Armed Police were out in their uniforms. A man dressed prosperity casual: a zip-neck pullover under a blazer. Fake-leather jackets. A Mao suit jacket. Burberry pants.

There were *"Jia you!"* T-shirts with accompanying *"Jia you!"* thundersticks, for volunteer rooters. The shirts had a new cartoon mascot on them: a curlicue-headed figure named Dongdong, meaning "Thump-thump."

The racewalkers looped back and forth, and the heat increased; I wandered back inside and strolled the concourse, taking in the futuristic details: the deep-red paint job on the seating bowl; the translucent, alien-botanic hanging light fixtures; the cartoonish signage and logos, like something drawn up by A Bathing Ape. The bathrooms had glossy black paint on textured walls, and gleaming black floors, from which a worker wiped tan footprints of Beijing dust over and over again.

And everywhere around, veering off and coming together at

different angles, were the huge tangled silver columns of the nest, the avant-garde steelwork I had seen rising for so long. I walked up to one and touched it, then rapped its surface with my knuckles. It had made a dull, stifled *tap*.

Tap? I mulled over the sound, in confusion. I was not a metallurgist or a structural engineer, but it felt as if I had knocked my fist against a big chunk of concrete. Not steel. Or not what I would have expected steel to feel like. But what did I know?

Reporting in China had always meant groping along through an epistemological fog. Language was part of it (and a big part, in my case), but there was something more fundamentally elusive and opaque about fact-gathering. People and institutions were not used to the experience of being reported on. It's not merely that they could be secretive or uncooperative or obstructionist, unprepared for the glaring light of a truly free and inquisitive press, and so on. It was that even people who wanted to cooperate—who may even have been affirmatively trying to put out a news story—didn't quite know how to distill and transmit information.

The organizing committee struggled with this. One spring morning, the press gathered to meet the director of the committee's project management department. A handout dutifully explained in English that the director's duties were to "provide services for . . . decision-making," "coordinate the compilation of overall operational plans," "carry out research . . . on leading subjects," and "frame preparation policies." What followed, after a long opening silence, was the reporters asking, reasking, and finally badgering and pleading with the guest of honor to explain, with one or two specifics, what sorts of things he actually had decided or coordinated or prepared. ("First," the director replied, after a particularly desperate entreaty, "I would like to say a few words about project management.")

Maybe steel felt like concrete when you tapped on it. What did I really know, beyond what I'd been told? The racewalkers lurched their way into the stadium, one at a time, and onto the final standings board. Jared Tallent of Australia won with a time of an hour and twenty minutes, with Wang Hao of China fourteen seconds behind him. Wang was listed on the scoreboard as representing Inner Mongolia; for diversity's sake, the Chinese entrants were listed by their provincial or other athletic affiliations: Heilongjian, the People's Liberation Army, Shandong.

The crowd thinned out as the finishers straggled in. A young Chinese man in a Nike visor struck up a conversation with me in English. He'd gotten his tickets from a friend on the organizing committee, he said. His cabdriver had had trouble figuring out how to get to the stadium, because the signs weren't clear. "I think surely there are a lot of things we need to improve in the future," he said.

He said his name was Michael Wang, and he was originally from Sichuan—from the hometown of the pandas, he said. First he had wanted to move to Shanghai, because it was a new city, but Beijing was "the core of China." He had majored in English—"not a good major, I think." No? "English is just a tool. . . . It's only a language." He went into international trade, and struggled at first because he hadn't learned business terminology in English.

A Sri Lankan racer entered the Nest, thirty-four minutes off the pace. The scoreboard read "Congratulations." "Sometimes, I think the last one deserves more applause," my companion said. "Because he has no hope of getting a gold medal, but he still has to finish the Games."

On the way home, the cabbie lit up a cigarette. A citywide smoking ban was due to take effect on the first of May. At least, that was what had been officially announced. By the time the day came, the ban had been revised to allow smoking to continue in restaurants, clubs, Internet cafés—more or less anywhere (except the hospitals) where people might want to smoke.

The hundred-day countdown was at hand, but instead of being in China, I was in China's waiting room. And with three months to go till Beijing would host the world, the mood in the waiting room was grim and angry. The visa hall at the Chinese consulate in New York was packed with people, every seat taken; the line for problem cases at Window 1 stretched all the way to the back.

The family had reached the limits of Beijing's hospitality. Christina's visa could be renewed open-endedly, but the baby's and mine could not. For all the trappings of stability—the new sofa, the Pampers, the organic maple-arrowroot baby cookies—our papers still said we were short-term visitors, and every six months, short-term visitors had to get out. I could only imagine what the city was doing without us, the things Beijing was changing behind our backs, while we were stuck on the old, familiar American side of the world.

The reason for the backup emerged when I got to the window and presented the clerk with a new set of the routine visa paperwork. It was not enough, the clerk said, in disgusted tones. There needed to be an airplane ticket, an itinerary from a travel agency, a bank statement showing sufficient personal funds, and a documented hotel reservation. When had the rules changed? These were the rules, she said, shoving the papers back.

This was China's greeting to would-be visitors as the Olympics drew near. Rather than expediting the process of getting into the New China, the consulate was taking the role of a guardpost on a hostile border. The first bureaucratic duty of the visa office was not to grant visas; it was to reject applications that didn't satisfy the rules.

And the rules had been changed without notice, so that every applicant would be rejected at first—so the hall was backed up not only with people arguing about their rejections, but with all the applicants making a second or third visit, till the people on both sides of the glass were infuriated with each other and the clerks were rejecting applications out of spite.

Not that the Chinese didn't have reason to be crabby. When I came back to the far West Side to pick up the passports, one or two dozen demonstrators on the other side of the West Side Highway were waving Tibetan flags and a sign with skulls inside the Olympic rings. "Bloody Olympics!" someone yelled. On the near corner, just across Forty-second Street, Falun Gong supporters were demonstrating. There was an arc of splattered red paint on the building, and glass blocks in the façade were broken. What protesters couldn't do in China, they were doing in the streets of New York.

In downtown Flushing, I came across a demonstration on the other side: a group of young Chinese people rallying outside the library, wearing T-shirts that said "One China." The map on the back of the shirts included both Tibet and Taiwan. One of the young people, wearing a hoodie and a stocking cap, said repeatedly, with a heavy New York accent, that his group was not affiliated with anyone in particular. It was a Facebook group for supporters of China. Outside a grocery market, a white man was talking into a cell phone: "They resent that the Tibetans aren't appreciative," he said.

Terminal 3, Beijing's vast, coppery-roofed new gateway, was open. We flew back into the newest airport in the world, 10 million square feet of internationalism, if you could get a visa for it. A train led from one sprawling lobe of the building to another, connecting the gates to the baggage claim, passing on the way through the dimness and bare concrete of a yet uncompleted middle section. The short hop to America had helped make the familiar in Beijing unfamiliar again: the thick air of evening, the trees pruned back to poles, the shapes of the guardrails and the streetlights, the tiny size of even a new Hyundai cab's backseat. The gait and pace of the people, and the dimness they moved through. There was a flashing arrow in lights at the mouth of the alley—we *had* missed something happening, right there—and blue metal fencing had surrounded the public restroom.

We had been gone long enough to get jet lag. It was May, and the sky brightened to deep blue well before five, on its way to a yellow-gray morning. The building where the bicycle store had once been was being renovated, with drywall and new wiring. Roofers were on top with flaming torches. A man smashed the concrete-and-brick curb with a sledgehammer. People peeked through the fence gaps at the restroom. A brick-lined pit was going in beside it. The phone and DSL were off, because we'd missed the payment date while we were away; the bank on the corner where we'd paid the bills was gone. *"Ban jia,"* a gray-haired woman in a long denim jacket said—it moved. There was an afternoon press conference on building an environmentally friendly city. By then, not quite twenty-four hours after returning, I had a burning feeling in the back of my throat.

A few days later, on a cool morning, a crew arrived to refurbish our own building. They lowered themselves down the inner face of the building, over the courtyard, on seats on ropes, using paint rollers and buckets of water to wash the surface. Cracks were patched, and some of the worst sections of paint were stripped away. By afternoon, the northwest corner had a patch of new paint, a bright margarine color where the old paint had been cream. *"Si tai zhong,"* a man said, looking up at it. The color is too strong. Someone must have agreed, because the crew disappeared for the next few days, leaving the bright spot as it was.

The wall at the corner by the public restroom was knocked down, and a front-end loader shuddered in the alley like a rhinoceros in a cattle chute, swinging back and forth in the tight space with loads of dirt. People strolled right past it.

And now, all around the city, the walling-off of everything was reversing itself. Construction fences were starting to come down, opening up the near and middle distance. Air and light filled my peripheral vision where there had been the constant, almost forgotten, press of walls.

New façades were going up on shops—blocks and blocks at a time—with uniform plastic characters replacing the old assortment of hand-painted or cheaply computer-rendered signboards. Run-down or irregular storefronts vanished behind a tidy, regular skin of silvery plastic-aluminum composite panels. Everything was squared off and gleaming, if only a half-inch deep.

There was a new feature on the aural landscape, too. To celebrate the hundred-day mark, an army of pop stars had recorded a song, nearly seven minutes long, called "Beijing Huanying Ni." Singers traded off lines, in the manner of "We Are the World," as a long, quiet verse promised a new atmosphere, morning light, the floating aroma of tea. The front door of our home is open . . . All are guests, from near or far . . . Make yourself comfortable . . .

Then Jackie Chan (atop the Great Wall, wearing white, in the video) belted out the opening of the refrain: "BEEEI-jinng HUANying NIII . . ." Beijing Welcomes You! Heaven and earth open for you! Mainland and Hong Kong and Taiwanese singers made the promise; American and Korean ones, even. A Peking Opera performer broke into the pop tune with a classical, nasalized wail:

"Beeeei-jinnnnng huannnnn-yinnnng nnnnii—YAAH!" On and on. That pentatonic hook was everywhere: cab radios, DVD shops, wafting over the streets. Beijing Welcomes You! The constancy of it all but guaranteed it would be the ironic backdrop to whatever might go sour in the course of a day. Coughing fit? Traffic jam? Argument with the authorities? *"BEEI-jinng HUAN-ying NIIII . . ."*

The Lantern Courtyard, however, would not be opening its front door to greet anyone. The fire marshal of Xicheng District would not grant a permit to Big Mack's hotel project. The fire code said that a hotel couldn't have exposed beams. There were no sprinklers. There was no second exit, and it was architecturally impossible to make one. By definition, a traditional courtyard house could not pass inspection.

Some forty other projects were held up in the district for similar reasons, Mack said. The fire marshal had added, cryptically, that he wouldn't chase after the Lantern Courtyard group if they went around him, but there was no legal way to open the hotel without the fire certificate.

Most of the renovation work was done. A damp-looking spot lingered on the paving stones in the first courtyard, making the new blocks darker than the old ones. The inner courtyard had been repaved, too, over the newly constructed cesspit and sewer lines. In the hall at the front, the old low ceiling was gone and the fire marshal's unacceptable beams were a rich brown overhead. New tiles on one end marked where the kitchen would have been.

The side rooms were largely finished. The bathrooms at the rear had been reconstructed and retiled, and a bathtub, running lengthwise, had been installed in the less-small one. Wires and plumbing hookups sat waiting for the lights and toilets that would never come. Mack was dissatisfied with the floor tiles in the smaller bathroom. The color didn't harmonize with the walls, not that it mattered.

"Well, the landlady should be happy," he said. They had spent 200,000 yuan on the renovations, he said, plus seven or eight months' rent.

He and his partners had managed to make some friends in the district government, but that had gotten them only a better explanation, not relief. In Dongcheng and Chaoyang districts, in the more visitor-friendly eastern part of the city, there were official programs to develop business in the hutongs. They had special business-licensing rules there, including fire regulations for courtyard houses less stringent than the national code. Xicheng had no such exemption. If the fire marshal were to approve a courtyard hotel, it would mean that he had personally lowered the standards, with no bureaucratic or political coverage.

So when the marshal invited them to bypass his office, Mack said, "he's just telling us that you have to use your connections." And their group didn't have good enough connections. It would take someone big—"like the commerce-bureau chief," Mack said, "or the mom of this guy, the fire marshal." It might become possible to do the hotel after the Olympics, when low-level bureaucrats were less afraid of drawing attention to themselves. Then, an irregular hotel pitched to foreigners might get by. "But I lost interest now," he said.

The American guy who wrote the book *One Billion Customers*—a bestseller about doing business in China—was right, Mack said. It was all about *guanxi*, your connections. This was the sort of thing that the expats would say to each other all the time, in stentorian tones, as a running gag: *Success in China is all about* guanxi. . . . *The Chinese place great importance on the concept of* mianzi, *or "face"*— all the received truisms about the Way the New China Really

Worked. Now here was Big Mack, the master problem-solver, glumly citing a business writer. "It's all about *guanxi*," he said.

We went back out to the alley. Around the corner, another courtyard house was being reconstructed. Old Beijing was getting yet another incarnation—the city had finally grasped that people valued the idea of a nondemolished hutong, and preservation had become a municipal goal, like slum clearance had been before it. So the neighbors were getting a renovation of their own, paid for by the government. Their house had two main buildings, north and south, and a little kitchen between. Wooden door and window frames were going into the rebuilt brick of the north building; the south one was done. The woman of the house was seventy-one, a retiree from the municipal building department, and she was paralyzed on her left side. She sat in a chair in the courtyard, by a pomegranate tree and a jujube tree, working her bad arm with her good one. Her husband was partly paralyzed, too, Mack said. They had four grown children, three daughters and a son, and the youngest lived with them. Another neighbor poured tea from a metal pot into paper cups. While the house was being rebuilt, the family had lived together in the kitchen, with an ayi to look after them. The whole neighborhood was being redone this way.

VI.

中国加油

GO, CHINA!

16.

起来 Arise

On May 12, around two-thirty in the afternoon, I took a sip of water in my fifth-story Chinese language classroom and felt suddenly, fleetingly queasy. The teacher felt nauseated, too, but neither of us said anything. Though we didn't realize it, the skybridge we were in was swaying invisibly. A friend of my wife's thought that something had slipped or broken in his office chair.

Nine hundred fifty miles away, in Wenchuan County in Sichuan Province, the Longmenshan geologic fault had ruptured. The earthquake measured 7.9 on the Richter scale. An early report on the *China Daily* website announced that there were 117 dead and that Premier Wen Jiabao was rushing to the scene. Then a report said that "up to 8,500" people were dead.

A week later, the death toll was in the tens of thousands. One way to try to envision tens of thousands of dead might be to stand in the midst of tens of thousands of living people. I couldn't say how many people were on Tian'anmen Square on May 19. I usually am not bad at crowd counts—cut out a section by eyeball, tally heads, multiply by the space—but the people spreading back from the flagpole on the north end of the square were an indivisible mass. The square was vastly wide and flat, and from down on the ground among them, I couldn't possible take all the people in, which was probably as good a way as any to stop and think about the earthquake.

A Chinese reporter guessed there were 30,000 people on the square, if we understood each other right. He may have been talking about the death toll itself. Saying 30,000 meant rounding 2,476 dead people off the count that was in the morning newspaper, or rounding 20,000 off the estimates that day of what the final number might be. Something like 50,000 people had been killed in Wenchuan County, Beichan County, and the surrounding areas. Nobody knew for sure. Eventually, the estimates would add almost another 20,000 to that.

After I got home from the mourning ceremony, I read that 158 rescue workers (or 200, depending on the report) had died in mudslides in the quake zone. One hundred fifty-eight more dead people didn't budge the needle. They weren't even killed in the earthquake; they were killed by the side effects of the earthquake.

The crowd arrived on the square from the south, filing past Mao's mausoleum and the obelisk of the Monument to the People's Heroes toward the top of the square, where the flagpole faces the Tian'anmen itself, across Chang'an Boulevard. The sky had a hazy white glare to it. The breeze blew from the south, and the red flag was flying in it at half-mast, which I had never seen before.

In America, the flag gets lowered at the first hint of tragedy. It was tempting to suppose that China's usual restraint meant that the Chinese must be inured to mass death. Dozens of people had died in a high-speed train wreck earlier in the month; coal miners died all the time by the scores. Our history books (though not always China's) recount millions and tens of millions of Chinese lives lost to famine or war or political turmoil.

But 32,476 dead—or 50,000 dead—was a staggering number, even against a background of 1.3 billion people, and China was staggered by it. It took a while to recognize what had happened. If you took China again to be more or less the size of the United States, the part of Sichuan where the quake hit was more or less where rural Missouri would be, if rural Missouri towns had 100,000 souls in them.

It was the tarps that began to tell what had happened. American news coverage, describing the scene, mentioned that some of the victims were being covered by red-white-and-blue tarpaulins. That referred to a very particular thing: a kind of striped fabric, a plasticky burlap, that was ubiquitous on the Chinese landscape. Sometimes it came in other colors, but the red-white-and-blue was the most common. This was the material of curtains on the windows of gut-renovation construction sites, of rain covers on the fruit stands, of cargo covers in the beds of the tricycle rickshaws and the blankets over the cargo-rickshaw drivers when they took a nap. It made tents in the migrant-worker encampments. Sewn into square-sided bags, it was the luggage of peasants arriving at the long-distance bus station. The week of the earthquake, I could look out the kitchen window and see a sheet of it laid in the courtyard as a dropcloth for the painting crew at the apartment. It was the fabric people used for the cheapest and commonest everyday jobs, and in Sichuan they were using it to wrap the dead and wounded.

How do you react to something like that? The practical response was immediate: the People's Liberation Army swung into action; helicopters and earth movers and rescue teams began working their way toward the epicenter. International relief organizations and foreign disaster squads followed. The symbolic response came together more slowly. China had not developed the American rituals of instant, willed grieving—candles, teddy bears, trauma counselors. Wen and President Hu Jintao did appear on television amid the rubble, as national leaders ought. But there was no coordinated expression of national sorrow in the beginning. The morning after the earthquake, the Beijing Olympic organizing committee had yet to prepare any official statement on the disaster. No one had thought about what to do if May became more important than August. A representative of the committee thanked the press for showing concern and took a question about the state of the torch relay as a technical matter: "The earthquake-affected area is not on the route of the torch relay, so it will not be affected." The Olympics could consider only the Olympics.

What took shape over the following week was considerably more raw than the American version of public grief. The Chinese press, shaking off the usual official censorship to swarm the quake zone, did not fall back on self-censorship. There was no consensus of tastefulness like the one that led to photos of jumpers and body parts being memory-holed shortly after 9/11. On the radio, as part of an earthquake broadcast, a child survivor sobbed while describing limbs sticking from the ruins of a collapsed school. The May 19 *Beijing News*, announcing the beginning of three days of official mourning, offered a front-page blowup of a photo of a dead and blackened fist clutching a broken toothbrush. I flipped the paper over for relief, and the back-page photo displayed a girl in a hospital bed, viewed from above, with a Barbie doll in her arms and a red stain spreading out from under her blanket, from where her left leg used to be.

The three-day mourning period itself was to begin with a three-minute nationwide observation, starting at 2:28 p.m. on Monday, exactly seven days after the quake. Citizens nationwide would stop what they were doing and stand silently, while motor vehicles laid on their horns and air-raid sirens sounded.

On Tian'anmen Square, the buildup was dizzying—people strolling or hurrying north, in crossing paths, till they ran out of room to walk. When 2:28 arrived, the pause itself felt curiously inadequate. The vastness of the square worked against it: the horns and sirens came from far off, a faint disturbance carrying across the open space. Camera shutters clicked and clicked. A silver-haired woman in a wheelchair bowed her head, and the photographers moved in on her.

Then it was over, officially. China had stopped—the entire nation, as instructed—and something had to come next. The crowd held its place, murmuring, considering. Near me, a man broke huskily into song: *"Qilai! Qilai! Qilai!"*—Arise! Arise! Arise!—the words of the national anthem. The singing faltered. A chant began: *"Zhongguo jia you!"* The sports chant, apostrophized to the whole country, Zhongguo, the Central Nation. Go, China!

For a few minutes, the singing and chanting continued raggedly, at odds, among different knots of people: *Arise, you who refuse to be slaves . . . "Jia you! Zhongguo! Jia you!" . . .* Then, swiftly, the crowd made up its mind: *"ZHONGGUO! JIA YOU!"* Thousands of fists pumped in unison, amid phones and cameras held aloft. Newspapers, their front pages done in somber black-and-white, bobbed along. A call-and-response developed: dozens of people, leaders of their vicinity, offering *"Zhongguo!"* and tens of thousands returning *"JIA YOU!"* A small man rode above the crowd, clutching a flag and a poster and a flower, thrusting his arms up over and over again in a Y of rapture.

After five or ten minutes, the chanting gave way to applause. A new call immediately picked up: *"Zhongguo!" "WAN SUI!"* Ten thousand years!—the old cry for wishing long life to Mao. Off across the crowd and across the street, the Great Helmsman's portrait looked down from the gate, but the masses were hailing their own country, themselves. *"Zhongguo!" "WAN SUI!" "Zhongguo!" "WAN SUI!" "Sichuan!" "WAN SUI!"*

The crowd milled, not pressed to the front any longer. People snapped pictures of each other, of the most fervent demonstrators, the elderly, children, pretty girls. Cameras pointed in my face. It occurred to me that I was an obvious foreigner in the middle of an impromptu nationalist rally, but that was too specific and intellectual to be a real worry. It was enough that I was in a numberless, agitated crowd, one that hadn't figured out what it was doing. "Country?" a man demanded, after snapping my picture. *"Meiguo,"* I said. America. He grinned and gave a thumbs-up.

Waves of chanting came and went, for twenty minutes, half an hour, on and on. Men were raw-voiced or panting with exertion. Uniformed police officers moved among them, with no obvious concern or emphasis. Then someone unfurled a large Chinese flag, and people began to push in toward him in excitement. A middle-aged man in a blue-on-blue dress shirt moved toward the flag-bearer, unobtrusively, and said something to him, and the flag began to retreat to the south and east, pulling part of the crowd with it. Another middle-aged man, wearing a blue pullover, held a walkie-talkie down by his side and watched.

Then the whole back of the crowd broke into a march, a river of people flowing from west to east, where the flag had gone. "China rising! China rising!" a gaunt young man in lensless hipster glasses called out in English, grinning, as he passed me. The river eddied into new vortexes of chanting: "Sichuan!" *"JIA YOU!"* The sixty-year campaign for international recognition, the hundred-year dream of hosting the Olympics—these were nothing next to the 5,000-year struggle of human civilization against heaven and earth. The man in the blue-on-blue shirt appeared again, steering a white man and woman out of the thick of one vortex. The chanting carried on.

It was more than an hour before the authorities finally decided to end it. The normal method of clearing the square, if an event required it, was for a line of soldiers to march down from the north and sweep it clear. This time, the soldiers worked their way south at a stroll, in no formation, wearing pale-green shirtsleeves. A baby-faced NCO took some pictures. The crowd began to move along. One man turned back and tried one more yell: *"ZHONGGUO!"* The plainclothesman in the dress shirt stepped over to him. Take a rest, he said, mildly.

Within two weeks of the earthquake, Sichuan was in the Bird's Nest, running and jumping. TV and radio were still full of disaster reports and fund-raising specials; orphans were everywhere. But it was time for the Good Luck Beijing Track and Field Open, with a mix of national, international, and provincial athletes. Tragedy and spectacle would make accommodation for each other. The Beijing crowd cheered pointedly when the stadium cameras settled on a Sichuan uniform, or when "Sichuan" appeared on the scoreboard.

Still, the Good Luck meet was above all a showcase for Liu Xiang. The hurdler had followed up his Athens gold medal by setting a new world record, 12.88 seconds, in the summer of 2006. He had become possibly the most famous person in China, beyond even Yao Ming. Now he was having a public rehearsal on the Olympic stage.

The overall national campaign for gold medals was principally about tactics and manpower, not individual heroism; the goal had been to find sports in which Chinese athletes could most feasibly compete, and train them up to win. If the gold medal count were going to be won, it would be won by an army of target shooters, weight lifters, and synchronized divers.

But Liu Xiang was an athlete in the Western, heroic mode. Chinese people had not believed that a Chinese competitor could possess natural superiority in running and jumping. Even when Liu had won in Athens, Chinese observers (and Liu himself) tried to credit it to his timing and technique, rather than sheer speed and muscle.

As Liu kept winning, people stopped trying to rationalize it and yielded to awe. By 2008, he was the subject of a commercial and popular personality cult, ubiquitous beyond comprehension. If he wasn't hurdling something on a billboard for Lenovo computers or Haier appliances or Visa credit cards, he was drinking Coca-Cola; if he wasn't drinking Coca-Cola, he was drinking Yili-brand dairy products. The face and legs of Liu Xiang soared over the entire landscape. *China Daily* would report before the Games that his commercial endorsements had fused together in the public's mind such that 15 percent of the public wrongly assumed that he must have been associated with Pepsi, too.

Before I saw Liu Xiang, I had business with the Bird's Nest itself. Down in the basement, outside an empty press conference hall, I finally put my finger on the stadium problem. I mean this literally. In front of me, plunging at an angle from the ceiling to the floor, was one of the stadium's columns, like the one I had rapped on at the Racewalking Challenge. On one edge, the silvery surface had been chipped by some passing object. In the chip, a dark gray was showing. I pressed my fingertip into the chipped part. When I pulled it back, there was concrete dust on it.

By now, I had been reading and writing about the stadium structure from various distances for years: "a lattice of interwoven steel" (*The New York Times*) . . . "a tangle of steel trusses" (*The Times*) . . .

"mesmeric steel frame" (*The Guardian*) . . . "monumental steel thatching" (me). Describing it was like reviewing restaurants and groping for ways to say "tasty"—it was a bird's nest. Made of metal. The end.

The weight of the whole edifice was hanging over me. I had come there in the deserted afternoon between sessions of the Good Luck Beijing Track and Field Open for a seminar on Olympic reporting, presented by the organizing committee, to be held in the stadium's press conference hall. This had been yet another inoperative piece of information, a red herring, a wild goose: the room was vacant and undisturbed—almost sterile—rows of white plastic seats under blue-tinged lights, flanked by coolers with every shelf full of untouched water bottles.

Out in the hall, by the columns, a stray venue volunteer suggested that maybe the session would start in half an hour. (It would not.) She went to check on it.

And then I took a look at the column, and the chip out of it. Does steel chip? And there was my left index finger, with concrete dust on it.

I began to review in my mind a rough list I had been making since the first tap on the pillar in April, the list of all the editors to whom I might now owe a correction. *Due to a reporting error . . . ? Due to impenetrable confusion about stadium-engineering techniques . . . ? Due to the fundamental unreliability of received information . . . ?*

But what would the substance of the correction be? My knowledge extended only an eighth of an inch below the surface. Maybe there was steel below the concrete. Maybe there was more concrete below the steel below the concrete. It was not a sensitive or controversial subject, as far as I could imagine, like the number of relocated residents was. The Chinese authorities were not trying to be obfuscating about it. Yet this basic point of fact was buried in layers of confusion. After more than two years of reporting on the New Beijing, I had no idea what the National Stadium was made of.

The reporting seminar had been canceled due to lack of interest from the domestic and foreign press. Time to get back to dealing with the facts on my own. I went home and rummaged through my notes. Deep in my clip file, I found an official story from the government's Xinhua News Agency, in English. It was an interview with Li Jiulun, identified as the "chief engineer" of the Bird's Nest. It described how Li and his colleagues had "stuffed the steel tubes with concrete bars" and "poured concrete into the tubes from underneath to custom-make over 1,300 concrete columns and trusses" ("which are three times as efficient as those made through foreign methods"). When I was done reading it, I had even less of an idea of how the stadium had been built.

I went back to the stadium in the evening, to cover the track-and-field competition. It was the night of the semifinal in the 110 meters, Liu's event. The crowd roared for his warm-up jog. A sepia-tinted replay of his highlights ran on the video board. Camera flashes and screaming. Liu false-started in his heat, in a group combining Chinese and foreign runners. It was charged to the field, so nobody else could try to sneak out of the blocks. The race was over by the time Liu reached the third hurdle. He won in 13.46, far off his record of 12.88. The stadium bowl emptied out as soon as he was done, leaving empty seats for the men's and women's 100-meter sprint finals, usually the glamour races. Deng Yaping—a two-time gold medalist in table tennis, who had once been the most popular athlete in China herself—would publicly criticize the crowd afterward for its bad manners toward the other competitors.

All the while, I pestered other reporters, face-to-face and by SMS:

What do *you* think the stadium is made out of? I think the whole surface is concrete! Does anybody know? Nobody did.

Down under the stadium, I asked two Australian sprinters from the ignored men's 100-meter final what they'd thought of the stadium and the air. In less than three months, Olympic athletes would be trying to get oxygen—if more of them didn't give up and decide Beijing was irredeemably polluted. "The air, huh!" Joshua Ross said. Ross had finished fourth. "A bit dusty. I dunno, it's just thick, thick air."

"It's a beautiful stadium," said Patrick Johnson, who had finished one-hundredth of a second ahead of Ross for the bronze, in 10.31 seconds. Johnson predicted, in what would retrospectively look like wild understatement, that the track would get quicker as it aged over the summer. "It's a bit polluted," he said, of the air, "but the reality is, everyone's got the same conditions. . . . If you decide not to come, then, fine enough, it's your personal opinion."

The underground concourse was big enough to drive a bus on. Full-sized buses had been driving on it, with room to spare. As the night was winding down, a band of people walked by, wearing what looked like saggy overalls—blue, red, yellow . . . These were the Fuwa, half dressed and uninflated. Right in front of me, they struggled into their uppers and fired up their backpack air pumps, the forms of Beibei, Jingjing, and Huanhuan swelling into shape. Giggling volunteers snapped photos as the Fuwa shook their newly inflated bottoms. The bottoms had round little mesh portals on them, right where an anus would have been. I was looking at the anuses of the Fuwa.

The next night was Liu's final, and the rest of the track meet struggled for the crowd's attention. Big cheers rose when Sichuan won a heat in the men's 4-by-100-meter relay; the anchor-leg runner looked into a stadium video camera and pointed to the characters for "Sichuan" on his chest. Poplar fluff and dead bugs and living bugs swirled in the stadium lights, raining down on the people below. In a duel for the women's pole vault title, Sichuan moved ahead of Beijing.

A roar went up for Liu toting his gear onto the track. Earthquake sympathy and the drama of the pole vault were forgotten. He was wearing a form-fitting red-and-yellow running outfit, with the Chinese flag on his right pectoral and the Nike emblem on his left, and with straps that came together in a skinny Y down his back, like a halter top worn backward.

Liu false-started again, to gasps from the crowd. This time the penalty was assessed to him personally. He would have to make sure to lag behind the starting gun, but it made no difference. He won in 13.18, with his teammate Shi Dupeng lunging hard at the end to get a 13.29. The interviews began down on the track. What did he think of the Bird's Nest? *"Bu cuo."* Not bad. He worked his way up through the gantlet of interviewers on the walkway out of the stadium bowl. Volunteers lined up with linked arms to keep the press in check. The women's steeplechase medal ceremony started. When the Chinese anthem began to play for the winner, Liu used it as cover to move along.

That just brought him into the second gantlet, the underground rope line of print reporters. I plunged in. Liu was eight feet away—he was surprisingly tall, and had acne on his jawline—but forty people were closer. Volunteers in coral-colored shirts and police in blue crowded around the exit, clearing a space for him. He worked his way through the line and out the far end, sticking to a wall, with a teammate swinging wide to screen him. As soon as he was clear, the volunteers broke ranks and went scampering after him.

Liu's press conference was scheduled for the very end of the evening. On the concourse, in the meantime, reporters had found J Parrish, the director of Arup Sport, the engineering firm that had worked on the stadium design. It was not a structured press availability, with handouts and interpreters; he was just there. Parrish was tall and bearded and loquacious, a person talking about what he did. According to his business card, the J had no period after it. He was politely telling a radio reporter that he had no idea what the opening ceremonies might involve.

What, I asked, apologetically, were the columns made of? Parrish looked around us. "Concrete," he said, indicating the nearest one, and continuing on, pointing as he went: "Concrete, concrete, concrete . . . steel."

I double-checked: Steel? The outermost layer of columns in the Nest, the key to the structure, was indeed steel, he said. Steel boxes, in cross section, of various thicknesses. The thicket of columns on the inside, crisscrossing the concourses, was concrete, mostly. All the columns were painted silver, to match.

You might need to hit them with a hammer, Parrish said, to tell the difference.

Liu was late to the press conference. Till that moment, the track open had run precisely on time. The press applauded as he entered. Were the false starts part of his strategy? The first one, the day before, had been deliberate, he said. "Today, I just started a bit faster than the gun," he said, through the official translator. What about the pressure and publicity surrounding him? "I just keep a balance mentally."

Who, a perky male reporter with an American accent asked, would he describe as his role model? *"Zhende hai meiyou,"* Liu said, beginning his response. ("I don't have any particular role model or idols," the translator said.)

He had expected to win the Good Luck event, he said. "The most important thing for me is in August," he said. A female reporter from Hong Kong had two questions: How would he handle the pressure at the Olympics? And would he be wearing his sexy gear then? "I think it all depends on myself," he said, about the pressure. As for the outfit, "I think this is only given by Nike for a trial."

It was near midnight when the press conference adjourned. Someone had drawn a heart around the characters for "Liu Xiang" on the white board by the door. I had a long hike ahead to get a cab. First, though, on my way out of the stadium, I veered back to the outer row of columns and knocked on one with force. It rang.

A giant rendering of Liu Xiang's eyes looked down from the Nike store on Wangfujing, the downtown street of department stores and shopping malls, where I was shopping for children's books for a baby shower. Inside the store, a mannequin in a Team China track outfit was posed leaping over a hurdle. China's athletic program had been subdivided among the international sports-marketing superpowers: Adidas had secured the exclusive rights to the uniforms they would wear on the medal stand, so Nike was investing heavily in the outfits for competition proper. The racks were full of Chinese national team gear; you could dress up as a Chinese wrestler, if you so chose. There were basketball uniforms, but in a fit of Western individualism, the only jersey was Yi Jianlian's. Yao Ming was with Reebok, now owned by Adidas.

Liu's victory in the Good Luck hurdles was the last win he would get in the spring. A week later, he dropped out of a meet in New York with a sore hamstring. In his next meet, he would be disqualified for a false start. Then, early in June, in a meet without Liu, Dayron

Robles of Cuba would win the 110-meter hurdles with a time of 12.87 seconds, shaving a hundredth of a second off the record. Liu Xiang was no longer the world's fastest hurdler. The public was not too concerned. By then Liu was off the circuit, resting and training for August, the only event that mattered.

17.

公安 Public Security

hen we finally got into an argument with the Chinese security, it was over an oddly American thing. We had gone to Urumqi, the capital of the Xinjiang Uighur Autonomous Region, on a short trip for Christina's job. Most of the troubles on the trip had been the usual Chinese ones: the flight from Beijing had been late because the whole plane, in this egalitarian workers' paradise, was held to wait for a tardy first-class passenger to show up. Someone somewhere on the flight had lit up a cigarette. There was violent, tossing turbulence. The beverage service ran out of water. When the baby finally started screaming from it all, the steward came back to our seats, near the pitching tail of the plane, and asked us to stop him from crying because the other passengers were trying to sleep. The way out of the Urumqi airport was clogged by an almost impassable pressing crowd. Because of the Olympics, our driver told us after helping us squeeze free, people were not allowed to wait inside the terminal for arrivals anymore, so they just formed a mob outside.

Then, as we headed back through the airport, for the flight back to Beijing, the security screeners pulled aside our diaper bag. The airport-security wringer was a fairly new feature of life in China. When I started traveling between the United States and the People's Republic in 2004, only one side of the trip had airports that felt like they belonged to a totalitarian state: America. The home of the Bill of Rights was where you had to strip off your shoes and belt, where checked baggage would be diverted and pawed through by inspectors, where guards would stop you if you tried to make a cell-phone call from baggage claim. Eventually, after the liquid-explosives scare, it was where you couldn't even bring a drink of water on the flight.

What was America's real contribution to global culture in the twenty-first century? In the airport line, as in so many other parts of modern life, China was catching up with the way things were done in the United States. While our actors and activists lectured China about how the advance of liberty cannot and must not be stopped, the American experience was sending out the opposite message: in a dangerous world, freedom and privacy must yield to the demands of law and order.

In March, state-run news had reported that a passenger or passengers had tried to bring down a flight out of Urumqi, using gasoline as the would-be weapon. The details of the gasoline plot were never quite clear, but the result was: soon after, China instituted an American-style liquids ban of its own.

It is necessary, in a campaign against terrorism, to emphasize insecurity. A worried public is more cooperative with its protectors. The rioting in Lhasa didn't undermine public confidence in the Chinese government's legitimacy; it fortified it: These are the kind of people we have to deal with.

China had pledged greater openness and adherence to human-rights norms, but it had also promised that the Beijing Games would be safe. And safety came first. Beijing was hosting a major international event, in what everyone agreed were perilous times. *The New York Times* had reported that American companies, including IBM, Honeywell, and General Electric, were supplying hardware and software to help Beijing build a state-of-the-art surveillance system to protect itself for the Games. Any terrorist who tried to disrupt Beijing would confront a security network of hundreds of thousands of cameras, programmed to automatically recognize suspicious people or detect unusual crowd behavior. That surveillance ability—to identify unwanted faces, to prevent the unexpected—would still be there after the Olympics were over, for the Public Security Bureau to use however it might choose.

On our way out of Urumqi, the X-ray machine said we were suspect people. Two officers, a man and a woman, were hand-inspecting bags that had flunked the scan. From the diaper bag, they produced two bottles of sunscreen, mine and the baby's. I constantly forget to put sunscreen in checked baggage. The last time I'd forgotten, it had just been the baby's sun lotion, and an officer had waved it through out of sympathy. But two bottles? I stood convicted of boneheadedness. The sunscreen (irreplaceable on the Chinese market) went into the bin by the officers' feet, with other fliers' cast-off bottled water and snacks.

Then they pulled out the two jars of baby food.

Technically, baby food was illegal under the new Chinese security rules. This marked one of the key differences between Chinese and American security procedures. In America, the rules might be intrusive, inconvenient, and pointless—and they could be foolishly and inflexibly applied—but customers expected there to be, at bottom, some sign of reasonableness. Passengers need to be able to take their medicine on a plane, or take out their contact lenses. Babies need to eat.

The Chinese rule makers and enforcers, on the other hand, didn't worry about whether or not people thought the text of the rules was reasonable. The rule banned fluids. Baby food was fluidlike. Baby food was therefore banned.

The male officer at Urumqi was ready to let the food pass. There was a baby; there was the baby's food. It was sealed in its factory containers. But the woman overruled him: No baby food allowed. The jars would have to go in the bin.

What had once been easy had now skipped past American-grade difficulty, into the impossible. It was a little before six p.m., the baby's dinnertime. If he didn't eat, he would scream all the way back to the capital. We offered to feed him right there, at the security checkpoint. None of the baby food would go onto the plane, except inside the baby. But the officers were inflated, petty authority seizing a petty problem. Baby food was not allowed. It had to be confiscated.

Somehow, while I argued with the female officer, my wife got her hands on one of the jars and began spooning fruit into the baby's mouth. The baby did not burst into flames. Unimpressed, the officer held on to the second jar. Perhaps the blueberries were a decoy, and the strained peas were the real explosives.

Was terrorist attack against the Olympics a genuine threat? It was hard to know in Beijing, as it is in New York. Besides the reported airplane attack, there had been a bus explosion in Shanghai in the spring, and the government had reported raids in the west on heavily armed Uighur and Tibetan groups, including finds of weapons cached in Buddhist monasteries. The armed-monk plot sounded far-fetched to American ears, but it was not much more implausible than the kung fu terrorist cell our own government announced it had broken up in Miami, or the feebleminded alleged schemes to flood Lower Manhattan or cut the cables of the Brooklyn Bridge with wire nippers.

In Beijing, the police were stopping foreigners more and more frequently on the street, even in expat-friendly neighborhoods, and asking to see their passports and visas. Every outsider was a potential security threat. Visa renewals had replaced air quality as the inescapable topic of conversation. The year before, declaring you wanted to get out of the country for the Olympics was an affectation, a way for old China hands to express their dismay at the thought of a once challenging city being overrun by soft hordes of first-time tourists. But it was becoming a practical decision—better to wait out the security squeeze back home than to put up with the new annoyances.

We managed to pry the peas away, and we shoveled them into the baby's mouth. Our terrorist co-conspirators in the baby-food industry had outwitted security, replacing the explosives with harmless vegetables. Mack finished the entire jar. When he was done, we tossed the dripping jars back into the confiscation bin, as hard as we dared, and were rewarded with the sound of breaking glass.

The press briefings kept coming. The Beijing Tourism Administration announced that the city of Beijing now had 815 star-rated hotels, 5,892 lodging places overall, 336,000 guest rooms, and 660,000 beds. In 2001, the city had promised the IOC 350 more star-rated hotels, for a total of 800 by the time of the Games. Two hundred thousand staffers would receive training in foreign languages and etiquette. The color of towels, and the softness of those towels, would be standardized citywide. There would be a city tourism manual and a television channel dedicated to tourism. There would be a hotline to a tourists' call center.

Would there be tourists? The forecast was for 450,000 to 500,000, no more than there would be in a normal summer. The Olympics was driving off as many people as it was attracting. What about the problems people were having getting tourist visas? "Well, all Olympic host cities will strengthen security measures during the Olympic Games. . . . Beijing has done likewise, and we have strengthened reviews on tourist applications. I believe if the applicants follow our requirements, for example identification of their hotels, I believe they will get their visas smoothly."

What were the reservation rates at the moment? For the five-star hotels, the rate was 77 percent. For four-stars, it was 44 percent. The shortfall was "not entirely" due to the security measures. Three-star and lower hotels "have plenty of rooms." The wintertime shortage of reservations, it now appeared, was failed speculation.

Then came the press conference on medical preparations. There would be 5,800 hospital beds available, and the city was laying in a supply of blood types suitable for foreigners. Less than one percent of the Chinese population had Rh-negative blood. The public health system would be prepared for black plague and food poisoning alike.

What about transparency in the handling of health matters? "Open, fair, and transparent is the responsibility of our government." Jin Dapeng, the party secretary of the municipal health bureau, was a heavy-faced man with wavy hair, a touch of gray at the temples, in a blue suit, blue shirt, and blue tie. He spoke slowly and oratorically. His eyebrows were impressive. He had gone into Tangshan, where an earthquake killed something like a quarter of a million people in 1976, as a twenty-nine-year-old medical staffer, he said. Unlike the ongoing spectacle of Sichuan, the extent of the calamity in Tangshan had been a mystery: Mao was on his deathbed, the Cultural Revolution was falling apart, and the death toll was treated as an internal matter. "At the time, the government wasn't open enough to release the information," Jin said. "This time, in Sichuan, you could witness the openness and transparency."

"We will prepare ourselves for all kinds of daunting difficulties," Jin said. "We will dedicate ourselves to achieving our goal, despite all kinds of difficulties. . . . We will go through this historical moment, and history will tell others that our medical team is capable and professional. . . ." He went on to a booming finish: "Just as the Chinese people have demonstrated in the earthquake. They have shown their strong character. We will also show our strong character."

Across from the alley mouth, the corner store and the corner itself were in total disorder. Inside the market, the cold case was all that remained of the grocery section. The rest had been gutted; torn-out ceiling tiles lay on the floor. The old overhead signs, announcing the "Family Planning" and "Little Edible" departments in English, were gone. All the surviving grocery goods had been crammed into the middle, where the fruit and eyeglasses used to be. A curtain of the striped plastic fabric imperfectly separated the work zone from the checkout, where the cashier was coughing from the dust.

The public toilet across the intersection was now four-fifths demolished, with only the east end standing. The newsstand had been shuttered and moved, in its entirety, a few yards to the rear. The vendor had set out papers and magazines in the open, on racks and a table, next to where the stand had been. The bicycle repairman who used to work alongside the toilet had set up shop on the amputated tile floor of the newsstand itself, inside the abandoned half-octagon foundation.

For Mack's first birthday, we took him to the zoo in the morning to see the Earthquake Pandas. Officially, they had been booked as the Olympic Pandas, but the Sichuan earthquake had struck the heart of the panda reserve, sending the collection of young pandas north ahead of schedule, as refugees.

The earthquake recovery remained the ongoing counterpoint to the Olympic preparations. Christina had found another ballet class to go to, a self-organized band of amateur dance aficionados—a shipping-industry logistics worker, a cabdriver—who would find empty studios and convene via text message. One of their preferred sites was the studio of the dance corps of the Chinese Coal Mining Association. Like other Chinese organizations, up to and including the People's Liberation Army, the coal association maintained a cultural wing. Since the dancers were frequently away, entertaining the coal miners, the studio was available. One night, there was a fund-raiser going on there, with genuine Sichuan orphans as the guests.

On the taxi drivers' radio station, an announcer was saying that taxis ought to make it possible for passengers to use child safety seats. By now, we had guiltily gone native; Mack had outgrown his infant seat, and lugging a larger version around from cab to cab was too much to contemplate. Also, the radio warned, one should be careful not to blow cold air on the babies.

People lined the windows in the Olympic Panda House, waiting for the pandas to show up. Around eight a.m., keepers wearing rubber boots began strewing armloads of bamboo around the enclosure. Then, to cheers, the pandas were released from a door in the rear, eight of them in all. They were two years old, a bit taller on all fours than knee-high to an adult human. Appearing all at once, they gave the impression of actually, adorably, tumbling into view. Panda abundance was new to me; I was used to the display at the National Zoo in Washington, D.C., with the expensively leased pandas displayed in individual settings, like the Hope Diamond, to be contemplated by reverent viewers. A young female keeper, skipping and clapping, led the pandas forward and spread them out at different piles of food, so everyone could see. The surge of panda admirers pinned me against the window frame.

We retreated to the outside. Next door and a little downhill was the Asia Games Panda House, built in honor of the 1990 games in Beijing. Outside it, in a pit with a sliding board and teeter-totter overgrown with weeds, a full-grown panda was sitting in near anonymity. People gave it a glance as they hurried toward the Olympic Pandas. "The Olympic Pandas can't be that lazy and dirty," someone said.

Away from the pandas, at a photo-taking station, a young chimp in a rugby shirt slumped between two zoo staffers, who were also slumped. The gorilla habitat was empty, with painted Chinese masks on the wall leering at the space where the apes would go. People plucked leaves off the shrubbery at random and fed them to the animals. Around one fair-sized glass enclosure, with open mesh at the top, a small crowd watched some exotic animals from abroad showing off their climbing skills: *huanxiong*, or "washing bears." *Procyon lotor*. The raccoon.

Ice dancing was playing on the sports channel once known as CCTV-5, now renamed the CCTV Olympics channel. Odd hours of the TV day that might once have brought snooker or bullfighting now delivered Olympic preliminaries and Olympic retrospectives. One special consisted of footage of opening ceremonies from the past, including a slow-motion replay of the moment in Seoul in 1988 when a few white doves, lingering after a mass release early in the ceremony, perched in the stadium's cauldron and were incinerated by the lighting of the Olympic flame.

So the ice dancers twirled and glittered on dozens of televisions at once, all along the shore of the scenic lake called Houhai, through the open windows and French doors of dozens of bars. Houhai, part of a string of landscaped lakes leading north and west from alongside the Forbidden City, was a phenomenon of the New Beijing—a quiet stretch of parkland devoured in less than a decade by a nightlife land rush. A few bars where the hutongs met the lakeshore had attracted expats and Beijingers with money to spend, and those bars had attracted imitators, and the imitators had attracted more people, more money, and more imitators. The chain reaction would run out of shoreline before it ran out of fuel. There were restaurants in the mix, and a Starbucks, and a plaza at one end where middle aged and elderly Beijingers would waltz in the open air. But those were grace notes against the frantic, eagerly debauched air of a boardwalk during spring break—tinged by the interethnic May-December satisfaction of Chinese-expat couples on the make.

It was warm out. A vendor sold T-shirts with flickering graphic-equalizer displays built into them. Live heavy metal came from an open bar front, a cover of "Country Roads" from another. Touts trolled the strip, murmuring invitations to this or that "lady bar." "Lady bar, lady bar."

I was talking to a woman named Eva Shen, who had stepped outside of the club she co-owned. It was not a lady bar, though it could have been mistaken for one; it was a place where couples or friends might go for drinks. Over the door, in glowing characters, was the Chinese name of the club, Yuwang Chengshi; above that, in larger letters, was its other name: SEX AND DA CITY.

The movie of *Sex and the City* was opening in America, and the sign on the bar had made me curious about the outpost of intellectual property. I had long since discovered that my job for *The New York Observer* was too recursive and confusing to explain to people in Beijing—a newspaper reporter who reported on newspapers and reporters?—but I recognized that people would be excited and satisfied if I simply told them it was the paper where the "Sex and the City" column was published.

But in what shape had this stylized concept of New York life arrived on the shores of the imperial lakes? "Of course, nobody wants to be Samantha," Shen said. It was a warm Saturday night. She spoke English and wore yoga pants, a white T-shirt, and flip-flops. ("I do yoga a lot," she said.) Her hair was reddish and pulled back. Around her, the night was full of women in short-shorts, teetering heels, sparkly things; among the women were all the men looking for women.

Sex and Da City opened in 2003, Shen said. She and about a dozen friends had been out at a nightspot called the World of Suzy Wong Club, and everyone agreed they might as well open a bar of their own. When they convened to discuss the idea again in the daytime, the group had dwindled to five. When it came time to talk about investing money, Shen said, it was down to four women.

That night, she said, she went home and watched HBO. And right there was a show—she had already been a fan—about "exactly four girls," pursuing independence and glamour in the big city. Before Shen and her partners went to the bank, another one of them dropped out, but she had already settled on the name. Replacing "the" with "da" was, by Chinese standards, a fairly respectful nod to trademark rights.

Shen said she was looking forward to seeing the new movie. "Maybe my husband already bought the DVD," she said.

Shen was born in Chairman Mao's Beijing, in Haidian district. "I never imagined that I could open a bar like this," she said.

Sex and Da City was a modest-sized club, with a square floor plan and a square bar in the middle, with a two-story mural of Marilyn Monroe above the liquor bottles. Jodi Xu, a reporter born in Shanghai and bound for journalism school in New York, had met me at the club to help with Chinese-language interviews. A DJ booth was playing hip-hop, loudly. Marilyn's face looked into a three-sided loft where tables were 500 yuan. The drinks menu was long and included an "Absolut Astronaut Shooter," a "Sex and Da City Absolut Cosmopolitan," and an "Olympic Cocktail." The last was orange-ish and fruity, and it came in a big martini glass with a cherry notched onto its rim.

On each side of the bar was a shiny metal pole, running up to the facing of the loft. Around eleven p.m., a young woman in a snug black dress and shiny boots that rose past her knees climbed up on the bar and began dancing around and on the pole. The dancer had a cheery smile and wore square-cut bangs down past her eyebrows. She danced in a matter-of-fact style, wrapping it up by shinnying up the pole, as if in gym class, and doing a back bend.

Another dancer, skinnier and in a blousy, shorter dress, took the next shift. Men paused outside in the lane, goggling through the clear part of the glass door. Shen said she added the pole dancers in 2005. "Actually, there is a school, a pole dancers' school, in Beijing," she said. Occasionally, she said, the district police would come by and tell them to make sure nobody did anything too provocative.

Inside, a Chinese couple in their twenties were having a drink at one of the tables. The man told Jodi and me that they had come to the club because of the pole dancers. It was the only pole dancing on the whole street, he said. The dancers used to be more sexy, and they had more moves, he said, but the police had made them cut down on the erotic dancing for the Olympics, to keep the city from seeming sleazy.

The DJ played "Let's Get It Started," and people whooped and began to dance. On top of the bar, the woman in the boots—now wearing a blue pleated skirt and a T-shirt reading "All Good in the Hood"—kept moving at her previous calm pace.

Up in the loft, by the top of the stairs, the other dancer was slouched in a chair, wearing earbuds. She took them out to talk to us about Sex and Da City. She came to Beijing from Shanxi Province two years ago, she said, and she had been an instructor at the Beijing pole-dancing school. She danced ten minutes a shift—she held up her index fingers to make a cross, the Chinese symbol for "ten"— eight shifts a night, till one a.m.

"I studied dancing since I was a child, so that's why I like dancing," she said. "But at the same time, I need to make money." Living in Beijing, she said, created a lot of pressure. "If there's no money, you can't survive, and it's hard to find a job."

She confirmed that the police had asked them to dance less sexily, more low-key. She fiddled with a cigarette lighter in one hand and a shiny cell phone in the other as she talked. How old was she? Twenty-seven, she said. "Don't ask about my age."

Downstairs at the center of the bar, a Chinese woman in a dull-patterned dress had been sitting for a long time with her back to the door, talking to no one, stooped over a lowball glass. A bartender set a bottle of Corona beer, with a lime in the neck, beside her. Then he put fresh ice in a glass and poured the beer over it for her.

Another thing about Chinese people would be that Chinese people love Kobe Bryant. The NBA Finals were on, Bryant's Lakers against the Celtics, and Ma Jian was hosting a viewing party at a sports bar.

The bar took up the third floor of a hotel outside the Jianguomen interchange on the Second Ring; across the roadway and a little to the north was a surviving piece of the city wall, topped by the platform of the Ancient Observatory and its bronze astronomical implements, or replicas thereof. The original implements had been looted by Western powers during the Boxer Rebellion, and only some had been returned—an early one of China's accumulated twentieth-century historical indignities.

Ma was still working on the financing for his sports-education plans. Meanwhile, he had been doing NBA announcing work for a new sports network called CSPN, a collaboration among provincial TV stations. The network, whose logo lettering bore a strong resemblance to that of ESPN, would carry the satellite video feed from America, and Ma would supply Chinese commentary over it. CSPN was not available to viewers in Beijing, but the studios were down at the south end of the city. I'd joined Ma there one frigid winter morning, as he broadcast one of the most boring matchups imaginable—Yi Jianlian and the lousy Milwaukee Bucks against the awful New York Knicks. People wanted to see Yi, even if there was nothing else worth watching about the game. The studio was cavernous (the largest sports studio in Asia, Ma said), cold, and deserted: no receptionist, no one bringing coffee, no lights on in the lobby or stairwells. The Bucks took a commanding lead in the third quarter, then gave it all back. Ma narrated the action—"*You le!*" he called as a shot went up. Got it!—and supplied occasional notes on strategy, as much as he thought the audience could tolerate. "They're not very knowledgeable about the game," he said, ruefully. "I wish they could understand." If they were technically minded, viewers would have wanted to see some other game. Yi scored four points and sat on the bench in the final minutes as the Knicks finished their comeback.

The NBA had vanished from Chinese television after

the earthquake, under a national mourning ban on lighthearted programming. Now the NBA had reportedly donated 14 million yuan to earthquake relief, and the grief had eased enough that the Finals were back on TV, and the league was sponsoring a party for 200 people to watch game four, with a breakfast buffet.

Ma was in a curtained-off VIP lounge, preparing to announce the game for the party guests. He wore jeans with a Kobe Bryant jersey over a pink polo shirt. The jersey was cut to be fashionably baggy on someone much smaller than Ma; on his actual player's build, the proportions were snug and short-waisted. His cohost, Gu Yu, was younger and skinnier, and he wore a Paul Pierce jersey. On the way to the hotel, there had been a billboard of Yi Jianlian. Twenty years ago, Ma said, he could have been the player on the billboard.

To emphasize its goodwill toward China, the NBA had sent over a platoon of Miami Heat cheerleaders. They arrived in sparkle-trimmed warm-ups, toting black-and-white Heat bags. Bananas and bottled water were sitting out, and the cheerleaders asked very politely if they could have some, their manner so winsome and multiethnically all-American that I felt a pang of homesickness for the first time in months. Ma tore off a banana and handed it over. One of them plugged in a curling iron, and it heated up fast. We warned them that the Chinese current was 220. They had already burnt out one curling iron on the trip.

Chairs had been set up facing a stage, where a full-color NBA Finals backdrop was flanked by two big projection screens. Roving spotlights projected Lakers and Celtics logos. Before the game, public-service announcements for earthquake relief played over and over; LeBron James and Yao Ming spoke somberly into the camera, wearing plain gray sweatshirts. Sichuan's tragedy belonged to the world.

Ma and Gu warmed up the crowd, then sat down in the front

row with microphones to comment on the action. The big screen
was bleary, and they quickly relocated off to the side, where Ma could
follow the action on a smaller, crisper television. The crowd cheered
as Los Angeles surged out to a big lead. A fan borrowed my pen to
go get Ma's autograph.

During one of the breaks, the Miami cheerleaders came on and
danced to "The Heat Is On," wearing string-bikini-style outfits and
hats with the Heat logo. They danced with the force to project to a
15,000-seat arena, and it was impressive, and a little alarming, to be
in a small space with them.

A woman in a halter top and satiny pants sat down by Ma. She
was a friend of his, she said, and she worked for a modeling firm
that hired European models for shoots in China. For the Olympics,
she would be working with another company, one that projected
advertising onto inflatable domes. It would be installing a big setup
in Chaoyang Park for the appliance company Haier. "I didn't know
he was so famous," she said, as Ma worked the crowd from the stage.
"When he was famous, I wasn't born yet."

The Lakers were in the process of blowing the biggest lead in
NBA Finals history. Back in his seat, Ma kept his eyes on the screen,
twirling a basketball on his finger as he sat. The ball was autographed
by the NBA commissioner: "NBA China: Where Amazing happens!
David J. Stern."

The Olympics were less than two months away. New street signs
were up on the major roads, directing the way to the athletic venues.
When we took Mack to the hospital for a checkup, the massage
parlors across the street were shut. A friend bought a bootleg copy
of No Country for Old Men, and the paper sleeve inside the package
had the Beijing 2008 logo on it.

Olympic iconography had crept into everything, even where it made no sense. The company that delivered Pampers and baby wipes would throw in a bonus toy if we spent enough money. One of the prizes was possibly the most unsafe toy ever created: a ball made of two clear plastic hemispheres tinted a sickly glowing green, its surface studded with soft, thimble-like plastic cleats, which pulled off easily and appeared to be the perfect size to clog a child's windpipe. When you tugged a nail-like metal pin sticking out of the ball, an off-center-weighted electric motor in the middle would begin spinning, causing the ball to hop and flip and skitter around the floor on the cleats, while LEDs inside flashed and the thing played an off-tempo, flat-pitched version of "Axel F." There were five irregular-shaped vent holes on each side of the twitching, flashing, tootling ball—holes cut out in the tiny, unmistakable, counterfeit silhouettes of Beibei, Jingjing, Huanhuan, Yingying, and Nini.

Out by Dongzhimen Bridge, the giant bronze vessel had vanished. Its pedestal was wrapped in red-white-and-blue tarps, with rubble peeking out the top. On our alley, down at the corner, the newsstand was rapidly losing its new piece of ground. The digging closed in on it, till it stood alone on a little peninsula, surrounded by trenchwork. Then, one day, it jumped diagonally across the intersection, to the corner in front of the now vacant bank. The public restroom was completely demolished, but when I reported to Christina that it was gone without a trace, she challenged the premise. No trace? Was the smell really gone, too? (It was not.)

I had begun, over time, to have a tenuous sort of faith in the promises of improved air quality for the Olympics. Unquestionably, since 2004, the air had been getting better—not only in the "blue sky" count, but in the number of days when the color of the sky was objectively blue. "Better," in this case, meant "less bad," but that was the point: with nowhere to go but up, things did seem to be going up. In May, the authorities had presented the details of their plan to get clear air for the Games: by August, even more industry would be shut down; half the private cars would be off the road each day; construction—or at least excavation and concrete work—would be halted.

As June stretched on, though, I wondered if I was being a Pollyanna. Construction showed no signs of slowing; crews were already digging and pouring the buildings that would open after the Olympics, when Beijing's future continued. Cement mixers had been lining up at the construction pit, ten or more at a time. Dust clouds rose to mingle with the haze. The air quality reached the don't-go-outside level, then got worse.

On a particularly gray afternoon, I set out for English class. Thanks to an introduction by Big Mack in May, I had fallen in with a group of retirees in the Dongsi neighborhood, a designated Olympic Community, who were studying English in preparation for August. Showing up in the classroom had automatically made me a sort of adjunct instructor, available to explain why was it preferable to say "had never imagined" rather than "have never imagined," and why you would say "How long have you studied English?" instead of "How long have you learned English?" In return, the students were providing me with their own advice and opinions: I should take the 106 bus or the 24 bus from Dongzhimen to get to class; my community, Hujiayuan, was a very famous one, with rich and colorful activities; a daytime ayi like ours should be paid only 1,000 yuan a month.

English improvement, like pollution control, was not a matter of straight-line progress. A banner in the third-floor classroom read "Public Welfore English Class or Citizens of Dongsi Olympic Community." This was better than I would have done trying to render that sort of phrase in Chinese, but it did capture the problem. The official line on English was that embarrassing errors in signage would all be rectified before the Olympics. There were, in practice, two difficulties with that plan. The first was in the strange, pedantic not-quite-accuracy of the language police. An official municipal magazine, presenting a top-ten list of errors in public signage, named such celebrated examples as "Racist Park" (for "Minorities Park") and "The Slippery Are Very Crafty" (for "Slippery When Wet"), but also gave, as self-evidently hilarious solecisms, "Room Price" in a hotel for "Room Rate," and "Eye Hospital" for "Ophthalmology Hospital." (The last was evidently based on a misunderstanding of why there had previously been merriment over an "Anus Hospital.")

The other trouble was that new English signs were spreading too fast for any correction effort to keep pace with. No matter how plentiful the correction squads, they would always be outnumbered by the sign installers. The new plastic-lettered storefronts, still multiplying in all directions, were a trove of typos and befuddling usage: "FOOT AND DADY MASSAGE"; "Different quality trade clothing"; "CLG A RETTE SHOP"; "Meat Patty Explode." A trashcan at the Imperial Academy was divided into bins for "Recycled" and "Organism." In the Olympic Panda house, all the signs and banners rendered "Beijing" itself as "Baijing."

Outside the classroom, in the community office compound, a countdown sign said there were forty-nine days till the Olympics. It felt further off that that. When I got upstairs, the lights were off and only one student was there—the electricity to the compound was out and the class had decamped for a different community center, on the next alley to the south. I trailed along behind the college-student instructors through a maze of cross-lanes to get there.

The substitute classroom was in a renovated courtyard house, around a big table in one of the subbuildings. A CCTV crew was filming, and the space along the edges of the room was packed. A sign on the wall read "Great the Olympics / Learning English / Go with 2008." I had been spending most of my time with Sha Meiyuan, an oval-faced woman who was retired from her job as a quality inspector in a watch factory, and with her friend Hu Yuesheng, who had curled hair, smiling cheeks, and sharp eyes. "My brain is no good," Hu had told me last time, cheerfully, making a study example out of self-deprecation.

I sat down with them on the far side of the table, and they brought out the words and phrases they wanted to know about: "uncomfortable," "sweltering," "humid." We worked some in reverse, from Chinese to English: *shi* . . . humid; *men* . . . stuffy; *men re* . . . muggy. Then more English. "The room feels cool." "It's cool in the room." There was rain in the forecast. How do you say that in English? "There will be a storm." "There will be thunderstorms" (or: "a thunderstorm"). "There will be heavy showers." Tea was served in paper cups. "The tea is too strong." Were we burnishing Beijing's credentials as a cosmopolitan city? The ladies were using language to say what they wanted to say. "I am sleepy." "I will take a nap." More: "I take a nap after lunch every afternoon." "We learned many sentences, but we can't remember them."

After class, Hu walked me out to the main street, wheeling her bicycle alongside. The frame was sturdy and black. It was Phoenix brand, from Shanghai. She had had it for thirty-eight years, she said.

In the evening, I met Jodi Xu in one of the sleek white towers of the Jianwai Soho complex, at the offices of Soojin Dance Team, the cheerleaders from the baseball exhibition. I had kept the business card of the director, Soojin Cho, and e-mailed to ask if the dance squad was involved at all in the Olympic cheerleading.

"I'm the director of the basketball tournament," Cho said. What she meant was that she was in charge of lining up the non-basketball part of the program in the basketball arena. The entrance to her office suite was lined with bags and bags of cheerleading equipment and costumes, with spangles and pompoms spilling out. She wore a Guess T-shirt and red gym shorts that said "Junior Varsity"; far below the shorts was a pair of low-top sneakers. Two little dogs ran in and out of her office. Their names were Mikey and Mini, she said. A carton labeled "Kimchi Ramen" sat in one corner.

Cho spoke in Korean-accented Mandarin, with Jodi translating whenever a break in the narrative stream happened to present itself. She hadn't been sleeping lately, she said, because she had been fighting with the construction crew that was supposed to be building a new dance studio for her. She had paid 90 percent of the price—the renovations were costing 200,000 yuan—but she wouldn't pay the last 10 percent till the work was done, and the workers said they wouldn't finish till she paid the last 10 percent.

The Olympics, she said, would be a good chance to promote Asian cultural elements in the dance program, "instead of just letting the good-looking girls with big boobs show their cute faces." It was the first time there would be performances during the Olympic basketball games, she said. Asian-themed dance would be part of a spectrum of international arena-class entertainment: Ukrainian cheerleaders were coming in to perform, and she was planning to have a trampoline-dunk squad.

Cho was born to a "pretty poor family" in Korea, she said. "My dad was a taxi driver," she said, and the family lived in a basement apartment. She wanted to study dance, but there wasn't enough money for dance school, so she took aerobics classes instead. After high school, she became an aerobics instructor, and a trip to Sydney for an aerobics workshop convinced her life would be better outside Korea. "It's been changing," she said, "but when I was living in Korea, the society would rate women by how well they married. . . . I don't want my life to be decided by someone else."

Her choice of a land of opportunity was limited by her budget: China was close, and it was cheap. So in 1994, she moved to Beijing, with $4,000 to her name. When the money ran out, after half a year, she got a job teaching aerobics in a small gym for 50 yuan, or about six dollars, an hour. "I needed to teach in Chinese," she said, "so my Chinese improved fast."

Her classes were popular, and she put effort into designing her clothes and giving a lively presentation. By 1999, she was working in bigger gyms, earning 2,000 yuan an hour, and appearing in exercise programs on television, and she was hired by the Chinese Aerobics Association as a foreign expert.

That was her first career peak, she said. Then her relationship with the state aerobics administration soured—they found her teaching style "unprofessional," she said—and she clashed with gym management. "A lot of the bosses asked me out at night to go to karaoke bars with their investors. I said, 'I'm a gym teacher, not an escort.'"

She quit the gym work and started her own team to perform aerobics demonstrations. When the World Cup came to Korea and Japan in 2002, she sent the team as a cheering dance squad for China—China's first cheerleaders. "The Koreans felt it was kind of unpatriotic to represent another country," she said. When the plane with the dancers returned to China, photographers were waiting. "I felt like a celebrity," she said. She published an autobiography in Korean.

The Chinese Basketball Association invited her to develop cheerleaders for the league. "I didn't understand basketball," she said. Sometimes, when the game stopped for a quick substitution, the dancers would jump out on the floor by mistake—Cho acted out a false start, by way of illustration. Fans were unfamiliar with the dance-team entertainment concept, too; out in the provinces, they assumed the women had come from Beijing to cheer against the home team, and pelted them with sunflower seeds.

So Cho made her first trip to the United States, to see the Laker Girls in action. She gazed upward, remembering. "I paid a lot of attention to the dancing. I said, 'I promise, CBA cheerleaders will be catching up with NBA cheerleaders.'" She began to incorporate Chinese themes—ethnic-minority dancing—into the team's work.

Then the CBA fired her. One of Korea's major exports to China is drama; its various soap-opera series, dubbed into Mandarin, are usually running on several stations at once. Jodi ventured that Cho's story sounded like one of those. Cho said she never watched the Korean shows. "All those TV dramas are always talking about how you love someone you're not supposed to love, and then when you get together, the person is dying." (This was, for someone who didn't watch Korean soaps, a pretty accurate summary.) "My life is more of a TV drama than the TV dramas, so I don't need to watch," she said. "Even though my love life wasn't the juiciest for the last couple of years . . . everything in my life is not less dramatic than Angelina Jolie's."

A reporter for the *Southern Metropolis Daily*, a major paper down in Guangzhou, wrote a story about her dismissal, under the title "Good-bye, Basketball Baby." Other publications approached her for interviews. "I said, 'I'm not worth anything, because I'm not employed.'"

The replacement cheerleaders, she said, were no good. She launched into an extended narrative of their shortcomings, crowding out the translation, talking with her hands. In the middle of it, she reached up and lifted an imaginary object off her shoulders, tucking it under her arms—one of the Ducks mascots, removing its head on court. Cho had been as dismayed by it as I was.

The dance squad kept performing at functions for business enterprises, which paid as much per person as a CBA game paid the whole squad. And Cho did choreography for dancers promoting Coca-Cola and other corporate clients. But she had wanted to find a way to contribute to 2008. "Even though I'm not a Chinese person, I felt like I wanted to prepare for the Olympics," she said.

The organizing committee, however, told her that they had already lined up cheerleaders—Cho's old nemesis, the Chinese Aerobics Administration, had gotten into the cheering business on its own. "I said, okay, if you don't want me to get involved with the Olympics, I'll go off on my own." As the Good Luck beach volleyball event approached, though, the organizers had doubts—senior leaders would be there, and the official dance squad was underwhelming. Cho, at a cheerleading competition in Hong Kong, got a call with two weeks to spare. She flew to Korea and bought 400 pounds of costumes, and slept in the office. Cho pointed to the spot on the floor where she'd lain.

What I'd seen at the beach volleyball grounds—one set of cheerleaders performing while the other looked indifferent—had been a showdown between the competing squads. Afterward, the beach volleyball and basketball cheering duties for the Olympics were awarded to the Soojin Dance Team, with the other team going to other events. "They saw who was the best, and they gave the job to them," Cho said.

The triumph at Chaoyang helped Cho force another dance-off, this one to get her team back into the CBA. The chairman of one of the league's corporate sponsors, Cho said, was dead set against letting her team perform, because he thought her dancers weren't pretty enough. "The team leaders of the other teams were standing by him like bodyguards," she said. "They were treating my team very differently from the other ones." She told the chairman that men like him were the reason Chinese women became mistresses, why the generation born in the eighties would sleep with someone for money to buy a cell phone. "I was very angry leaving the room," she said. "At the entrance of the building, there was a cleaning lady who was sweeping the floor. She said, 'If we had a vote, you were the best team.' When I heard that, I started to cry." Cho acted out the moment, the way her team had gathered around her, while she had pounded out furious text messages to the chairman through her tears. He began sending her text messages back, apologizing, and the CBA duties were divided three ways, with the Soojin Dance Team alternating with two teams from the aerobics authority.

Cho had a saying, she said: "TIC: This Is China." "China is very sexy," she said. This was a generalization about China I had not encountered before. It looks very simple from outside, she said, but once you've been in the country a year or two, you realize—"*Mo bu dao,*" she said. You can't get hold of it.

"They didn't give me a budget," she said. "I have to figure out the budget by myself. . . . I feel like I'm a volunteer."

The usual tone of deference one heard from Olympic participants was not forthcoming. She brought up the subject of the corps of women who made the medal-presentations—young, maidenly figures, selected for symmetry, height, and poise, whose training photos were saturating the press. In front of the cameras—Cho pulled herself upright and smiled overdemurely, holding up a pretend medal with both hands. Away from the cameras—she flopped back against the window, slovenly, puffing fiercely on an imaginary cigarette. "Also the mascots," she said. "I don't understand why those five mascots were released. The purpose of the mascots is to be liked by all the people. They're not serving this need."

Outside the tower, dusk and pollution were annihilating the view. A violent downpour was on its way. "I used to be a very typical

Korean girl when I was in primary school," Cho said. "Very quiet, very introverted. . . . I became something that is not a woman, not a man. Something in between. . . . When I was training students, I beat them up.

"Army training," she added in English, with a smile.

She cued up a video clip of the sort of dancing she preferred. It was from the Good Luck basketball tournament. Her dancers were in severe black costumes, with bare feet. They brandished red fans. The music was drumming. Fans snapped, feet stomped. It got a roaring ovation.

Her ambitions went beyond dancing. She pulled out a proposal for a reality show, to be called *Cheerleader Fever*, in which women would work to become CBA dancers: "As girls from the sophisticated cities such as Shanghai and Beijing bump up against girls from rural inner China, sparks fly as cultural and regional differences become evident." Another write-up proposed *The Cho Show*, a talk show hosted by "Oprah Winfrey with Tyra Banks's figure."

But first, the Olympics. "Olympics," she said. "Blah blah blah blah."

18.

拉拉队 Cheerleaders

Before the Olympics, we had had to make one last visa run. Returning with our visas, entering the new Beijing, our final descent was into the familiar featureless gray haze. The opening ceremony was twenty-eight days away, but clouds and pollution were pulling the dusk forward into the day, now as before. On Terminal 3's brand-new people-movers, people were not walking. Welcome back.

We cleared baggage claim and customs, with Mack perched atop the luggage cart, and exited into a thickening swarm of photographers. A stout little girl ahead of us had a bouquet thrust into her hand as shutters fired. The mainland and Taiwan had begun allowing direct flights, and we had arrived at the same time as the first return flight from Taipei. Men pushed carts piled high with cartons labeled "Made in Taiwan," as camera crews focused on them.

When we'd left, the outbound plane supplied us with a copy of

China Daily: "Visa policy will not deter visitors," a front-page teaser said. "Those who apply to come to China for justifiable reasons will be given every convenience," an official said in the story, on page three. The official "also denied reports that the visa policy had led to low hotel occupancy rates. He said hotel occupancy is affected by many factors, such as room prices and market fluctuations."

In other news a Foreign Ministry spokesperson had said that Tibet was not open for discussion at international conferences. Hedgehogs and squirrels were finding their way into the Olympic Forest Park. (Hedgehogs?) A wire-service story credited democracy as one of the reasons Denmark had polled as the happiest country in the world. China's results were not listed. (I later looked up the results: China was in the lower middle of the pack, between the Czech Republic and Mali—a little below Taiwan, a little bit above Hong Kong.) An annual plague of locusts was spreading through Inner Mongolia "in the region's three areas close to Beijing. . . . But there have been no reports in recent years of any swarms of locusts in the region flying to Beijing."

Another paper greeted us on the flight back. A business-section story reported that companies not sponsoring the Olympics had been making inroads in customers' consciousness, causing them to misidentify companies as sponsors. Besides the cloud of confusion around the tireless Liu Xiang, it quoted a Nielsen official saying that Adidas, the Olympic-certified brand of athletic wear, was barely more associated with the Games than the ubiquitous and home-grown Li Ning brand, a nonsponsor—"with identifying rates of the two at 34 percent and 29 percent respectively," a Nielsen official said.

Out on the expressway, the newest tufty saplings were still propped up, their puffs of leaves fading green against the gray light. The left lane had been painted as a reserved lane for Olympics vehicles, with alternating white and yellow dashes and the Olympic flag painted in the roadway at intervals. Olympic banners hung from the light posts. We closed in on home, past apartment towers that were still empty concrete shells. As our cab reached the Fourth Ring, a wash of decorative lights came on, sweeping a cream-colored glow across a flyover ramp, then more white lights on the overpass, and then red lights on the pillars beside us as we passed under. There were new flowers in beds by the road, and people strolling in the park beyond. Public exercise equipment was in use.

The Yuyang Hotel, no longer gutted, had its sign lit. The approach to it, still strewn with construction material, was flanked by a shiny galvanized construction wall; a half-installed chandelier showed through a window. A man in a pink polo shirt walked down the steps, cell phone held to his ear, as workers kept laboring around him.

On the alley, the row of portable toilets that had replaced the restroom—squat-style toilets, with mounds of feces around the holes— had been taken away. A plain brick wall wrapped around the corner, as if that were all that had ever been there.

The next day was clear and blazing, the streets desolate in the baking sun. What people were outside were under parasols: silver ones, a yellow one, a pink one. The fruit bus was closed. The street leading out to Dongzhimen had been widened, and the roadway had been extended north across the center of the main Hujiayuan community compound—cutting all the way to the rear gate, plain asphalt where a plaza and fountain and benches had been.

Out back, to the west, the demolition crews had come through at last. I had begun to think the area might survive, but Beijing was too thorough for that. A Hyundai digger was parked on the north side of the street and a Komatsu on the south. The Peugeot service center back there was gone, as was the kitchen supply store and the stereo store—nothing but rubble on vacant lots, all the way out to the cross street, and beyond, a clear vista to the new Moma Linked Hybrid and its skybridges, as celebrated in a copy of *The New Yorker* that had arrived while we were gone. The light-green buses from the depot passed, one after another, out in the open. A bird fluttered by. A few people sat in the shade of a mature tree that had been exposed by the demolition. There was something oddly pastoral about it. The demolition zone wrapped around the corner. A giant statue of a roasted duck had emerged into view, on a surviving restaurant set back from the road. Men sorted through a tangle of shredded metal, brilliant silver in the sun.

Along the Third Ring, the potted evergreens from Christmastime had been replaced by potted palms. I began logging the surviving shabbiness: tattered awnings here, a slummy retail strip there. A scrim of shiny panels had gone up in front of the slummy strip, and there were scrims going up on apartment buildings, silvery gratelike things to hide the air conditioners and crumbling parts.

On Monday, Mack was going to preschool day camp. We rode there in a cab with the windows down, with Mack on my lap. On Outer Dongzhimen, I smelled something familiar—an acrid, sweet smell, which I mistook at first for the smell of welding and renovation. Why was I smelling it out on the boulevard? Then I saw the spray truck—pesticide again, being hosed onto the trees and the traffic alike at a quarter to nine in the morning. I dived for the window crank; a spray of insecticide drops splattered against the window as I closed it. The front window had stayed half open; I could taste the stuff. I swore and spat across the backseat, as the cabbie calmly flipped on the wipers to clear his windshield.

The old Beijing organizing committee media operation had shut down, to restart as the Olympic press center for media that had registered to cover the Games themselves. To get myself into future briefings and press tours, I picked up a noncredentialed Olympic journalist's credential at the Beijing International Media Center, the press operation away from the Olympic Green. It was where the organizing committee press center had been two incarnations before—the shabby hotel now wholly renovated and clad in bluish-white glass, with numbers and letters etched into it in the various scripts of the world. On the way there, I passed still more apartments with new scrims hiding their air conditioners. The rows of the cover-ups were not entirely even, and with the old building surface showing in the gaps, the towers looked like thirty-story battered air filters.

The underpass to the media center was damp, with a smell like new sneakers sweated in for the first time. On a big television in the reception tent, I could see Wang Hui addressing the press. At the south end of the tent was a bookstore for foreign press: Paulo Coelho, Anne Tyler, Agatha Christie, Philip Roth. *Yao: A Life in Two Worlds.* One shelf featured photo books with such titles as *Artists' Nude Models*—distributed through a cultural loophole in the antipornography laws.

Then it was off to the police substation to reregister as a foreigner. The officer at the registration desk had exchanged his usual uniform for a T-shirt that said "Get Pepsi for Surfing." And he had acquired an assistant, a skinny young woman in a vest and a Levi's T-shirt with a cartoon of a girlie-girl on it. The shaky radio signal of my Chinese comprehension was tuning in: Get me some tea in my mug, he told her. It's the one with the little bear on it. The assistant brought him a cup with a bear on it. Maybe we were getting used to each other, the police and I.

The ayi was teaching Mack to clap along with a chant: *"Huanying, huanying!"* (Clap, clap, clap-clap!) *"Aoyun jia you! Aoyun jia you!"*

(Clap, clap, clap-clap!) *"Zhongguo jia you! Zhongguo jia you!"* (Clap, clap, clap-clap!) Welcome, welcome! Go, Olympics! Go, Olympics! Go, China! Go, China!

Soojin Cho had resolved her troubles with the renovation crew. The new studio, labeled Soojin Dance Team—Soul of Dance Academy, was on the top floor, the twenty-ninth, of Jianwai Soho's Tower No. 17. It was glassed in, decorated in white on white, with mirrors on two walls. There was a loft overhead, reached by spiral stairs at one end and a straight open stairway at the other. Cho was away when I arrived, but more than a dozen dancers were there, most wearing Soojin Dance T-shirts, and a photo shoot was under way upstairs.

The dancers, in formation, went through routines to blasting music: "Sexy Back," "It's Raining Men," "Let's Get Retarded," "We Will Rock You." Spin, kick, front roll. Then they sat on the floor in a circle and a dancer in plaid shorts, a lieutenant of Soojin's, divided them into teams for a competition: two dancers, with silver-sequined purple tops tied over their eyes for blindfolds, groped for a set of keys on the floor while their teammates shouted instructions. After a few rounds of blindfold work, the circle broke up and the dancers sat down facing the mirror, with their backs to the window, and began putting on makeup. Ballads played on the sound system.

Upstairs, off the loft, there was a deck area open to the sky. A dancer in purple, with an iridescent white cowboy hat, was posing for photos with an iPod Touch. It was clear and bright out, and behind her, through the glass wall, was the loop of the CCTV building—fully formed now, the planning model rendered on the real skyline. Behind the solid surface, though, the icon of Beijing's future was empty and unready inside. CCTV had hoped to rig up a studio on the interior, so the new building could at least host broad-

casts during the Games. But time had run out. The epochal architecture would only be a decoration.

The dancers downstairs had been primping for a good twenty
minutes: eyelids, foundation, lashes, eye shadow. Gradually their
complexions were becoming tanned and unreal, their eyes lengthen-
ing into startlement. Their faces glimmered. Around the twenty-
five-minute mark, they started applying blush.

The cheerleader in purple was doing leaps in the sun with the
iPod, over and over. The photographers were from *Nanren Zhuang*,
a men's magazine; there were three still cameras and two video cameras. The cheerleader was not leaping very high. The lead photographer, a man in a blue tank top and flip flops, with a samurai ponytail,
demonstrated the desired jump: a running leap that left him staggering to a halt, slapping the wall. A female assistant, in tartan shorts
and knee-high stockings, with a pierced nose, darted out to blot
sweat from the cheerleader's lip and lower eyelids.

Besides the magazine people, there was a South Korean photographer for a Chinese publication as well as a Korean TV crew. The
makeup kept going on, forty minutes of it now. Yet another team of
reporters showed up. It was getting hot in the studio, and the ratio
of dancers to other people was near one-to-one. There was a loud
thump as a dancer, trying to enter the studio, walked headfirst into
the glass wall. She found the door and entered, with laughter and
chagrin.

At last, Cho arrived, with a bandanna on her head and a gray
T-shirt with a winged Superman logo. She talked with the press in
Korean, English, and Chinese, handing out business cards as she
moved. How was she doing? *"Mang,"* she said, with a shrug of
exhaustion. Busy.

The dancer who'd walked into the glass read off a list of names
and gave instructions. Eight dancers trooped upstairs and returned

wearing orange and white. The music came on: Chubby Checker and the Fat Boys. Link arms, hop, kick—windup . . . clap and yell on the turns. The routine was over in moments. A second team, dressed in blue ruffles, took over, dancing to "Proud Mary," rolling their arms, tossing their hair.

Then came new outfits—shiny red dresses, with loudly snapping fans to match, and red elbow-length gauntlets. The dresses were halter dresses, with Mandarin collars and with pleats at the back, some idea of Western meeting some idea of Eastern at the outer limits of sartorial terminology. Cho had wrapped up a round of interviews upstairs, and stood watching with her back to the mirrors. A squad of dancers in white bell-bottoms was on. *"Cuo le,"* Cho said. Wrong. She watched them repeat it, her arms loosely folded, eyes tracking the left side of the formation. Then she dashed over to the sound board and cranked up the music, making them repeat it again. She grabbed a cameraman and repositioned him. The dancers posed for still photos, holding stuffed penguins. Cho showed them how to cuddle the penguins.

At the foot of the stairs, I talked with a dancer named Sun Zheng. She was an advertising student at Beijing Technology and Business University, she said, and she had found the Soojin Dance Team on the Internet. "I love dancing, so I wanted to join them," she said. "To be a cheerleader, it's a proud thing for me. I'm very proud."

What was it like to study under Cho? She was very—Sun couldn't think of the English. She wrote down the Chinese characters: *yan li.* Stern, severe. "For example, our movement, when we do this"—she stuck out one arm and held the other back by her head, then corrected the angle. "She is professional. Like our hairstyle and how we do makeup and all our clothes are the best. . . . Before a show, she is very kind. She likes to help us, and she is a funny woman."

"I think Soojin is the best team, so we have a responsibility during the Olympics to be the best," she said. "And I think not everyone can join Olympics as a cheerleader, so it's a very good chance." After these rehearsals, the team would spend the rest of the month in seclusion in Hebei, an hour away by bus. There was nothing to do but practice and wait.

VII.

倒计时

COUNTDOWN

19.

蝎子 Scorpions

The last night of the old, normal life, July 19, was mild and beautiful. The air was clear, even though the Olympic rules would not take effect till the next day: the driving ban, alternating daily between odd- and even-numbered license plates; the halt to digging and concrete pouring; the closing of Olympic traffic lanes to unauthorized vehicles. Tomorrow, by plan, the Olympic city would be in place.

I had spent the morning and early afternoon eighty-some miles away, in Tianjin—the Newark to Beijing's New York. I had in mind that I would return on the brand-new bullet train, but the bullet train wasn't open to customers till August 1. Neither was the new Tianjin train station, so I waited in the old one, an enormous, unclear shed above the tracks.

It was getting easier and easier, staying within the busily improving capital, to forget what the ordinary infrastructure of China was like. Tianjin brought back the Beijing of 2004. Hand-painted train-announcement signs and LED ones contradicted each other; information moved through the sea of travelers by word of mouth or herd intuition. The crowd-mind absorbed the news that the 3:46 express to Beijing was delayed twenty minutes—thirty minutes—ten or fifteen minutes more—finally (a surge toward the stairways) boarding.

The train itself was clean and modern and completely sold out. I rode standing up, looking out the window in the train door at the tedious landscape. In America, I usually enjoy the view from trains, the shacks and junkyards and industrial wreckage of the country's backside. But China was already one big rail bed; the backside of the country was everywhere. If anything, the railway scenery seemed tidier than average. In the train car, a seated passenger was reading a magazine article with the headline, in English, "Keep Fit While Learning English / Simple Ways to Suppress Your Appetite."

Construction was still in full swing on the approach to the Beijing station. Inside, the hallways had been given over to endlessly repeating lit-up advertising posters of the Fuwa: *Beijing Huanying Ni . . . Beibei Jingjing Huanhuan Yingying Nini . . . Beibeibei Jingjingjing Huanhuanhuan Yingyingying Ninini . . .* The cab stand was jammed; I filed along to the front, then squeezed my way back down the line of parked taxis to sit in one, unmoving. *"Zhongguoren tai duo!"* the driver said. There are too many Chinese people! Standard disgruntled observation number one. The real problem wasn't the numbers but what the taxi stand was doing with them, feeding people into the traffic jam rather than waiting for empty cabs to come up.

I had come back from Tianjin early in case the new subway lines had started running. A few days before, the Olympic press center had called a sudden news conference—a "flash"—to announce that the final Olympic subway lines would be opening . . . soon. Probably before the end of the weekend. As usual, a reporter who was there told me, such specifics as a date or a time went unoffered.

A text message arrived from a friend: The subway was open. Another, from a different friend: The new Apple store was open. "People keep pulling the security cord off the laptops, setting off alarms . . ."

With Big Mack, I swung by the Donghuamen night market, the organized center of Beijing street food—a row of clean, standardized stalls under striped awnings, stretching westward from the Wangfu-jing shopping street. Donghuamen was largely a stage for a culinary-theatrical carny hustle, on the theme Crazy Things the Chinese Eat: self-consciously exotic displays of skewered snakes and skewered frogs and skewered centipedes and skewered testicles pulled in the passersby, native and foreign alike—while other vendors in between offered the thrilled gawkers a chance to buy fried banana balls, minced-pork sandwiches, or *chao mian*. Authentic street food!

On a corner across from the food stalls, a young Chinese woman in a black polo shirt stopped me—Would I take a survey? The lanyard around her neck said "Nielsen." She held up a tiny, featherweight notebook computer. I clicked through the questions. How long had I been in China? (Longer than a year.) Did I recognize the Olympic slogan? ("One World, One Dream.") Did I agree, disagree, or not know whether each part of the three Olympic concepts was accurate: Green Olympics (agree; for public transit alone), High-Tech Olympics (agree; the surveillance system was astonishing), People Olympics (didn't know). Had I bought any Olympic merchandise? (Yes.)

Did I think that the Olympics would be a success? (Didn't know.)

Mack and I had been going to Donghuamen to investigate the boundary between the performative and the edible. Also, I was hungry. A would-be participant in foreign folkways couldn't help but notice that the Chinese themselves would giggle and pull out their cell-phone cameras before trying the leggiest and crawliest morsels. And many of the things laid out on skewers were flatly impossible to chew off a stick with your teeth: How could you gnaw on a whole crayfish? Or a starfish?

We headed to stall 56, where a red cloth flag certified that the operations were a model of sanitation. The proprietor, Zheng Zhong-bin, had the market's legal monopoly on fried scorpions. He had been at the market since 1991, and had put scorpions on his menu in 1996. Vendors who came up with a new recipe or new food could get a specialty license to be the exclusive vendor. "Everybody knows about scorpions, but no one thought to sell them here," he had told us.

The scorpions presented one of Beijing's mysteries. A friend of mine, living in a courtyard house on a hutong, had been stung by a scorpion in his bed once. He caught and killed it, and though the neurotoxins hadn't seemed to be spreading beyond his leg, he went to see a doctor. The doctor, a Canadian, said there were no scorpions in Beijing. He suggested that the scorpion (indisputable: a scorpion, dead, in a plastic bag) had hidden in my friend's luggage during a visit to Spain, and had made it into his bed that way. This satisfied the doctor, but it didn't explain why the authentic Beijing food market sold fried scorpions, or where those scorpions might have come from. It also didn't explain why the cat caught another scorpion in the same courtyard house later on.

Zheng's scorpions came from a can. Due to hygiene regulations, he used scorpions packed in brine. "No doubt, the live ones taste better than the canned ones," he said. He prepared them by soaking them in fresh water, then giving them a preliminary fry in oil to make them look nice. When a customer ordered a skewer, he would give it a final fry in oil—too long, he said, and the taste gets bitter; too short, and the flavor doesn't fully develop. The oil was a standard cooking mix. "If you fry them with pure sesame oil, they will taste even better," he said.

Zheng had large, shiny black scorpions, three to a skewer, for 50 yuan, and an assortment of other arthropods—crickets, silkworm pupae—but he recommended the small, drab pincer scorpions, for 15 yuan. "Of all the food that I sell," Zheng said, "the scorpions sell and taste the best. And whoever comes to my stall, I tell him that the scorpions are the best. It doesn't matter if they're foreign or Chinese."

The press loved his scorpions. He held up his hands to show how big his photo had been in *The New York Times*. A lot of Korean TV stations had come through, too, he said.

Before 1991, he said, he had no fixed job. His parents were from Dongbei and had once owned a photography studio, "but during the Cultural Revolution they were suppressed," he said. "It is a historical matter."

Some people bought the scorpions for fun, Zheng said; others bought them as medicine. "Some people eat them because they have pimples. . . . In Chinese medicine, it's supposed to reduce heat, or cleanse the body."

Foreigners would buy one three-scorpion skewer at a time, usually. Chinese people might buy ten, Zheng said. Sometimes he cooked scorpions for himself at home, he said, and had them with *erguotou* liquor that he'd infused with herbs. Big restaurants like the Quanjude duck chain might sell scorpions, too, he said, but they didn't get enough regular practice cooking them.

"I'm not trying to talk big," he said, "but I am confident in saying that, when it comes to frying skills, I'm the best in this market."

The little scorpions came off the skewer perfectly crisped, tasty fried bites of nothing much. I moved on along the rows, eating and taking notes as I went, on fried bees, a fried starfish, a bowl of pork-intestine soup. The starfish was full of a gummy gray mass like fla-vorless, overcooked fish eggs, and was so messy to pry open that I gave up after two of the five arms. Everything else was fine.

When we got into a taxi to leave, the cabbie confessed he had no idea how to get from downtown to Dongzhimen. He was fresh from the countryside, and he had been driving a cab for less than ten days. Big Mack and I got him to the Second Ring Road, then gave him a quick tutorial on the layout of the Northeast as we went: Chaoyang-men interchange, then Dongsishitiao, and finally Dongzhimen. His driving experience was no more extensive than his geographical knowledge; the cab flinched in and out of lanes. In less than twenty days, Olympic visitors would be trying to hail his taxi.

There was still time to catch a ride on the subway. I took another cab out to the Third Ring, under which the new No. 10 line ran, and entered at the Liangma Bridge station. The hallways were a tasteful gray, and a breeze was blowing through them. I bought a one-ride card—at a cost of about thirty cents—and rode one stop to the Sanyuan Bridge station, to see if I could transfer to take the new airport express train home. I could, the station attendant told me, but it would be more than ten times as expensive—twice as much as a taxi ride. I was not that curious. I surfaced and got a cab.

The 20th was hot but clear and clean. The inner driveway of the apartment building was lined with now banned cars, their plates ending in 9 . . . 3 . . . 9 . . . 7 . . . 5. But in the construction pit across the alley, a crane was still moving.

Toward evening, we went to Sanlitun, the old embassy-district bar street a few blocks east of home. The west side of the street had been redeveloped into a series of shopping complexes. In a white Moorish-style building, we found a new branch of an Asian chain selling Western kitchenware: tri-ply copper-stainless cookware, silicone cake molds and basting brushes, pepper mills, enameled cast-iron casseroles. A year ago, a place like that would have been unimaginable. We had been cooking with a hodgepodge of pans and utensils collected from supermarkets, the corner store, and parts unknown.

In the courtyard outside the kitchen store, Tex-Mex music was blaring from a restaurant with a cactus on the signboard. Workers were finishing store interiors. At the front of the building, signs announced that an American Apparel was coming soon.

Farther down Sanlitun, at the corner with North Workers' Stadium Road, was the new Adidas superstore, the world's largest. Next to it was a nearly finished Uniqlo. The two marked the south end of the Village, a collection of retail buildings drawn up by avant-garde architects, all steel and angled glass walls and gold-tinged materials. Farther into the compound was a Nike store, and then the Apple store: a glowing white logo on a gray box, two or three stories above an open square dominating the scene—the old Macintosh "1984" commercial perfectly reversed. Inside, a clerk greeted me in English so flawless that I didn't notice it was English till a second clerk did the same.

It was getting dark. Back outside the Apple store, a billboard-sized video screen announced: "The paint is almost dry, and the first villagers are moving in." A slapping sound echoed off the walls. Up on a scaffold, a worker was gluing tall purple letters to the glass, rising from left to right, thumping each one into place with his hands. He was just putting the N on "STEVE MADDEN."

There were seventeen days to go. The full security lockdown of the Olympic Green was still a few days off, and the press center there was holding a briefing on forestry. On the way, we hit a traffic jam, on the Second Ring. The left lane was closed to regular traffic, as one of the reserved Olympics lanes, and through some sort of traffic-engineering algebra, half as many private cars driving in two-thirds as many lanes worked out to much worse traffic than usual. When he saw me looking at my watch, the cabbie began fighting his way around the traffic, tapping his horn with his thumb. To keep demonstrating his concern, he continued tooting along the Third Ring when we got there, even though there was no Olympic lane and the traffic was moving.

"The Olympic things are only convenient for the Olympics," I said, in a flash of Mandarin competence. "For everyone else, they're annoying." The driver clapped a hand over his mouth and held it there theatrically. Then he put it back on the steering wheel. "Understand?" he said.

The on-site press center was less plush than the off-site one. The renovations at the latter were cushy, the elevators so lavishly mirrored, inside and out, that it was hard to tell when the doors had opened. Outside the biggest press conference hall, a uniformed employee tended a silver dispenser of ice water, with lemon in the water.

The front end of the Olympic Green center, on the other hand, was built to serve as a convention center after the Games: broad concrete hallways, with exposed pipes and ductwork in a black-painted ceiling. Then, right before the largest of the press-conference halls—Hall No. 1, the "Plum Blossom" hall—visitors crossed over

into the part of the building that would be converted into the five-
star InterContinental Beijing Beichen Hotel after the Games. There,
off to the right, was a soaring lobby with multistory wall art, and
polished surfaces everywhere (except underfoot, where gray industrial carpet awaited a monthlong trampling). The seats in the Plum
Blossom hall were red, and there were some eight hundred of them.

There were wireless translation receivers available for the international press, with a whole counter full of volunteers to meet the
demand for them. The headsets did something to breach the language barrier, but not enough. The translation was smooth during
the scripted part of the forestry briefing: in accordance with Beijing's
master plan, there were now 12,600 hectares of parkland along the
ring roads and major arteries; 43 percent of the city was green space
now, up from 36 percent in 2000; 40 million flowers were being
prepared for the Olympics.

In the question-and-answer period, though, I wanted to know
specifically what varieties of trees had been planted in Beijing. The
vice-director of the forestry bureau explained that they had different
kinds of trees for different areas, and began listing some, briskly, in
Mandarin. Over the earpiece, the translator reduced it in English
to "poplar and other kinds of trees." The online transcript in Chinese
left out the list altogether, though it included a photograph of me
asking the question. The gesture of providing an answer had been
enough.

Sixteen days. The international press was settling in and discov-
ering that the Internet was blocked, even in the press center. The
foreign anonymizer site I had been using as a slow, ad-filled work-
around at home had finally been shut out, too. The morning briefing
was about security: during the Games, an official announced, there
would be authorized zones set aside for protests in three city parks.

Reporters huddled afterward to figure out where the third of the three parks, World Park, which nobody had heard of, was located— halfway out to Hebei Province, according to the street atlas. But the other two, Purple Bamboo Park and Altar of the Sun Park, weren't bad. Was China really making space for dissent?

20.

收拾 Tidy Up

ifteen days. An airport express train pulled into Dongzhimen station, and the doors opened on the far side to let arriving passengers out. There would be a lag of between fifteen and thirty seconds before the doors opened on our side of the platform, David Feng told me.

The Dongzhimen station complex above us was the hulk of an empty promise, its hastily installed glass skin still missing in places. The Olympic goal of smooth intermodal access, of baggage checked through to the airport, was unmet. But the trains were running.

Feng, a tall and tidily dressed young man, had met up with me to take a ride out to the airport, for the sake of taking a ride to the airport. I guessed, correctly, that this would be a draw for him. Feng was the author of a website called Beijingology, a Wikipedia-style project to document transit and transportation in Beijing. "Wikipedia wasn't ideal," Feng said. Wikipedia wanted citations, not original research, and Feng's enthusiasm was for seeing and recording things himself. All things: "The Line 2 part of Yonghegong Lama Temple station," the site reported, "takes the shape of two tan boxes (exits A and B) or an exit built into a nearby building without the Subway logo (exit C). The Line 5 part are either integrated into nearby buildings (exits B and C) or are two boxes with alternating glass/grey stripes (exits A and D)."

Yonghegong was the station I'd been through the previous fall, when Line 5 had opened, adding seventeen miles to the Beijing system. I had wanted to see what it was like to ride a brand-new train. At the time, I had been reading in *The New York Times* that, back in the United States, the federal government had just agreed to supply New York with part of the financing for the beginning of the construction of the first leg of a Second Avenue subway line—so that by 2014, someone could in theory ride a train from Sixty-third Street to Ninety-sixth Street. Or you could walk.

Meanwhile, on Line 5, which broke ground in 2003, I had rolled smoothly north toward the Fifth Ring, with flat-screen displays listing the stations along the way. As the train rose aboveground into the sunshine, there was a twittering of birdsong, evidently from someone's mobile ring tone. The stations had fantastical canopy roofs on them, each a different shape: beams strung together at acute angles over one platform, an undulating blue roof over another.

For the ride to the airport with Feng, the air outside was gray and smoggy. "The bit I love the most about the Beijing subway of course is the fact that it's expanding," Feng said. What had been a sleepy two-line system was on its way to being "transit nirvana," he said, with the city scheduled to open a new line every year till 2012, on its way to 561 kilometers (or 350 miles, if you're willing to round). The year 2008 was a mere transfer station to 2012 and beyond. "That's the day we're not going to be seeing any more of this, you know, less than optimal weather," he said. By 2050, he said, depending exactly on how plans worked out, the system might be up to 1,053 or 1,032 kilometers.

The ride to the airport took less than half an hour. As we walked into Terminal 3, Feng spied an English label on a trash can—the word "Waste," in a typeface he identified as Arial Black. "Use any font but Arial," he said, disgustedly. Beyond his subway expertise, he was head of the Beijing Macintosh User Group, and he had strong feelings about design. His interests came together in his own subway maps, rendered to his own tastes. He called one up on his iPod Touch to demonstrate.

Feng was originally from Beijing, he said, but his parents had moved the family to Switzerland when he was a child, and he was a Swiss citizen now. He said he could speak German, French, Italian, English, and Chinese fluently, along with "a bit of Japanese, Korean, Romansh, Latin, and Spanish." The Beijing Planning Exhibition Hall would call him in as a tour guide if they were getting groups who spoke German or French. When he left China, he said, he knew 2,000 Chinese characters; in Switzerland, "I lost eighteen hundred characters." The ones he remembered were those that had been on road signs on the Second Ring. The character *dong*—the sun behind a tree, meaning "east," and appearing in terms such as "Orient," "thing," or "force of good"—was for Feng the character from "Dongzhimen Bridge."

Now he was living in Beijing again, and the city was rewarding his devotion. "Who won't want to live in Beijing, if getting from A to B is that easy?" he asked.

Of the Olympic architecture, he liked the Water Cube more than the Bird's Nest, he said. When the colors of the bubbles changed at night, he said, "I think they should change it so they cycle through the whole Beijing subway colors." He ran through the colors of all the lines, present and future, off the top of his head. Then he discussed the pet names that rail enthusiasts had for the lines in online forums: Line 13 was "the cat," because the cars looked like a cat from the front. He had his own names: Line 5 was the "Mozart Line"—"because when it opened, all the music it played was Mozart serenades."

Was he planning to see the Olympics? "I may not go to one of the games," he said. But Line 8 of the subway, which would eventually run north and south through the city, was opening for the Games as a spur connecting Line 10 to the Olympic Green, for spectators only. "I might be grabbing a ticket just to go into Line 8," Feng said.

An entire edition of the *Beijing News* was pulled from newsstands—it had printed a photograph of the Tian'anmen Square incident from 1989, word was. Our home-delivered paper had escaped the recall, and we hunted up the offending image. It was on page C15, down at the bottom, in a series of black-and-white photos accompanying an article about a longtime photojournalist. The pictures had simple captions in Chinese: "roller skating," "young people on patrol," "love," and then, at the bottom, "the wounded": stricken bodies on the bed of a speeding cargo tricycle. Reportedly, someone had pulled the photo off the Web to fill in the layout and, because images of the Tian'anmen crackdown were so unfamiliar, hadn't realized what it was.

Fourteen days. The final batch of Olympic tickets was released for walk-up sale to the public. This was the fourth round of Chinese ticket sales, each one having been a case study in how not to sell tickets. In the first online lottery, the one we'd entered, we ended up with tickets to two nights of track-and-field. While other ordinary buyers had also limited their requests, so as not to be awarded too expensive a batch of tickets, brokers and would-be scalpers had used the system of multiple requests and multiple fallbacks to snap up tickets in bulk.

The second round, to compensate, was limited to tickets for two events, with no fallback choices. It was to be first-come, first-served— and the computer system crashed irretrievably under the strain. A third round eliminated the rush, but kept the two-event limit, so that nobody was willing to bid for anything but the most popular events.

The chance to buy tickets directly, at last, drew lines a mile long, with tens of thousands of unruly customers. Police blocked reporters from approaching the scenes of chaos at the box office, and the *China Daily* carried a mystifying after-action story saying that a photographer from Hong Kong's privately owned *South China Morning Post* had apologized after "breaking through a barricade" at a Beijing sales site and "kicking a policeman in the groin."

Under the pressure of the impending games, the *China Daily* had dropped its usual quirky, gothic tendencies and had become the sort of mouthpiece foreigners would expect a state-owned newspaper to be. English headlines now announced news such as "Games to Be a Great Success: Survey" or "President Boosts Athletes' Morale." This was not the time to be undisciplined or off-message.

The new air-quality measures had been in place for nearly a week, and they were not bringing new air. Day after day, the same old air had been sitting over the city, getting dirtier. Facing another thick, white day, a redundant-looking press conference on something environmental was scrapped in favor of a hastily scheduled briefing on traffic and pollution control. On the stage, the assembled officials wore white shirtsleeves, for serious work on a hot day.

The measures, they said, were working. All of them. Air pollution was down 20 percent from the same period last year. There were 2,000 more buses in service, and on the first weekday of the driving restrictions, an additional 3.9 million people had used public transit. Reporters were suffering from a simple misapprehension: we were looking for results following the traffic and construction bans of July 20, but there were other air-quality rules that had started on the first of July, so the relevant comparison should account for the entire month. And this July, as a whole, was better than last year's. The traffic flow wasn't worse, either. It was just less obviously better in some places, such as the Second Ring. The traffic jams and foul air were not what they seemed to be. Beside the help desk, overlooking the lobby, a white board said "Today's Weather: Sunny," accompanied by a drawing of the sun spreading its rays.

Twelve days. The first athletes, forty-two members of the Polish delegation, arrived on a morning flight. With the haze still hanging over the city, the municipal traffic-control department opened for a tour. Traffic was light, at least—because it was the weekend, my cabbie told me. At the Second Ring on-ramp, a towering floral starburst had been installed, with cutouts of the Fuwa capering around it. *"Piaoliang!"* the driver said. Beautiful! Then he went the wrong way, but made up for it with a disquisition on street names: Outer Drum Tower Street, where we were trying to go to catch the media bus, used to be Zhongzhou Road. He had taken Old Outer Drum Tower Street by mistake, so we were cutting across along Ande Road, so named because it ran from Andingmen to Deshengmen. The cartography of the invisible.

In the traffic center, a three-story video wall presented a color-coded map of the city's traffic flow, flanked by more maps, computer graphs, and live video from roadside cameras. Most of the arteries were green. Three dozen workstations faced the map, but only eight people were sitting there. Above them was a double tier of glassed-in balconies—studios for traffic programs, overlooking the center. A Chinese reporter stopped me: Could I do an interview for Beijing Television's *Traffic Light* program? This was the program that had been marking 2008 with a daily segment in which camera crews tailed drivers, looking for civilized or uncivilized behavior at the wheel. The well-behaved drivers could win a free tank of gas. The show aired three times a day, she said, live in the mornings and early evenings for commuters, then a late show on tape at quarter past ten. "Almost all the drivers in Beijing watch the program," she assured me.

Eleven days. All through the Olympic preparations, the years of hasty demolition and hasty construction, people in Beijing, Chinese and foreigners alike, had kept offering the same analogy: It was like tidying your house in a hurry before company comes over. The clutter gets stuffed into cabinets or under the bed; you wipe down the bathroom the guests will be using; you hide the dirty dishes and dig out matching forks and cloth napkins. The buildup struck outside commentators as Potemkinism, a spectacle put on to fool the visitors. But what host doesn't try to show guests something better than everyday life?

The last frenzy of covering things up was at hand. By the Sanyuan Bridge, a banner with a fifteen-story-high picture of a field-hockey player was hanging over the gaping concrete-slab face of an unfinished building. More giant athletes lined construction sites along Chang'an Boulevard. At the foot of Wangfujing, another unfinished building had been slipcovered on all sides with a picture of a finished building's façade, complete with images of people in some of the windows and a strip of blue sky along the top. More sheets of fabric were up at Chaoyangmen, with pictures of plants on them. Mottled red cloth framed the window arches of the Yuyang Hotel, where the surrounding red stonework stopped.

To resolve the problem of nonsponsors encroaching on the Olympics, the government had removed or covered over all public advertising everywhere, save for sponsor ads. An illuminated Kappa sportswear sign, on a roof by the northeast bend of the Second Ring, was shrouded in white; the InterContinental sign on the Main Press Center was hidden by rainbow-colored fabric. The eyes of Liu Xiang were gone from the Nike store, replaced by a Beijing 2008 billboard— part of acres and acres of billboards, "One World, One Dream," covering anything that even faintly resembled an advertisement, up to and including the names and logos of construction companies on building-site fences. Blue tape and paint on newsstand canopies blotted out the titles of magazines and the logos of China Mobile and the postal service. By the time the Games began, every toilet and urinal on the Olympic grounds would have a strip of duct tape covering the manufacturer's name. The state's enforcement of the Olympic commercial contract was so total it felt like an exercise in no-logo anticommercialism. Beijing would be an advertisement for itself alone.

Ten days. Clouds moved in, bringing cool, clear air with them. A brief, heavy shower washed down the roads, and then the sun came out. The Liangma River by the apartment looked clean and inviting. The buildings looked clean, too. At Tuanjiehu Park, on the east side of the Third Ring, where a former industrial kiln pit had been turned into a lake, couples twined on the benches in the afternoon light. Cicadas screamed from the trees; dead goldfish floated in the water.

World Trade Center Tower Three, the city's new tallest skyscraper, poked into view over the top of a willow tree, framed by apartment buildings.

Nine. Food-safety briefings were always the worst. The media-relations office couldn't avoid discussing the subject—China's food industry was constantly being caught selling adulterated, contaminated, or drug-laced products; *The New York Times* had reported on a chicken breast so full of steroids that an athlete could flunk a doping test by eating the meat—but it was too sensitive a subject to allow any honest disclosure. In a too-small room at the municipal agricultural bureau, officials told the crowded press what they always told them: first, that testing had demonstrated that the entire ordinary food supply of Beijing was clean and untainted; then, that a whole separate food-supply system had been set up to protect athletes from tainted food. It was not politically feasible to make the two messages conform to each other, let alone to logic or the truth.

Then came a bus ride of nearly two hours, to get to a special organic farm for Olympic athletes, which was unnecessary because the general food supply was already perfectly safe. Rows of greenhouses were growing green peppers. Peppers after peppers after peppers after peppers, clear down the row, almost to the end, where a few greenhouses were full of basil. Camera crews swarmed through the doorway to surround a woman in a straw hat, stooped over, snipping basil with scissors. The athletes would have fresh basil.

Eight. Zheng Mojie, the deputy director of the translation-defeating Office of Capital Civilization Spiritual Construction

Commission—the office that had been trying to stop spitting—gave a briefing on the city's manners. Reporters were presented with paper bags, in which were manuals on correct behavior, packets of tissues for spitting into, and stuffed dolls of the three cartoon mascots of the civility campaign: Wo Canyu, in green with two green pigtails; Wo Fengxian, in red with a red double topknot; and Wo Kuaile, in orange with an orange single topknot. Their names meant I Participate, I Contribute, and I Enjoy. With the five Fuwa, the Paralympic Fu Niu Lele, and Dongdong the cheering mascot, the number of Olympic-affiliated characters was into double digits.

Manners were no less subject to numerical targets than anything else. Four-point-three million households had received books on proper behavior, Zheng said. Twenty-two thousand, seven hundred fourteen ordinary citizens had been honored as models of civility. People had been guided in lining up at 1,805 bus stops.

One foreign correspondent, Zheng said, had written that he had spent a whole day looking for spitters without seeing any. Zheng had had the same experience, she said: "I believe that due to our rigorous campaign . . . such cases are declining." She evoked the image of a host greeting guests, too—mending clothes and putting on nice things. "It is a great pleasure to welcome friends coming from afar," she said. "Our streets are clean. Our environment is beautiful. Our flowers are in bloom."

On the way out of the press conference, a man pushed his way into the elevator before I could get off. Guards by the exit gave me a stony glare. A minivan on the alley blasted its horn while passing me.

At the Dongzhimen interchange, the pedestal had a giant bronze vessel atop it again—not the same bronze vessel, but a more squat one, with four legs instead of three. This was another bit of rectification: in the taxonomy of ancient Chinese vessels, the slender old tripod had been a *ding*, while the new four-legged one was a *gui*. The inner avenue, Guijie, was Ritual Vessel Street instead of Ghost Street.

Six. Overnight and unexpectedly, the cabbies began wearing a uniform: yellow short-sleeve shirts, blue-and-yellow clip-on neckties, and dark trousers. Red lanterns were going up along the roadside, and Chinese flags. What looked like metal-and-glass cattails had been added along the airport expressway.

When I went to the new bank location to pay the phone bill, the bank was offering a guidebook for visitors, including useful phone numbers. The phone line for the weather offered the temperature on the pavement. It was 45 degrees Celsius, or 113 Fahrenheit.

The DVD store a few blocks south of home had almost no contemporary movies, and the inventory it did have was dominated by Russian titles. Hollywood had been protected into near noncxistence. In the absence of the usual bootleg merchandise, most of one wall had been given over to sex-instruction videos, sex-themed thrillers, or anything that could pass for something titillating—a copy of *The Governess*, with a skin-intensive cover; a World War II–themed exploitation movie called *Comfort Women*. The usual movies were gone because of the Olympics, the woman at the counter affirmed. Facing her, the TV showed white-clad superstars, singing "Beijing Huanying Ni."

Five. White pickets were added down the middle of the widened roadway back to the alley, as if it were Chang'an Boulevard, making it impossible to cross the street at the usual convenient jaywalking angles. With that, two-way traffic finally began.

I rode through the new traffic pattern, heading out to the 798 arts complex, a compound of imposing mid-century factories that had become to the Chinese contemporary art scene what Times Square is to musical theater, or Freeport, Maine, is to outlet shopping. Bohemian adaptive reuse had swept through 798 so fast—from the furtive squatter stage through official quasi-recognition as a municipal asset—that there were still factories doing factory work among the studios and galleries (and cafés and shops). The art made for an ongoing study in what could be construed to be contemporary, or Chinese: ironic juxtapositions of the Mao-and-Big-Mac variety, photo-and-narrative documentary art about prostitution, a gallery full of Nike sneaker art.

A few weeks before, in one of the galleries, I had come across a work filling an entire wall, a photo-manipulated grid of little black and white boxes. There were more than a thousand of them, and they had tiny images in them. Most were of people, some photographed on the street, some posing nude, some collected from published images. For contrast there were occasional other things: a leopard, butterflies, a bear. And more or less in the middle—twenty boxes in from the left and ten up from the bottom, just below eye level—was Liu Xiang, in mid-hurdle.

Now I was going to talk to the artist Zhao Bandi, who had a store and an office in 798. In 2004, Zhao had staged his own Olympic opening ceremonies, in Bern, Switzerland, as a work of performance art. "The whole title is *Too Impatient to Wait*," he said.

Zhao was a slightly built man with rounded shoulders, longish hair, and droopy eyes—earnest, harmless looks that protected him from coming off as a smart-ass, even when no other explanation than that he was being a smart-ass came readily to mind. He wore snug-fitting clothes, black pants and a black T-shirt with gray sleeves, with bright white sneakers and a blue Al Jazeera ball cap. His most famous work revolved around being photographed with a stuffed toy panda, in comical or provocative or sinister situations; he had already taken pictures with his panda in the rubble of Sichuan.

In Bern, Zhao Bandi had replaced the city flag, which had a black bear on it, with one with a panda, had relabeled the streets with Beijing street names, and had gone running through the city with a torch, with the stuffed panda riding on his shoulders. He measured the mayor and supplied him with a Sun Yat-sen suit, the kind with a jacket that buttons up to the collar. CCTV had showed a program about the whole thing.

Europe was eagerly receptive to Chinese art projects; in the summer of 2007, Ai Weiwei had sent 1,001 Chinese people—including, independently, Big Mack and a Uighur woman who worked in Christina's office—to live in tent barracks at an art festival in Germany. They were accompanied by 1,001 antique chairs, which Ai had then sold off. Now Ai, the son of a poet exiled by Mao, had helped design the Bird's Nest, only to turn around and denounce the Olympics to foreign reporters as a "fake smile," saying he was "disgusted" by his role in creating the stadium.

But Zhao was promoting the Olympics, or himself, or some opaque combination of the two. Participation and publicity were inseparable from the art. Downstairs from us, in his Bandi Panda shop, he was selling his own set of mascots: five stuffed pandas, each one with markings in a different color of the Olympic rings. "I always asked myself . . . Why doesn't Zhao Bandi, the artist Zhao Bandi, create a mascot?" he asked. A box of Bandi 2008 mascots—he had opted against calling them "Olympic," after a factory objected—went for 499 yuan.

The factory had produced 10,000 mascots, he said, and he expected to order 30,000 more by August. "I gave a lot to the children in the area of the earthquake," Zhao said. "I think they loved them." He pulled up pictures on the computer of himself in the camps of survivors, distributing colored pandas, with his own panda on his back.

The Fuwa, he said, suffered from being designed by committee. "They tried to mix many ideas," Zhao said. "My one is very simple. Because everything I designed by myself. I like the simple things. I like clean and simple things." After 2008, he said, "the Fuwa will be finished. . . . So the color pandas can be growing."

Zhao said he had been trying to give his mascots to as many people with Olympic connections as he could. He pulled up pictures of himself delivering colored pandas to the female medal-bearers: from the ping-pong arena, from the baseball stadium. He had given pandas to the shooting-arena attendants, identical twins who had become minor celebrities because they were scheduled to present the first gold medals of the Games. He was hoping to give pandas to reporters and athletes, too. He wanted to see what people thought of his work, he said: "Beautiful or not, you can judge. Maybe you don't like? No problem." Did I know anyone he might be able to give pandas to? I found an extra business card from Soojin Dance in my bag and handed it over.

After all this waiting, Zhao said, the atmosphere was not what he had expected. When the city won the Games, seven years before, the streets were full of celebrating people. Now, he said, the mood was "not as warm as I believed. . . . It's empty. The street is a little bit nervous. The feeling is a little bit strange." I agreed; the city was unhappy and subdued. Maybe on August 8 things would come to life, he said.

Outside, there was the whine of power saws from somewhere within the complex, and the pulsing shriek of cicadas. Zhao's car was parked nearby, an Alfa Romeo Spider convertible, the metallic yellow of a foil-covered chocolate coin. A spare stuffed panda sat in the driver's seat.

I arrived at the Soojin Dance studio minutes after a class of Fuwa trainees had left. The mascots were from the martial-arts academy, and they needed to learn antics and dance moves to go with their acrobatics. A male assistant of Cho's told me in Mandarin that the Fuwa suits came in three varieties: inflatable, athletic, and cute. The most demanding mascot jobs would be at the basketball arena—there, the Fuwa would have the greatest number of routines to learn.

Cho was working on a routine using the red fans, along with a team of eight dancers. They pumped their chests, bounced down and up, tossed their heads, and broke into a wedge formation, snapping the fans when they hit the final mark. Cho counted them off, over and over again. Then she ordered them into a single-file line—"Yi pai!"—and showed them how to sift the line apart and back together, cocking their heads and hips to alternating sides.

In the middle of this, the studio door opened and Zhao Bandi appeared, accompanied by another artist, Mozarte Zhao. It was less than two hours since I'd handed him Soojin's card. They had with them a bulky translucent bag full of colored pandas. The dancers gathered around and collected a panda apiece, and Zhao Bandi briefly addressed them. The red panda, he told them, signified love. The green one meant family. Yellow was enjoyment of life, black meant having friends, and blue meant surpassing oneself. The dancers posed for group photos with their pandas, with Cho smiling proprietarily at the edge of the group; Zhao reclined in front of them, propped on one elbow, like an odalisque.

"I'm always asked by people, 'What's the meaning of the different colors?'" he told me when he was done, as the dancers ate sandwiches. The Fuwa, he said, had meanings for everything, so he had meanings for his mascots, too.

Dancers in faux-leather shorts and death's-head insignia started practicing, hips working: left, right, left-right-left; right, left, right-left-right. Cho watched for a while, then stopped rehearsal and began lecturing the dancers. They were not learning well enough; they were not making progress. The dancers stood very still. I could tell they weren't the Miami Heat squad, but they seemed to know what they were doing. In the middle of the dressing-down, her phone rang. Cho took the call, then came back and picked up the thread. *"Mei ci, jiu baifen zhi bai,"* she said. A hundred percent, every time. Finally she called them in, to form a circle, hands in. *"Yi! Er! San!"* One! Two! Three! "Yeah!"

"I've spent so much time teaching them," Cho said, when they'd left, the coach still trying to prod her charges into greater achievement, even in absentia. *"Mei jinbu."* No progress.

Four days. The air was dirty gray again. The Second Ring ramps had been blocked off into a new traffic pattern, and the cabbie I was with missed the adjusted turnoff for Dongzhimen. When he tried to reverse course at the next interchange, we got stuck on the exit ramp where a BMW had rear-ended another taxi. "Beijing Huanying Ni" played on the radio as he missed the light to get back north.

Three. Mack went toddling across the living room toward the ayi at top speed. You're like Liu Xiang! she told him.

Two. Traffic was stuck on the Third Ring. It was the torch relay, the cabbie said. The flame had made it back to Beijing and was traveling around the city for two days. He had the best English of any driver

I had ever encountered. He had heard that George Bush would be coming to open the new American embassy soon, he said.

At the exit for Outer Drum Tower Avenue, the bridge was lined with spectators. City cops, the People's Armed Police, and security guards blocked traffic. I climbed up to join the crowd, standing on a concrete ledge, a twelve-foot drop behind me. A torchbearer-to-be, a man with glasses and a receding hairline, waited in the street with his unlit torch for his little piece of the Journey of Harmony. Joggers in blue-and-white outfits, the paramilitary Guardians of the Flame, came toward him—and then the flame itself, in a quiet and anticlimactic handoff. The security lines slackened, and I climbed down. Canteens and olive-colored bags and water bottles lay in neat rows in the underpass leading south from the bridge, where the People's Armed Police had left them. An old woman paused and stooped to examine the bottles. When she came out of the tunnel behind me, she was carrying an armload of them. Sunlight was losing out to filth.

One day. The uncredentialed-media center was selling an extremely limited number of tickets to events, first-come, first-served, starting at 8:30 each day. At 4:30 a.m. I crawled out of bed and hailed a cab, looking for a lone basketball ticket. The predawn streets were dark and otherwise empty. Only a skeleton crew of volunteers was at the media center, most of them dozing. But in the back hallway outside the ticket office, two bleary-eyed Chinese reporters, a man and a woman, were already sitting in the chairs. What were they there to buy? I asked. Swimming, the woman said. Basketball, the young man said, with a sheepishly triumphant smile.

When did you get here? I asked. Three a.m., he said.

21.

八月八日　8/8

The day Beijing had waited for dawned white and dusty, with a feeble sun. This was it. First, we had to take Mack to the doctor. He had woken up with a cough and fever. My own sinuses were clogged, and my eyes burned when I went out into the dirty air. Everything was breaking down. Out in the alley someone had thrown tea dregs on the pavement. The morning was lifeless. We got a cab. A low-speed accident was stopping traffic, and a traffic cop stood by, ignoring it. The clip-on fastener for our cabbie's necktie was hanging down under the back of his collar, and he had his uniform trousers pushed up above his knees.

By now, we figured we knew what to expect from the doctors. We had been through this—like many preemies, Mack tended to get an inflamed respiratory tract when he got a cold. Bronchiolitis. They would give him some spray medication for the wheezing, and we'd wait it out. Premature babies get colds.

How many times had Mack had the wheezing? the doctor asked. Oh, three, four, who knows—happens a lot, right?

When it happens this much, the doctor said, we call the baby an asthma suspect. We're going to start treating him for asthma.

Our son had asthma. There was no use pretending it was the squeaky-clean, sensitive, upper-middle-class kind of asthma. He had the asthma that ghetto children come down with, because they live in the dirt. He was wheezing because at last, today, on the morning of the Olympics, the filth of the city where he was born had gotten into his tender lungs. He was sick because we had let him live in Beijing.

When I went out to buy meat, at the French-style butcher's, the pollution and glare were like being kicked in the bridge of the nose. Everywhere, the city had the unhappy, busy, strained feeling of wedding preparations. Many sausages were being wrapped up, in advance of somebody's party or cookout. I bought a chicken to cut up for soup, for the illness. The cabbie was pleased to see that the road to the alley had become a two-way street. He tried out his English on "Turn left" and "Stop here."

It was time to go see the opening ceremony. China's big moment was at hand. I arranged to meet friends at Ditan Park, the Altar of Earth, to watch the show in public. A magpie squawked as I headed down the alley. Food sizzled in one of the shacks, behind a curtain of strips. A man with a terrible dye job, a classic Beijing dye job, came the other way.

Those were the last signs of everyday life. On Outer Dongzhimen Avenue, half the lanes were closed off. Policemen and the People's Armed Police were standing guard all along the street. The paramilitary police were wearing uniform jackets, despite the heat. The street was nearly empty except for them and a few taxis. The Second Ring Road was squeezed down to one lane. The city had been scoured clean of anything that could conceivably disrupt or even distract from the day's singular purpose, as if all Beijing were a vast dust-free microprocessor plant—or as if it were under quarantine. Or—and despite my efforts not to see contemporary China through Western conventions and stereotypes—as if this stifled atmosphere, with police on post everywhere, was what Beijing had been like in 1989, under martial law.

The video screens were on a plaza inside the north gate of the park, with security screening at the entrance. Ninety minutes before the ceremony, the space was already loosely filled with people, sitting on the pavement on newspapers and blankets (mostly newspapers). We took up a spot at the back, between side-by-side entrance and exit gates. The big screens showed people filing into the Bird's Nest. Up ahead in the park, a surveillance camera jerked to life and spun on its pole, scanning the scene.

Cheers went up in the middle of the crowd, around a foreign man who was wearing red tights and a red-and-white radially painted hat. I watched the flow of people through the entrance gate. Forty people in one minute. No sooner had I counted than the police and security guards began allowing the new arrivals to overflow the paved plaza and sit on the grassy parts of the park. This far away from the real Olympic action, security was stretched thin, and the hired guards far outnumbered the real law-enforcement officers. But there was still the camera, pivoting this way and that with lurching, robotic purpose.

Someone made a scouting trip to the refreshment stands. There was Budweiser in cans and another single-microwave popcorn operation. I took a stroll through the crowd and ran into a camera crew. Where was I from? What did I think of being with so many Chinese people to celebrate? Did I have anything to say to my country's athletes or to China? Not really, I said.

Around half past seven, one of the screens went dead, then came back. The security forces decided that the center of the plaza was too full and formed a line to block it off, sending the new arrivals cutting sideways across the grass and the flower beds, right through our camping spot. A city policeman chewed out a scrawny security guard on the line, for some infraction or other. "Do you want to be laid off?" he yelled. The Vision Beijing food movie played on the televisions. The begonias were being trampled.

At 7:52, an establishing shot of the Bird's Nest appeared, and a roar went up. The Olympics were nigh. The cameras found Hu Jintao, and the park filled with applause. We could see the haze in the lights of the stadium. The crowd in the park was in the thousands; a man in front of us had climbed up a tree for a better view. Another roar greeted the Water Cube, colors shifting across its face.

The particulars of Zhang Yimou's ceremony had been fiercely guarded. After a Korean TV crew had posted video of a rehearsal on the Web, all press had been barred from the final dress rehearsal. Now it was beginning: a mass of drummers, their drums strobing on and off with the strokes, each person acting as an anonymous pixel in a mass display. The symbolism would not be missed by the global audience. The drummers formed numbers—and Chinese characters—for the final countdown: four, three, two, one . . . Olympics! It was 8:00 sharp, after all, not 8:08. One piece of misinformation resolved.

Now it was time for the ceremony to embrace the whole city. The view cut to Tian'anmen Square, where an opening volley of fireworks went off. Then came an aerial tracking shot of more fireworks, each burst shaped like a footprint, marching up the central axis toward us. And then—boom!—our share of the pyrotechnics was bursting off to the west, over the treeline, behind the screens broadcasting their perfect god's-eye view of the glowing trail advancing on the Olympic Green. "Unreal-looking," I scribbled, "—but there are the fireworks." I had seen it with my own eyes. The Bird's Nest went up in a wreath of blinding light. "CGI feel," the notebook said. Next note: "singing child."

Bamboozlement, all. The news would report, over the next few days, that what looked like CGI had in fact been CGI, a faked-up set of fireworks prepared for fear that the real ones wouldn't translate on TV. The singing girl was not singing, or, rather, the girl who was doing the singing was not onstage, a Politburo member having deemed her insufficiently pretty and too crooked-toothed to be the public face of China.

At the time, all there was to do was take the ceremony as presented: the flawless-faced little Han Chinese girl sang, and a squadron of children in minority costumes dutifully carried the national flag toward her. Then a goose-stepping squadron of adult soldiers intercepted the minority children (who were not, it later emerged, real minority children) and took the flag away from them.

The spectacle unfolded glacially, through lush and improbable and slow-moving tableaux. Zhang was indulging his maximalist tastes. It occurred to me that perhaps the loss of Steven Spielberg was more than a symbolic setback—the awe was untempered by entertainment values. The Chinese clichés of Chinese culture rolled forth: scroll calligraphy, ancient musical instruments, movable type—the field of performers, caged in boxes, acting out the role of movable type!—the Great Wall, peach blossoms, the Silk Road. In front of us, someone was on a cell phone, in irritation, trying to track down someone else: "Tian*tan haishi* Di*tan?"*—Temple of Heaven or Temple of Earth?

At 8:35, the broadcast froze, then cut away to a tape of the torch-lighting ceremony in Greece. Had the Free Tibet forces stormed the field? Had the vise grip of vigilance and preparedness somehow slipped? And then the picture came back, live, as before—the unsurprising, staged as the unimaginable. Lang Lang played the piano. A globe filled the center of the stage, changing colors, ending up on red. The 2,008 smiling-face fireworks that organizers had promised went off. Ethnic minorities danced, as ethnic minorities must.

Then it was time for the parade of nations. Israel got a big cheer from the crowd in the park. When Taiwan appeared—"Chinese Taipei"—the man next to me began hollering and banging water bottles together. Pakistan got a cheer, too. So did Spain, with the old fascist, the former IOC president Juan Antonio Samaranch. And Iraq, and Great Britain. As the evening had worn on, the crowd had been getting more and more white. Reporters kept washing up in our little backwater by the exits, accompanied by their fixers, looking for the reaction of the Chinese people. The expats cheered for America and Australia. Everyone cheered for Roger Federer.

Who was going to light the torch? The sturdiest rumor seemed to hold that it would be Li Ning, the gymnast turned sportswear maker. The torch-lighting was still a long way off.

I had worked my way to the front by the time the Chinese delegation came in. The cheers rose, and so did the hands, fists and cameras thrusting up. People were jumping up and down. *"Zhongguo!" "Jia you!" "Zhongguo!" "Jia you!"* The cheering surged again for Hu.

No production values could squeeze out the bureaucratic necessities, though. It was speech time: These would be the Green Olympics, the People's Olympics . . . I would never get a cab if everyone left at once. As the speechifying went on, I retreated. IOC president Jacques Rogge urged the assembled athletes to "reject doping and cheating." Then, by bureaucratic standards, the moment of moments—the Olympics, Hu declared, *"kai le!"* Have opened! Officially!

It still wasn't over. The Olympic flag entered the stadium, taking its time. By now I had slipped out the exit, onto the pathway out of the park, to watch through the trees. The Olympic anthem played, slowly. Enough. If I moved fast, I might see the torch get lit at home.

Outside the north gate, in the wan blue light, there had been a bicycle accident. The bicycle lay in the street, with a bag of groceries tumbled across the pavement away from it. A woman was limping around, and two men were studying the scene. The bicycle lock lay in a puddle of soda. Old people sat in an alley mouth, not watching.

There were empty cabs still. All the way home, the police were still standing at their posts. Along the alley, people huddled around TVs, indoors and out. Out the window of the cab, I saw a televised figure—Li Ning—running in midair, on wires, with the long-traveled torch. Then the white flare of the flame. Outside, in the night courtyard, the fireworks rumbled through the city air.

VIII.

开了 OPENED

22.

比赛 Competition

The Games proper found us while we were eating brunch. Outside the lantern-covered twenty-four-hour dim-sum restaurant, just south of Ditan Park, the roadway was being cordoned off. We were meeting a friend who had spare tickets to the rowing, being held out by the farms and luxury villas of Shunyi District, but here were the Olympics already: a road-cycling race course, in the glare of sunlight through dirty white haze.

The International Olympic Committee had now joined the local officials in claiming that the press was mistaking normal humid mist for pollution—the old lie dragged out of retirement and pressed into emergency service. "The fog you see is based on the basis of humidity and heat," Jacques Rogge had told the press. Meanwhile, despite the security crackdown and the tourism slump, the Free Tibet folks had successfully showed up, protested, and gotten themselves arrested.

And now—a text message arrived, over tea, from a reporter out at the shooting range—Du Li, the 2004 gold medalist, had been beaten in the morning's air-rifle competition. China had faltered. The identical-twin attendants would be delivering the first gold medal of the Beijing Olympics to a Czech woman.

The restaurant's televisions were tuned to women's weightlifting, the other event where China had been favored for a quick win. But the competitors on the screen were from Canada and Japan. Outside, the peloton of road racers went whizzing by, trailed by little silver station wagons with spare bikes on their roofs. More than a third of the riders would quit before the end of the race. The majority of their post-race quotes seemed to blame humidity, rather than pollution—but then, the United States road-cycling team had already been rebuked, and had apologized, for wearing filter masks as they got off the airplane.

The weightlifters dropped out, one by one. A contestant from Taiwan lifted 112 kilograms to take the lead in the clean-and-jerk round. Only then did the Chinese lifter, Chen Xiexia, appear on the screen. The event was for women up to 48 kilos in weight—a little under 106 pounds. Many of the early-round lifters had been almost slim. Chen was shorter and wider. She faced a 113-kilo barbell, her first of the day. And she lifted it. Applause filled the restaurant. Then Chen—shouting *"Jia you!"* to herself—lifted 115. Across China, 155 million people were watching the broadcast.

The Taiwanese lifter, attempting 115, staggered and fell. No one else was left. China had a gold medal. The bar was loaded to 117, and Chen lifted that, too, to close out the scoring. Then she skipped off the stage. She hugged her coach, her broad back to the camera, a pink scrunchie in her hair.

By the time we left for the rowing park, the road-race barricades had broken up. The route out to Shunyi was sleepy. On the rural

White Horse Road, there were traffic lights for the nonexistent traffic, and a volunteer booth waiting by the empty fields. The road melted into a gray mirage-puddle in the distance, from the haze and glare.

Gangs of students in school uniforms, who had been offered surplus tickets the day before, thronged the gate of the rowing park. The line to go through security was roped off and folded back on itself; the Chinese spectators cut corners in the switchbacks and tried to form a passing lane to sneak ahead. Inside, the nearest refreshment stands were all out of water.

In the stands, I discovered bird droppings on my shoulder. It was baffling. There were no trees, and the sky was oppressively empty of everything but smog. The TV screens on the far shore showed blue water and blue sky, through some miracle of color filtering. There on the scene, it was hard to imagine how a body of water could look more like a parking lot.

Before the rowing-venue construction, this had been the site of Maxingzhuang Village, home to some 2,300 people. The residents had reportedly protested their relocation. Meanwhile, the local Chaobai River, from which the rowing stream was built, had run dry from overuse for nine years in a row, the Xinhua News Agency had reported. So a pipeline had been built to bring new water eight miles from the Wenyu River, at a cost of nearly $60 million.

We lasted something like an hour before the watery paradise defeated us. I was sweating profusely and my lungs hurt. The boats were slow-moving, and the only drama was the occasional battle to stay out of last place and elimination in the heats.

Hundreds of other people had reached the same conclusion. The line of people to flee the venue was far longer than the line of buses to take them away. We tried to catch a cab, but cabs were too few. Later, there would be reports that the Shunyi venue had begun to forbid cabbies to pick up Chinese people. For a moment, it seemed as if we might be able to cadge a ride from a van occupied by people in T-shirts that read "I feel sLOVEnia," but we settled for the bus line. By the time we boarded, we had spent more time trying to leave than we had spent watching the Olympic competition.

The K-19 bus, on its way back to town, carried us back into 2007. Either the bus route had been accidentally left off the beautification checklist or someone had guessed that foreigners would be smart or rich enough to hire cars. There was green dust-suppression netting over a rubble field, amid unfinished demolition. There was an alley of ramshackle buildings, and then blue-metal fencing.

Just as we were reaching our final stop—named for a subway station, but nowhere near one—a text message arrived on my phone: there had been a murder at the Drum Tower. Chinese perpetrator, American victim. Two more people wounded, all with a knife. The killer had then jumped to his death from the tower, to the plaza where the pedal-rickshaws and tour buses were perpetually idling, and where the American writers were usually nursing coffee mugs. None of the reporters at the scene were getting anything from eyewitnesses. All the technology and manpower of the security state couldn't lock down violence after all, but it could still lock down information.

23.

金牌　Gold Medals

The next morning's press session was about the weather, and a cleansing downpour had obligingly begun to fall. The People's Armed Police had put on olive-colored rain suits, the first concession I had seen them make to weather conditions. In the floral starburst by the Second Ring ramp, new growth was starting to engulf the pictures of the Fuwa.

In the press hall, I studied a *China Daily*, looking for a mention of the stabbings. Chen Xiexia's picture took up the top of the front page. Down at the bottom, just above the box with the countdown to the Paralympics (twenty-seven days), there was a small headline: "US Tourist Killed in Beijing Attack." It directed readers to page 5, where a short thirteen-paragraph story said that a Chinese man had stabbed two American tourists, one fatally, and then jumped to his death from the Drum Tower. "Local authorities are investigating the case," it said. (The final three paragraphs began: "In another development, Chinese people condemned and protested against five foreigners for fomenting 'Tibetan independence' at Tian'anmen Square yesterday noon.")

Also on the front page, below the fold, a yellow box carried the news that on the night of August 8, the Weather Modification Office had successfully intercepted and suppressed oncoming rainstorms. Over the course of the afternoon and evening, 1,104 rockets had been fired to keep the opening ceremony dry.

Zhang Qiang, the modification office chief, filled in the details from up on the rostrum: the bureau had spotted clouds moving in from the west and the south during the afternoon. Around four p.m., they began firing into the western clouds, while also attacking a small convective system that was threatening from the northwest. Rockets went up from Fangshan, Mentogou, Haidian, and Yanqing. After ninety minutes, they paused for half an hour, then in coordination with the Baoding batteries in Hebei Province, they launched rockets into the southern and southwestern skies, continuing until around eleven at night.

The clouds had come within ten or fifteen miles of the Bird's Nest, Deputy Director Wang Jianjie said. On all fronts the goal had been to overseed the clouds so they wouldn't rain, rather than trying to precipitate rain before it reached the city. By the bureau's calculations, it had used one gram of silver iodide per square kilometer—a volume, Zhang said, that "would not cause any harm to the human beings or to the environment."

Even in triumph, Zhang was as judicious as ever: those cloud systems on August 8, she said, had been small ones. If the bureau tried to mitigate rain as powerful as what was currently falling outside, she said, it "might not be able to." Had today's rain been assisted by the bureau? I asked. "Today's rain," Wang Jianjie said, "is natural."

The *China Daily* had also printed two separate tables of the medal standings, both saying the same thing: China was in first place, with two gold medals; the United States was in second, with one gold, one silver, and one bronze. American media, at the same point, had the U.S. in front, with three medals to China's two. There was no official correct way of scoring the medal count, because officially the medal count was a regrettable jingoistic overlay on the pure athletic spirit of the Games. Especially if your country was losing. So China maintained that silver and bronze didn't count; the United States maintained that finishing third in an event was as good as finishing first.

A little after five in the evening, amid a renewed downpour, the power went out. Then it came back on. I tuned in the big television to watch Team China in basketball. Yao Ming hit a three-pointer; Sun Yue made a big shot early. Between the third and fourth quarters, the Soojin Dancers came out, brandishing their red fans.

Two days in, the murder story was already withering, as a story. At the time of the attack, it had seemed that something drastic and irrevocable had happened. But now, on the American side, it was developing into a story about tragedy striking the extended family of the national volleyball team—the murder victim had been a coach's father—the sort of tragedy that forces athletes to play on, valiantly, through their tears. Not a bad sort of tragedy, as far as the Olympics was concerned. And on the Chinese side, the moment of horror was obscured by the procedural and detail-free announcements of the local authorities, as they investigated. The killer was an unemployed and divorced man, forty-seven years old, from Hangzhou. A disturbed individual. There must have been video surveillance at the Drum Tower, but who wanted to know what the camera might have known? An unfortunate incident had happened, for no reason worth mentioning, and now it was over.

The rain had left the city clean, cool, and wet; the Liangma River was running high in its repaved banks. On a tip from a fellow American, I went looking for scalped tickets outside the boxing site, at the Workers' Gymnasium, a few blocks south of home. A thick-necked Liverpudlian tout with receding ginger hair—the very same scalper my friend had met, to go by his description—found me as soon as I stepped out of my cab. His colleague had a ticket to the current session, for 500 yuan, he said. I told him the price sounded too high, and we talked shop for a while: there were dozens of scalpers in town for the occasion, he said, and the resale market was busy. The cops were no trouble at all. Swimming was tough to get, he said, as was any sport with a lot of the Aussies in it. It was important to get good seats, he said, because some of the upper-level stuff people were selling was terrible.

We settled on 300 yuan, and another Brit swung by and handed over the ticket. This was, I discovered, a 900 percent markup over face value. Inside the Workers' Gymnasium, ushers and signs directed me up and up again—to a seat in the second row from the top, behind the ring of national flags hanging from the arena's upper rim. When I lifted my eyes from the boxers far below, I was staring at the bottom halves of the flags of Ireland and, unsettlingly, Georgia, where the Russian army was busily ignoring the tradition of the Olympic truce. The video screen was up there, too. On it, a boxer's uniform read ENIARKU, because I was seeing the back side of the projection.

The next evening, there was women's soccer at the Workers' Stadium. The stadium, like the indoor arena, had disappeared behind green mesh and scaffolding for months upon months during the Olympic preparations, but the renovations couldn't change the fact that it was a relic of the pre-entertainment era, with grim narrow concrete corridors and no built-in snack stands. The concessions were outside, in the parking lot, and they were overrun, with a deep formless mob crowding around the two stands closest to our gate.

The stands farther around back were less crowded, or people were at least standing in line at them. As I waited at one, Chinese people began sidling up to the counter at an angle, forming a competing auxiliary line. All the Lining-Up Days had failed to cure Beijingers' pushiness. This was the Olympics, the object of all the civilization campaigns. It was time to stand up for international norms. *"Pai dui ba!"* I barked. Line up! *"Pai dui ba!"* I jerked a thumb over my shoulder to show where the line began. Sheepishly, the line jumpers began clearing out. A Chinese woman appointed herself monitor and dispersed the stragglers.

I bought ice cream, some popcorn—prepopped, now, rather than coming from an overburdened microwave—and beverages. I had a sharp, atavistic craving: I was an American and I wanted some Coca-Cola. The beverages came without bottles, poured into wobbly oversized paper cups, so that no hooligan fans of women's soccer could throw them. Security again.

On the stadium video screen, computer-rendered Fuwa capered, glossy and plastic-looking, accompanied by the exhortation "Let's Do the Mexican Wave." This was the place where tens of thousands of Red Guards had gathered for rallies and mass denunciations in the Cultural Revolution, smashing the old society. Now men in tan button-front shirts and olive slacks, wearing white caps, sat in folding chairs around the track, with their backs to the field. This, I realized, was a new, dress-casual incarnation of the People's Armed Police. The uniforms might have been more soothing if the officer nearest us hadn't been sitting bolt upright and scanning the crowd with barely contained tension and alarm, like a Doberman on alert.

On the aisle to our left, there was a young man in a volunteer shirt who looked more muscular than the average college student. He surveyed the stands, then took a seat opposite a uniformed city police officer.

The cheerleaders wore blue-and-white outfits, cheerleader gear without a trace of Chinese cultural influence, and danced to "It's Tricky." The public-address announcer recited the medal standings—the "gold medal standings"—with China comfortably in front. At day's end, China led, 13 to 7. Or, if you preferred, it trailed, 21 to 20.

Bad news continued to trickle out. There had been rumors in the Beijing dance community about an accident during the opening-ceremony rehearsals, and the Chinese press confirmed it: Liu Yan, one of the country's most decorated dancers, had fallen from the elevated platform representing the Silk Road while practicing a solo, and she was apparently paralyzed. A report in the paper said that she couldn't feel anything in her legs, but that she believed that if a dancer had to go down, the Olympics was a good reason. According to the story, Liu said that she planned to find some other way of bringing beauty into the world.

Meanwhile, TV cameras were showing the world embarrassing expanses of empty seats. The ticket allocation had been so botched that sections of volunteer cheerers were being bused in to fill swaths of empty seats at the events.

Also empty were the official protest zones. No one had succeeded in staging a protest in the lawfully assigned areas; people who had applied to try to protest were being charged with "disturbing the social order." And the air was turning foul again. As I rode toward the field hockey venue, to watch China take on South Korea, I could barely see the tower of the newly built 7 Star Hotel, shaped like a dragon's undulating neck, marking the southwest corner of the Olympic Green.

As I reached my seat, Song Yi, the karaoke-singing Chinese team captain, scored a goal to give China a 2–0 lead. Korea quickly scored in response. Big Mack joined me in the stands. Without the Lantern Courtyard to deal with, he had found another project to keep him busy. Through the earlier part of the summer, he had been traveling around China with a Singaporean reality-TV crew, setting out as a fixer and then taking an on-camera turn as a camp chef for the show's contestants.

We were sitting next to a section of people in matching yellow shirts, with "Cheering from Beijing Workers" printed on their thundersticks—part of the emergency cheering corps. There were other color-coordinated sections around the stadium, where more empty seats had been filled. Swallows flitted by. As time expired in the first half, Korea was granted a penalty shot, and made it. It was 2–2.

Cheerleaders with little bells on their costumes came on and did a halftime routine. The last one off the field looked winded by the effort. Mack asked if I had seen the Internet video parody of "Beijing Huanying Ni," about the national men's soccer team. Chinese people hated the men's soccer team, he said. While European soccer players reportedly earned twenty-seven times the average European's income, he said, Chinese players got fifty times the national average. And they were dirty and uninspired players, whose principal highlight in these Olympics had been when one of them punched a foe in the crotch. The new song was "Guozu Huanying Ni"—"National Soccer Welcomes You." Our goal is open wide, the parodists sang.

The field hockey team was not doing much for national honor, either. In the second half, the Chinese kept fouling the Koreans, setting up penalty shots. Before each penalty, the players would go behind the goal and pick up headguards, then stuff protective cups down their pants. Korea took a 3–2 lead on a penalty, then went up 4–2 on another.

The crowd headed for the exits when Korea scored its fifth, and final, goal, with two and a half minutes to play. There was a reason field hockey was not one of China's sports of emphasis.

China's best boxer, Zou Shiming, had a bout scheduled for the afternoon. I had found another source of tickets, a reselling website with a shaky interface. There, the boxing tickets were marked up with only an $18 service charge on top of the $30 face value. The pick-up office was down in Jianwai Soho; a steady trickle of foreigners was flowing through the grassy plazas, among the white towers. Ticket reallocation was beginning to clean up the mess of ticket allocation.

My seat was low down in the first section, by the red corner. I could see everything. If I turned my head and squinted way up, I could even see my previous seat. Nearby fans chanted "Ka! Zakh! Stan!" With one bout to go till Zou's turn—a France–Uzbekistan matchup—there was a stirring on the far side of the seating bowl. Don King had appeared.

Zou, quick and self-assured, was taking on a Venezuelan. Cheers of *"Jia you!"* rolled around the arena, not quite in phase. The only drama was around whether the Venezuelan would land any scoring punches at all, or Zou would get a shutout. The Venezuelan trailed 8–0 after three rounds, and was wobbling. He came out in the fourth and scored with two punches, but Zou, backpedaling, had everything in hand. The final score was 11–2. Zou stood in the middle of the ring and blew kisses, one step closer to his share of China's medal count. In his yellow robe, he did a TV standup interview, hands folded behind his back. The crowd kept its eyes on him as he went down the row of TV cameras. A Dominican fighter arrived for the next bout, playing to the crowd by wearing a poncho made up of one Dominican flag and one Chinese one. The Dominican's bout was in the third round before Zou finally blew more kisses and exited.

Thursday brought thunderstorms, sending sheets of water rolling through the neighborhood streets. Rowing, softball, and tennis were rescheduled. The press had spread out into the city, looking for the authentic Beijing. On our own alley, I passed a crew from TV of Catalonia interviewing one of the shopkeepers. The Olympics were a week old, and Little Mack was still sick, with coughing and diarrhea through the night.

Friday morning was the best weather yet, clear and mild, under a blue sky with wispy white clouds. Looking west down North Workers' Stadium Road, by the tourist-thronged Yashow Market and the mirror-faceted Adidas store, I could see the mountains, blue on blue. Yingying the antelope beamed from the side of a pedestrian overpass, with the clean, beautiful scenery behind him. Beijing Welcomes You.

In the evening, there were empty seats all around the beach volleyball arena. We grabbed better seats than the ones on our tickets, and when some Chinese people approached, looking like the actual ticket-holders, an usher steered them away. The cheerleaders wore aqua bikinis. An Austrian duo beat a German one, and inflated Fuwa and extra dancers filed into the stadium. Jingjing and Nini clasped each other in a carnal, humping embrace. There were two dozen cheerleaders, half of them Soojin's Chinese dancers and the other half a team from the Canary Islands. To the strains of the Offspring's "Pretty Fly (for a White Guy)" they tossed their hair and did air-guitar moves, welcoming Chinese and Cuban women's teams. Then came "Whoop, There It Is." The Chinese team, Xie Chen and Zhang Jie, held off a Cuban rally in the first set, then won the second easily, to the shrieking approval of the crowd.

A bright white moon rose over the stands. The Chinese cheerleaders retired for the night, giving way to the Canary Islanders: bigger-looking hair, smaller-looking shorts. Some Norwegians ran a lap around the grandstands with their flag. Then three Germans and an Australian took a flag lap. Then some Americans and Canadians. The whole happy world was inside Chaoyang Park.

24.

美术大师
The Artist

Saturday morning was so clear we could see an airplane rising far away in the sky above the Western Hills, from the military and government airfield that all the maps omitted. Big Mack and I were on our way to join a group interview with Han Meilin, the Fuwa artist, at the Han Meilin Museum. Big Mack was not fond of the Fuwa, himself; he said he didn't see why Beijing couldn't have just reused Pan Pan, the panda mascot of the 1990 Asian Games.

The streets were quiet. All over town, elderly security volunteers sat by the roadsides, wearing white-and-red Yanjing Beer polo shirts and red armbands, but there was hardly anyone for them to watch. The construction ban had settled the debate over whether to send the undercivilized migrant workers home for the Olympics or to let them enjoy the festive city they had built: with no work for three months, the labor force couldn't afford to stay. Some Beijing professionals were choosing, when they could, to get out of town till the Olympics were over. The flight was called *biyun*, or "avoiding the Games"—a play on *biyun*, meaning "contraception." Longtime expat residents were taking a few months abroad, frustrated by the visa crackdown.

So many people had left, Mack said, that vendors were stuck with unsold peaches. And even if there were customers, because no out-of-town vehicles were allowed on the roads, farmers in Hebei couldn't bring produce into the city. Many markets were closed to prevent the sale of bootleg merchandise. The auto-parts bazaar Mack liked to go to, on the northeast bend of the Fourth Ring, had been closed down.

The media bus took us east and south, out along the Batong subway line. The bus driver stopped to ask people sitting by the roadside for directions. Then he stopped again, to flag a passing woman on a bicycle to double-check the directions. A GPS unit, ignored, was mounted on the windshield of the bus. The bus made a U-turn.

The tour organizer and the bus driver were discussing, with some heat, whether they were heading to the Han Meilin Museum or the Han Meilin Workshop. The bus had looped back around to where it had been before. More passersby were questioned. Then, a short way down the road, there was a gate, flanked by a pair of fancily rendered dragon statues.

We disembarked. Han was still in poor health, we were told, and this was the last time he would do an interview before he went in for an operation. We should please stay focused and keep it short, so he wouldn't get tired out.

The museum was modernist and new, with wood-grain marks in its concrete walls. Han Meilin was running late, so a young female docent in a Han Meilin–logo polo shirt, with the collar turned up to show a multicolored lining, led the group of journalists through the whole place. "Han's name has become a household name because of his small kittens, poodles, wolves and monkeys," the English portion of an introductory sign said. "Even when he has created huge works of art, he remains true to his cute, sweet, and charmingly naive small creatures."

The tour moved swiftly through the winding multiple levels of the museum, the pace emphasizing the proprietor's productivity: quickly past a multistory stone Buddha, a yards-long painting of horses with exaggerated circle-curves on their necks and flanks, a yards-long tapestry of panthers—and but also a room of huge ceramics, and another room of huge ceramics, and a wall of little teapots in little niches and another wall of little teapots in more little niches, and sketches and logos. A series of buxom bronze mothers embraced adorable bronze babies in various appropriated modernist styles. The emblem of Air China—the red letters "VIP," curlicued into a phoenix—hung alone in a spotlight, like a canvas.

We passed down a ramp lined with sketchbook drafts of the Fuwa: little pandas and monkeys, round schematic masks, capering cartoon figures. There were more than one set of what looked suspiciously like the multicolored dancing-bears logo of the Grateful Dead. Some pages featured sketches of nude women—narrow-waisted, high-breasted, and full-hipped—with little proto-Friendlies flitting around their curves.

The room for the interview was long and dark, with heavy drapes over a wall of windows and a table the size of a driveway running down the middle. There were loosely rolled sheets of paper at the near end, and the cloth on the table was blotched with ink. We took seats in armchairs at the far end of the room, and Han was ushered in to sit on a leather couch.

He was a small man, with rounded shoulders and double bags under his eyes, but his hair had been dyed a not-too-inauthentic black and he looked better than his age, let alone his advertised condition. He wore a blue polo shirt with a gray collar, and he was in a talkative mood.

"I feel sorry for these five Fuwa, because they have to wear such heavy hats," Han said. "If you asked me to single-handedly design this, I would definitely design it better, more fun. I wouldn't say this is my work. I have to consider a lot of other people's interests."

Now that the Olympics were safely under way, he said, he didn't mind telling stories. He held up a completed rendering of the abandoned Dragon Fuwa, in red, with round dragon-eyes glaring from its headdress. Then there had been the idea of using a crane. "I thought this was not a good idea," he said. A long beak would endanger children who bought souvenirs.

A reporter raised the fact that the Fuwa had been absent from the solemn artistry of Zhang Yimou's opening ceremony. "I don't care," Han said. "I'm very busy. Even my seats were changed. I was supposed to sit behind Hu Jintao. . . . I don't care about that. I'm famous enough. I'm so famous that I don't care."

"These are the little stories, small things," he said. "I haven't told you the big stories. I won't tell you the big stories, because I still love this country. . . . I maintain a positive attitude. I do not include sad feelings in my work. I look down on these people that have gone overseas and got educated and started to come back to China and criticize."

It is not easy to eliminate Chinese elements from culture, he said. The pinyin romanization system for spelling out words would never replace characters. Picasso had once said he wished he were Chinese, so he could have learned calligraphy. Han swooped his arm in a brushstroke. "Waaa!" he yelled. "You don't do calligraphy with brush and ink, you write it with your *qi*."

He brought out a copy of his book *Tian Shu* (Book of Heaven), a compendium of ancient characters, rendered in his own writing. "I collected all these during the most dark years during the Cultural Revolution," he said. "I got out of prison in 'seventy-two. . . . Then I started to travel around the country to research about cave paintings. I visited secondhand bookshops."

He offered a disquisition on the yin and yang symbol, explaining how he had sought to render it in three-dimensional form as a pierced jade disc, an example of which he had been fiddling with as he spoke. He drew a yin and yang on his sketchpad, and pointed to the museum logo on a staffer's polo shirt: a dot and a curling line. He drew an egg and sperm. Then he tore off a strip of paper and made it into a loop. A tai chi master had visited him, he said, and had told him he didn't believe Han Meilin could achieve the goal of making a satisfying three-dimensional yin and yang. The master drove a Mercedes 560, Han said, and he had thrown the keys on the table and said he would give Han the car if he succeeded. Han twisted the paper loop to make a Möbius strip, then flattened it into a triangle. And that was how he had won a Mercedes-Benz, he said.

With further refinement, he had smoothed the triangle into the disc, with one half of its face covered with a tapered groove, spiraling to a hole through its center and out the other side, an endless surface.

He began autographing copies of the Book of Heaven. "The most power comes from being humiliated," he said. "This is my biggest source of power. If you say that I can't do something, then I will not only do it, I will be the best." He was at work on a sculpture that would be 120 meters tall—the tallest sculpture in the world. A phoenix sculpture he had made had used 400 tons of copper, 500 tons of clay, and 4,000 tons of plaster. "That comes from the power of being humiliated," he said.

"China is like a piece of ceramic . . ." he said. "It looks beautiful and it feels hard, but it is easy to break."

He turned to the subject of modern architecture. The National Theater was a fried egg, he said. The CCTV building was a *you tiao*, a fried stick of dough.

A reporter asked him about a notion that had been circulating on the Internet, that the Fuwa were cursed, and that they corresponded to the year's disasters: Jingjing with the Sichuan earthquake, Yingying with the Lhasa riots—

"I'm not that smart, to predict all these disasters," Han said.

Han had been quoted recently in the press saying that he had only been promised one yuan in payment for making the Fuwa, and that he hadn't even been paid that. Now he said he had told that anecdote about the nonpayment at a banquet with officials, and Wen Jiabao had said that it showed that China still didn't respect knowledge or art. Not long after, he and his fellow designers had received 300,000 yuan as payment for the design, to be split among nine people. His share, as leader, was 80,000, which he donated to a schools project for rural children.

At the southeast corner of the Olympic Green, outside the Bird's Nest, humanity spilled out into the streets from the backup at the security lines. The evening sessions of track-and-field didn't need volunteer cheerers to pad them out. Everyone, including me, was holding up a camera to record the chaos.

Volunteers urged spectators to get on a shuttle to Gate 8, where the lines would be shorter. We got on the bus and rode off and kept on riding, and riding, and riding. Gate 8 was uncrowded because it fed onto the Olympic Green somewhere north of the International Broadcast Center, which was north of the Digital Beijing building, which was north of the National Indoor Stadium, which was north of the Water Cube, which was north of the Bird's Nest—a long hike back down the spine of the Green to the event. Along the way, we kept running into little girls with heavy green eye makeup—they were from the Dance Academy, two of them told Christina, and were performers in the daily Fuwa parade. Did we have any Olympic pins? they asked.

Our seats in the Bird's Nest were in the dark, at the back of the bottom deck, in Section L. Stickers saying "Beijing 2008" had been pasted over the molded oil-company logos on the seat backs. On the big screen, a computer-animated Yingying represented the 100 meters. We were at the top of the stretch, the sprinters heading away from us. Usain Bolt of Jamaica ran a 9.85, in gold shoes, to win a heat. Tyson Gay of the United States finished fifth, eliminated from the final. On the slow-motion replay, his face held a pained expression as it flapped against the resisting air.

A boy with heart-shaped Chinese-flag stickers on his cheeks played with a PlayStation Portable in his seat. The women's shot put event was directly in front of us. Under the overhang, the air was getting close and mosquitoey. Three Chinese women and two Americans were in the final. The video screen was focused on the start of the 400-meter hurdles, but the crowd kept yelling *"Jia you!"* for the home country's shot-putters, till the public address announcer had to tell them to pipe down so the runners could hear the gun.

There was a certain lack of drama built into the shot put. Valerie Vili, a New Zealander, went nearly 20 meters with her first toss, and before long it was clear that none of the other women could possibly throw the shot as far. Round after round, she heaved it comfortably past the 20-meter mark, while only one other competitor even cleared twenty. Both Americans and one of the Chinese were eliminated in the first cut-down.

On the track, the women's heptathletes were finishing their event with the 800-meter run. The Chinese entrant, Liu Haili, was all the way at the back. "We're not asking you to win!" someone exhorted from the stands. "Just don't be last!" Liu obligingly passed someone, moving into next-to-last place. "Pass the next one!" the person shouted.

After a long mass victory lap by the heptathletes—a show of sisterhood and sportsmanship undermined only afterward, when the silver medalist was disqualified for failing a drug test—it was time for the men's 100-meter final. Bolt towered over the other finalists, his shoes gleaming in the lights. It took about two seconds from the starting pistol to tell that both U.S. runners were beaten, and as Bolt kept running away from us, maybe another two seconds to tell that everyone else was beaten, too.

Then came a sort of confused mass hypnosis, as 91,000 minds staggered together toward the same conclusion: He is . . . he just . . . the clock . . . point what? . . . point SIX?? The sign said: 9.68. Followed by, in understatement: "Olympic record."

Followed by: "World record."

The replay came up, and the crowd laughed, shrill with amazement, at the sight of Bolt breaking form and celebrating before he'd even finished. It was the greatest sprint ever. The Bird's Nest had hosted something immortal.

We left the stadium and headed back north up the Green, toward the subway station. The bubbles of the Water Cube glowed blue, then magenta, then blue again. More color-shifting lights flowed along a three-sided observation tower, crowned by the shining hoops of the Olympic rings. The pathway carried the crowd down into a sunken garden plaza, through a red-lit monumental arch. There were stone lattices and a wall made of illuminated red-and-white drums. It was the lurid, electric China at its most stunning, a vision of pure future, marred only by the odor of frying from the showpiece McDonald's, mingled with a whiff of sewage.

Little Mack was feeling better. I took him out with me to Ritan Park, the Altar of the Sun, looking for any sign of the official protest zone. The afternoon was gray, a rare clean and natural gray after rain, and it was quiet; a few sightseers wandered here and there. If there were undercover police among them, they weren't obvious. Toy motorboats zipped around on a pond. The protest space seemed to be as hypothetical as the protesters. The altar itself was flat and square, paved with plain square blocks. Mack stood on top of it contemplatively, sucking his thumb—Chinese people are scandalized by babies that suck their thumbs—then began toddling around the altar platform. The social order was undisturbed.

IX.

胜 TRIUMPH

25.

阿基里斯 Achilles

Liu Xiang was down. He had come out for a preliminary daytime heat in the 110-meter hurdles, and he had limped off the track before the race began. The crowd had drained out of the Bird's Nest with him. I was on my way to Jianwai Soho to pick up basketball tickets, and the radio in the cab was playing the press conference about it, in Chinese and English. ". . . unless the pain is intolerable . . ." the translator said. The press was asking about the pressure Liu had felt himself to be under.

I got the tickets and headed across town to Wukesong. Liu Xiang went by, an image on the side of a bus, then gazing out from a blown-up magazine cover on a newsstand. Liu Xiang was drinking Coke on every third or fourth bus stop on Chang'an Boulevard.

Liu Xiang was not going to run in Beijing. He was skipping his apotheosis. Instead, he was going to recover, rest his Achilles tendon, and train and run some other time, in however more years and meets were ahead of him. Liu Xiang, of all people, now belonged to the world after the Olympics.

It had been an obvious but unthinkable proposition during the whole long countdown: the Olympics would end. The Fuwa would have nothing more to represent. Beijing would stop symbolizing China's future and start inhabiting it.

There was a shopping frenzy at the souvenir stands in the arena. Inside, on the NBA-approved twenty-two-ton scoreboard, a computer-rendered Nini squashed a cigarette butt; Beibei chased down an animated camera and wrestled the flash attachment from it.

The Chinese men's team entered to a loud cheer—suspiciously loud, for how empty the arena was, with just twenty-five minutes till tipoff. I was getting too mistrustful. Maybe it was a trick of the acoustics; the music system had a strange ambient buzz-roar behind it, not just loud but overwhelmingly full-sounding, as if it had been tuned to the natural resonant frequency of the arena for maximum thrumming power.

The upper sections were more full than the middle; a knot of people with flags and cameras leaned over the railing of the top deck. The crowd cried "Ooo!" when Yao Ming tossed up an alley-oop pass in warm-ups, and gave a deep bass cheer when Yao was introduced. The cheers for Wang Zhizhi were not as loud, but sounded somehow deeper.

To my left was a middle-aged couple with a gleam in their eyes; to my right was a pair of young couples. One of the girls wore a Chinese flag—still creased from its packaging—as a shawl, over a lime-green dress, yellow flip-flops, and eggplant-colored toenails. Team China was playing Greece, with hardly anything at stake: both teams had already qualified for the medal round. If I wanted to see Chinese basketball live, I couldn't be choosy.

After a mutually sloppy start, the Greeks went on the attack. With

China down 12–7 and the crowd booing their play, Wang checked in for Yao. Greece hit a three-pointer. Wang faked a three, drove aggressively, and got the ball slapped away from him, with China keeping possession. Wang got the ball again, faked again, drove, stopped, feinted a pass, and banked in a turnaround jump shot off the glass. Whenever China had the ball now, the action was going through the old hero Wang, for good or ill—a drive for another basket, then a point-blank miss, then a loose ball Wang grabbed and put in.

But the Greeks were running out behind the defense, over and over, for easy layups. Down 38–17, China called time-out, and the announcer welcomed the "Beijing Dream Dancers," Soojin's team. The dancers wore red and silver, with some sort of stockings that gave their legs a weird sheen under the lights.

Yao took over for Wang. Now the game was going through him. He tried to make a move in the paint and a Greek took him down, Yao's seven-foot-six frame hitting the floor with a thud. The crowd booed. On Greece's final possession of the half, Wang, back in the game, blocked a shot. It was 46–24. China had attempted fourteen three-pointers, and had made zero.

The crazy-dunk team, as promised by Soojin, performed on a trampoline as the crowd clapped in rhythm to "In Da Club." Then the trampoline act ran off and came back in gray jumpsuits to do a *Ghostbusters*-themed routine, ending in a dunk over a three-high human pyramid. It was more professional than some ball-spinning routines I'd seen at NBA halftimes.

In the third quarter, China's three-pointers began falling. A deep three-pointer by Sun cut the deficit to 58 48, and the arena began filling with noise again. Greece stretched the lead back out to fifteen, then held for the last shot, but the Chinese defense smothered the play. The Dream Dancers came out for "Proud Mary": hair flying, bodies merging into a line, arms rolling, the skirtlike trim on their hot pants twinkling.

China would make one more run, with Yao and Wang sharing the court. Wang hit back-to-back three-pointers, sandwiched around an agile rebound. But Greece slipped away again. Yao retired to the bench to rest for the medal round, his seated form jutting above those of his teammates. Greece won, 91–77. There was duct tape hiding the manufacturer's logo on the sink in the men's room.

The farther around Beijing I ranged to watch Olympic events, the blurrier the periphery became. The city that hosts the Games is bidding to become Anywhere. Centuries of history and seven years of planning were reduced now to a series of arenas, like the various plates on a buffet line. On my way back to Wukesong the next day, to see the Chinese women's basketball team, I reached Zhu Zhu, the singer and baseball game hostess, on the phone. Her album had been delayed till after the Olympics. She had been doing segments about shopping and fashion for the *Today* show, she said, and she would be hosting a Sean Paul concert and another event, a party on Qianmen after the closing ceremony. She was getting her makeup done for *Today* as we spoke.

I went through security, putting the ritual dab of sunscreen on the back of my hand to show that it was nothing more dangerous than sunscreen. "Are . . . you . . . rrrready??" the voice from the PA asked. It was the quarterfinals, China against Belarus. The top deck was full again. The Chinese women did everything the men had not done: attacked, disrupted the passing lanes, forced steals. A boy behind me kept yelling *"San fen!"*—Three-pointer!—and was finally rewarded with one, after a patient possession.

The entertainment during the breaks was all new: European

dancers; performers on stilts with backboards strapped to their backs, who threw balls to the crowd and urged them to shoot. Half-time was for traditional culture: dancers in gold, with plumed head-dresses, carrying flags with ancient Chinese characters on them. To drum-heavy music, they paraded their cultural heritage around the hardwood. Later came breakdancers and then a ethnic-dance troupe, barefoot and wearing ankle bracelets.

The Chinese basketball team led all the way. Miao Lijie, number 8, was the best player on the court for either team. In the final minutes, she dribbled down the clock, drove down the right side, and got knocked down by a big Belarusian, who fouled out on the play. That settled it. At the end, Miao and her teammates danced in a circle on the court, then turned around and bowed to the audience.

A man near me was rattling a noisemaker shaped like an abacus. I went to the souvenir stand to try to get one for little Mack. There were three members of the ethnic-minority dance team on the concourse, with their costumes garment-bagged and their makeup still in place. They said they had traveled all the way up from Yunnan Province to perform.

The abacuses were not for sale. They had been giveaways. A girl of about eleven, in a red headband, offered one, still in its bag.

I had the unnerving realization that there was only a limited time to buy Fuwa. On the way out, I grabbed a cab away from upstream passengers by signaling first and more aggressively. The thing about Chinese people is, they have no taxi-hailing technique. As we headed east on Chang'an Boulevard, we passed a little silver Xiali with a couple kissing passionately in the backseat.

The magazine in the taxi's seat-back pocket had a day-by-day guide to the Olympics—"The Festival of Olympic"—in which the day designated for seeing the Bird's Nest was August 21—"Liu

Xiang's final contest." "Liu Xiang's final contest is attracted to everyone. Though the match is in the evening, you can come here early to visit the 'Bird's Nest' and spend the whole day here."

The cabbie who took me to the Peking University ping-pong arena had a second cabbie riding in the passenger seat, smoking a filter cigarette. I cranked down the window, and the extra passenger hopped out at the bus depot. The morning was sunny, hot, and vaguely brown. The on-ramps to the Second Ring were jammed again. We took the Fourth Ring, passing the Olympic Tower, its countdown clock gone dark, with nothing left to count toward.

An hour's slate of women's games was under way. At the far end, a player from Poland by the name of Li Qian was taking a point from a Belarusian in a flurry of big smashes. Li's style involved getting down below the table and swinging with the paddle flat, parallel to the tabletop. The Belarusian was ahead, three games to one. "Li Qian!" the cheer went up. *"Jia you!"* Li added enough gas to take the game.

The other women's matches ended, and players began arriving for the eleven-o'clock men's matches. Li kept playing. The Belarusian had been the better player, but she was visibly tired, and Li settled into a deliberate, patient rhythm, content to prolong the points indefinitely with those low, sweeping strokes. I started trying to count the shots: thirteen on a single point, then twenty-two soon after, as the men waited for the table. Li got to game point, at 10–6— but then her composure wobbled. The Belarusian began pushing the pace again, each shot harder and harder, to a conclusive smash. Suddenly the Belarusian was ahead, 11–10, and serving for the match. One shot, two, three, four, five . . . Li was holding on . . . eleven, twelve, thirteen . . . not the placid volleying game anymore, but kill shots and desperate returns . . . twenty, twenty-one, twenty-two . . .

the Belarusian hammering away, trying to end it until . . . twenty-six, twenty-SEVEN—Li finally gave way. The Belarusian sank to her knees in triumph.

The crowd was very Chinese. An Austrian named Chen Weixing faced a towering Indian in red and black, with a red bandanna. *"Zhongguo dui!"* the crowd cheered. *"Jia you!"* Go, Team China! In point of fact, there was no *Zhongguo dui* to be seen, at least not in uniform. Team China wouldn't be along for a few hours, till the top seeds played. But there was Chen the Austrian, and Lin Ju of the Dominican Republic, and Ko Lai Chak of Hong Kong. Chen won, and stopped to sign an autograph on the way out. Lin, the Dominican, lost. Hong Kong beat Greece.

The men's room had a squat toilet and a pee wall with running water instead of urinals. The water left a wet spray zone on the floor.

The next round, women again, included Li Qiangbing of Austria, Tan Wenling Monfardini of Italy, and Shen Yanfei of Spain. Li, the Austrian, won, and two white Austrian men yelled heartily and waved their eagle flag at her. More players came on: Wu Xue of the Dominican Republic, Stephanie Sang of Australia, Xian Yifang of France, Lau Suifei of Hong Kong, Gao Jun of the United States.

In the one sport where China had enjoyed a historical head start, the world was ruled by Chinese athletes. By the end of the Olympic tournament, the People's Republic of China would have collected every ping-pong medal it possibly could: men's and women's individual gold, silver, and bronze, and a gold in the team competition—which had replaced the old doubles competition, sparing the rest of the world the risk of being completely shut out.

Either the weather modifiers didn't care about beach volleyball or the weather was beyond their capabilities. China's Tian Jia and Wang

Jie were playing for the women's gold medal against the U.S. super-duo of Misty May-Treanor and Kerri Walsh, in the open air of the Chaoyang arena, but it was pouring rain all morning. The friend who had been bringing me a ticket was late. I scrawled the characters for *"Wo xiang mai piao"*—I want to buy tickets—on a page of my notebook and tore it out. There were deep puddles in the roadway along Chaoyang Park.

I stood with an umbrella and my sign, in the drenching rain. It was time for the match to be starting. A tan minibus rolled by into the parking lot, with Jason Kidd, taking a break from the basketball tournament, sitting by the window. There were one or two other signs in people's hands, going limp in the rain. The ticket-resale economy had shut down—too many people wanted to see China play America for the gold, and nobody wanted to get wet scalping tickets.

The United States had already won the first game by the time my friend and I splashed through the gates. The venue staff was distributing disposable full-length ponchos. Ours were pale blue. The second game was going on, and the stands were filled with other people's ponchos, in Easter-egg pastels: pink, blue, green, yellow. The ponchos and umbrellas served mainly to channel the pouring rain into rivulets in unexpected places. Water streamed off the poncho of the man next to me, finding a gap in mine and soaking the pants pocket where I had my cell phone.

The cheerleaders were dancing down below, out in the rain. Their hair was soaked. There was a medical time-out, and it fell to them to fill the time, clapping and dancing. Play resumed, and the rain pounded down even harder. The U.S. led 17–15, but China rallied back. Now it was 18–18. Feet hammered on the sheet metal of the stands. The U.S. team pulled ahead once more, got to match point, and spiked for the win. The players fell to their knees. Then Walsh formed a huddle with the cheerleaders and bounced up and down.

The dancers weren't out of the rain yet. For their post-match performance, they brought out their red fans. Carpeting and podiums were laid out. Workers with twig brooms swept off the platforms. There were twenty-four dancers, in four groups of six, in red bikinis with red cowboy hats. They came together in twin bowling-pin formation for "Celebration." Wave arms side to side; step right, left. Pass the formations through each other to switch sides. The rain kept falling on them. Turn, clap clap, turn again. Rotate the whole show one-eighth of a turn around the arena. The volume on Kool and the Gang got turned up. The formations got a bit ragged, then broke up to form a sort of J wrapping around the victory platform. Hats off, hair plastered down. "Blue Monday" played on the sound system; the announcer said that the victory ceremony was five minutes away. Another dance routine filled the time with big stomping steps, the cheerleaders pulling back into V's facing each other. Then, finally, they gathered up their hats and jogged off, heads down, behind the mob of photographers, as inconspicuous as two dozen girls in red bikinis could hope to be.

For the last night of track-and-field, we took the subway, the new No. 10 line, around the Third Ring to the Olympic spur. At the transfer station, the passengers were steered up out of the station, around the lot, through a screening checkpoint, and back down inside, free to ride to the Olympic Green. The relief of having cleared security, the sense of permission and belonging, is the motor oil in the engine of the control state.

Most of the corporate pavilions on the Green had lines too long to wait through, but we drifted through the Kodak one. People posed for victory photos with a stadium backdrop. Outside, a concession stand was selling self-heating meals: the operator opened a white plastic box, dumped a packet of meat and sauce over a bed of rice in a tray inside, put the rice tray on top of a flat white packet, put the lid back on the whole thing, and pulled a ripcord. The box sat quietly, then abruptly puffed out of shape and began steaming. There were bones in the meat, but they had been cooked so soft we could eat them. Convenience food of tomorrow.

A man in a ClimaCool mesh sportshirt and a licensed ball cap hawked and spat into the shrubbery alongside the sunken garden. The pavement of the Green was strewn with rolled-up mats, used for traction in the downpour the day before. Everywhere people were climbing up on the rolls to pose for photos, eager for the extra foot or so of elevation above the rest of the masses. On the big screen set in on the dragon's neck of the 7 Star Hotel, Zou Shiming was out-fighting an Irish boxer.

Our seats were up at the very top of the Bird's Nest, under the rim, looking straight ahead at the national flags. Far, far away, people ran and jumped and threw javelins. The Chinese women finished next-to-last in a heat of the 4-by-400-meter relay. A Chinese runner finished far out of the medals in the 5,000 meters. Jamaica dropped the baton in the women's 4-by-100 relay.

Then came the men's 4-by-100 relay, with Jamaica and Usain Bolt. Bolt had already added a 200-meter record and medal to his performance in the 100. We had seen enough relays by now to know that because of the staggered start, the thing to watch was when the handoffs happened. Jamaica was a little bit ahead on the first two legs, in the relative timing, and then the baton went to Bolt. Time became space, yards of space, opening up behind him as he swept around the curve at an inconceivable speed, delivering the baton to

Asafa Powell, who a little more than a week before had been the fastest man in the world. There was no one anywhere near. Powell crossed the finish line at 37.1, three-tenths of a second ahead of the old world record.

As we made our way out of the Bird's Nest, the Water Cube glowed ahead of us like stained glass. On the subway, a Jamaican boy, maybe nine years old, hunched over in his seat and buried his head in both hands, as if he were trying to keep happiness from splitting his skull. Then he reared up and threw some uppercuts at the air and began singing aloud, to no one in particular: *"BEIII-jing HUAN-ying niiii . . ."*

26.

同一个世界
One World

Here and there, as the end came closer, the Olympic rules were starting to crack. The migrant laborers were still missing, and the Uighur nut-loaf vendors, but traffic was getting thicker—rumor had it that government workers' cars were back on the roads—and a small construction team had erected a new white-and-blue barracks overlooking the alley, on the edge of the building site.

Even though there was scarcely anything left of the Olympics to prepare for, there were more than fifty people in the Dongsi Olympic Community Public Welfare English Class. Shao and Hu told me that they had been working for the Olympic security watch, the teams in Yanjing Beer shirts, four hours each day.

An Olympic countdown board was still outside, with a pig-tailed mascot on it—another mascot, this one, particular to the Dongsi Community. Its name was Dongdong, but with a different character for *dong* from that used for Dongdong the cheering mascot.

The class was on Lesson 47, which involved inviting someone to have tea. On the board were the words "jasmine" and "chrysanthemum." The teacher was named David and was young, a little heavyset, with a buzz cut. "Try some of," he read.

"Try some of," the class echoed.

"Our wonderful green tea."

"Our wonderful green tea."

"Try some of our wonderful green tea."

"Try some of our wonderful green tea."

The word "chrysanthemum," it emerged, was an almost impossible hurdle. David had a good, natural-sounding American accent overall, but when the dialogue reached chrysanthemum tea, it came out "kryzanzmum": "Kryzanzmum sounds interesting."

On break, the students came around to talk. The senior citizens had gone to CCTV to film a singing program on the twentieth, they told me. One old man, with thick square glasses and abundant nose hair, was new to me, and kept pushing up close. Did I know about class struggle? he wanted to know. And about opening and reform? Could I name the Three Represents of Jiang Zemin? In English, he called them the "Three Representatives." I could not name the Three Represents. He was exasperated, a satisfied exasperation, having caught the foreigner in a shortcoming. The Three Representatives were very, very important. Number one, the Party stands for advanced production force. Number two, the Party stands for advanced culture. Number three, the Party stands for the most people's interests. I wrote them down dutifully.

The teacher, David, approached. The students were wondering, could I demonstrate the pronunciation for them? I took the microphone. "Chrysanthemum."

"Krzyzanzmum."

"Chrys-"

"Khryz-"

Wait, where did the syllable breaks go? "-san-" Oops, I'd accidentally doubled the *s*.

"-zan-" It was dawning on me I had never really thought about how to say the word "chrysanthemum" in my entire life.

"-the-"

"-de-"

"-mum."

"-mum." There. Again:

"Chry-"

"Kree-" Yes, better.

"-san-" (Or was it "-santh-"?) Uh-oh.

"-san-"

"-the-"

"-the-"

"-mum."

"-mum."

"Chrysanthemum."

"Chrysanthemum."

Okay. "Jasmine."

"Jasmeen."

"Jas-min."

"Jas-min."

"Jasmine." I was entering one of those states where you contemplate a word for so long that it stops seeming like an intelligible word at all. But I was doing it up on a stage in front of half a hundred eagerly attentive senior citizens, people who had been through revolution, famine, isolation, the Red Guards. Someone off to the right had out a video recorder.

The more attention I paid to Lesson 47, the less sense the dialogue made. "Try some of our wonderful green tea," the Chinese host would say, and the foreigner would assent, and so why was the Chinese host then going on to push flower teas, after they'd already agreed on green tea?

Luckily the students were looking to study the real topic at hand. Could I write "I love Beijing" on the blackboard in Chinese? As a matter of fact, I could. *"Wo ai Beijing,"* I wrote in characters, to their approval. We put up the words "reporter" and "interviewer" for consideration. What sports did I like?

Once I was back at my seat, my political examiner came by for another visit. Did I know what the best country in the world was? He had read that it was Finland. China was too big. America was too big, too. Finland was small. It had lots of forests and lakes. Finland was the best country.

After he'd left, one of the women gave a dismissive frown. He was *taoyan*, she said—did I know *taoyan*? I went into the dictionary on my phone. First definition: "disagreeable." No, that wasn't it. Further down: "nasty." Yes. That was it. *Bukesiyi:* unbelievable.

The Bird's Nest beckoned once more: the men's soccer final, Argentina versus Nigeria. There was a spare ticket. I gathered up little Mack, so he could someday say he'd seen the Beijing Olympics. He dozed in his stroller across the regular-irregular flagstones on the way in.

The seats were down low, right by the field, just in the shade, directly behind the *New York Times* columnist and globalization guru Thomas Friedman. The state-approved cheerleaders down on the track wore blue and white, with pompoms. They were accompanied by Fuwa of different sizes—the big inflatable ones and the little plush ones. There were two Yingyings and two Beibeis—no, there were two of each. Ten Fuwa, jumbled together.

Mack woke up, gazed with interest at the green grass, and ate an ice cream cone. I was congratulating myself on taking my son to such a stimulating experience when Argentina broke loose and scored. Ninety thousand people leaped to their feet and started screaming. The roar faded down, and a single scream rose up in its place—a child's howl of fright and alarm. I wiped his tears and calmed him down. See? It's okay. Everything's fine. Then came another rush on goal, a shot, a save—ROOOOARrrrw from the crowd and waaaAAAAHHH from the baby. Enough. I bundled him off to the concourse, where the Olympic experience was darker and quieter, and watched the sliver of the field I could see from there, with televisions for reference.

Out on the plaza of the Green, the sun was powerful, and the mountains were visible through clear air. We traversed the imposing sunken garden one last time, passed the great red gateway and the McDonald's. A small Chinese boy stood just off the sidewalk with his pants down, urinating on a grate.

Jacques Rogge was giving his farewell press conference, summing up the Beijing Olympics for the gathered press. The People's Armed Police were out by the roads again, blocking the on-ramp to the Second Ring. My driver headed for the backstreets. The radio was playing a passage from *Romance of the Three Kingdoms*, a fourteenth-century epic novel about the wars to unify third-century China. The Three Kingdoms was everywhere this year; the last two times we had gone out to see a movie, we had ended up seeing different Three Kingdoms epics. The second time, we had tried to see *Hancock*, but the American alcoholic-superhero movie was sold out, so we grabbed what was available, entered the movie five minutes late, and gradually realized we were watching the actor Hu Jun doing exactly what we had seen Andy Lau doing before. Now that I had picked up the names of the multitude of main characters, I was able to tell it was always on the radio, too, a murmuring Chinese counterpoint to the internationalism all around. *"Liu Bei hen bu gaoxing,"* the radio said. Liu Bei (the good-guy leader in the story) was very unhappy.

In the Plum Blossom Hall, Jacques Rogge said the IOC was "extremely pleased by the organization of the Games." China had won the gold medal count, going away. The United States had barely come out ahead in the number of total medals, but unless you really did count bronze medals as equal to gold, China had surpassed the United States overall, too, under any known system of weighting the results. "I believe each country will highlight what suits it best," Rogge said. "We take no position on that matter."

Rogge took very little position on anything, and took even less responsibility. The blocking of the Internet? "We acknowledge that the situation has not been perfect." Reports in the press that China's gold-medal gymnasts, including the young-looking Jiang Yuyuan, might have been underage? "Eligibility of the athletes is the responsibility of the international federations, not the IOC." A reporter asked him about the fate of the latest would-be protesters, a pair of women in their seventies, who had been sentenced to house arrest for daring to apply to use the Olympic protest zones. The authorities had told the IOC, Rogge said, that "this is an application of Chinese law. The IOC is not a sovereign organization. We have to respect Chinese law."

And there were your international norms. The Chinese authorities were abusing dissidents, because abusing dissidents was an old habit for them. It was the IOC who had suggested setting up the protest zones, and it was only because the IOC was involved that people had accepted the invitation to try to protest. And now the people who had trusted Rogge and his organization were locked up. China had dishonored the IOC's promises, and Rogge was willing to stand up at the podium and accept the dishonor. One World, One Dream.

Hawkers outside the press center were trying to move pins and caps and shirts while they still could. Along the ground level of the Pangu Plaza, by the 7 Star Hotel, signs announced a "Famous Stores Corridor": one more coming attraction that had failed to arrive in time for the big event.

The cab ride home took a different route from usual, through a neighborhood decked with Olympic banners, in Chinese and English: "Seize the opportunity of the century to seize the dream of a century." "Brighten the Dream with Passion, Build the Olympic Legend."

27.

公共关系
Public Relations

The press—the grasping, curious, unpredictable free-world press—had penetrated Beijing, or a version of Beijing, and Beijing had come out fine. There had been stories of repression, pollution, and dislocation, showing that journalists were serious about China, and so what? The Olympics was a show, and the production values looked great on camera. The city gleamed, the drummers drummed, the Chinese flag waved in mechanical breeze over Chinese gold medalists, against mostly bluish skies. Tens of thousands of smiling volunteers had stood ready with smiles and freshly printed informational handouts and serviceable foreign-language skills. They were, as promised, ready.

"They took an antagonistic world media corps and turned them into purring kittens," Jeff Ruffolo told me, as the media operations wound down. Ruffolo, an American who had made himself into the native-Anglophone face of the Beijing media operations, was an

Olympics obsessive, a former radio sportscaster who had badgered the organizing committee into putting him on staff as a means of getting a role, any role, at the Beijing Games.

For the Chinese staff, he served as an emissary to the foreigners they would be dealing with and as a specimen of what they would have to deal with. His Chinese was nonexistent, his outlook sharply American; in the long runup to the Games, he had frequently either been exasperated with his colleagues or exasperated them—or both at once. "I have a high regard for them now," he said. "I didn't when I started. . . . These are true believers in the Olympics. I've never seen anything like it in my life."

In October, when the Games were over, Wang Hui was finally free for an interview, at the Olympic Tower, on the Fourth Ring. The morning was clean and warm, and the mountains were showing again in the west, down to the shadows on the surface of the slopes. The cabdriver was listening to a novel on the radio, cranked up to painful volume. In the story, a mother was telling her son that his father's illness was very serious. The ten-o'clock chime sounded, and the program switched to a reading of *Romance of the Three Kingdoms*. The Fourth Ring interchange sign iridesced in the sunlight. We passed a pair of brand-new black Audis with white protective film on their roofs and hoods, and with splashes of mud all over their sides.

The interview was in room 402. A double row of thick-framed armchairs—covered in cream-colored fabric, with oversized embroidered antimacassars—ran down each side of the room, a standard Chinese meeting-room arrangement, implying comfort while actually evoking stiffness and separation. On a polished side table by each armchair was a paper cup in a plastic cupholder, with dry tea leaves inside. Two more armchairs were at the head of the room, flanked by Chinese and Olympic flags. At the far end of the room were a few ceremonial objects on display, including a dark, flat carved stone with a shallow basin for mixing ink: a desk object enlarged to the size of a small tombstone. The tag said its name was Dragon Welcoming the Olympiad Ink Stone.

I was late, but Madame Wang was running even later—delayed in a very important meeting. "Madame" was how underlings or associates referred to Wang Hui when discussing her in English—no surname, just "Madame," as in "You should call Madame's assistant," or "Madame would like to schedule the interview for Wednesday."

Her assistant offered me a seat, and a housekeeping staffer brought in a thermos and poured hot water into my paper teacup. The assistant's name was Selena, and she said she had come to the Beijing organizing committee after getting her master's degree in economics from the University of Warwick in England. Her hair was bobbed, and she was dressed for work in a green velour hoodie, ruffled miniskirt, and tall brown boots with black tights. She had first come to Beijing from Hebei, to study at what's now called Beijing Jiaotong University. She preferred the older name, she said, Northern Jiaotong University, because it was more geographically ambitious, and because that had been the name bestowed by Chairman Mao Zedong.

Selena's hometown was Handan, in southern Hebei, one of China's multitude of minor, ancient former capitals. "It used to be a beautiful city, but now it's very dirty," she said. Her grandparents remembered a lovely river and forests, she said, but after the war, the landscape was sacrificed to development.

And Beijing? "I love here," she said. "I love here. This is the most beautiful city in China, I guess." The futuristic spectacle of Shanghai impressed some people, she said, but her preference was for the tradition of Beijing. "It's the capital city for six periods," she said. "I love history, and I think Beijing is a well-preserved historic city."

I took this less as a message from a propaganda chief's assistant than as the word of someone who had lived even closer than Beijingers to the leading edge of industrialization. "I feel most comfortable here," she said. "Especially in autumn. . . . One of my friends said, in autumn, the sunshine in Beijing is golden and most clear. . . . China developed very fast, but I think Beijing goes not too fast and not too slow." She said she had two apartments in the city—one by the Olympic Forest to the north, and one out east in Tongzhou district, a ground-floor apartment with a courtyard garden and a tree.

Madame Wang arrived, apologetic, accompanied by another staffer. She was wearing a pink dress just above the knees, with a cream-colored jacket that had pastel threads and flowers incorporated into the weave.

Before she took charge of China's Olympic press operations, Madame Wang was head of the Information Office of the Beijing Municipal Government, a post she was due to resume after her Olympic work was done. The Information Office is under the Department of Propaganda, which is not as awkward or ominous-sounding in the Chinese language context as it is in English, because the same Chinese word covers "propaganda" and "publicity." As far as the politics of language goes, this may be more hygienic than what we do with our own Public Information departments in English. Before the Information Office, Madame Wang had worked for Beijing Television, making documentaries.

Madame Wang settled into the armchair around the corner from mine. Had I taken a holiday after the Olympics? she asked. I said I hadn't gone anywhere, but I had relaxed for a while. Had she? She hadn't. "Maybe after two months," she said. With a by-your-leave gesture, she then switched into Mandarin, with the new staffer inter-preting. She spoke in long passages, followed by long pauses for the interpreter to provide an English version of each passage.

What I was trying to find out from Madame Wang, here in the end, was what the encounter with the rest of the world, through foreign press, had felt like from the Chinese side. "I have been involved with the preparations for about eight years, and my feeling is that the Olympic Games is not a sports event," she said, "it is like a media event." What had she expected, going in? "I hoped through the Olympic Games that the journalists would present a true picture of China to the world," Madame Wang said.

"It is a pleasure to explain to other people about my country," she said. For example, there was the issue of human rights. Journalists from developed countries couldn't see the progress that China had made, because China was in a different stage of development from that in the West. Likewise with air quality—"London also experienced serious fog during its industrialization," she said, using the old word *wu* for "fog." "Yes, we have the issue of pollution, but we are working very hard to improve air quality in Beijing, and I think criticism does not help. . . . It's a stage that you have to experience, because there is such huge economic growth going on. . . . Many developed countries, when they achieved their development, they used maybe a few hun-dred years to achieve their economic progress and to clean up the environment, but China did it in only a few decades."

Then she turned to Tibet. The problem with reporting on Tibet, Madame Wang said, was that many foreigners had the mistaken idea that Tibet was not part of China and that the Dalai Lama was a human-rights leader. "Fifty years ago, the Dalai Lama was the biggest slave owner in Tibet, and he used a lamp burning people alive," she said. "So no one in China believes that the Dalai Lama is a human-rights leader. . . . And everybody believes that Tibet is part of China. That's because people in China understand more about the history in Tibet and about the country.

"There are many other small issues," she said, "but these are some of the more important ones."

The biggest difference between the foreign reporters and the Chinese media, she said, was that the foreign reporters wanted information immediately whenever something happened. "This is quite different from what we're used to, working with the domestic media." The Chinese had learned to adjust. For example, she said, there had been an incident during the opening ceremony of the Paralympics, in which a woman got onto the field and tried to take off her clothes. "We released information about this incident ten minutes after it happened," she said. I had missed the incident entirely, and when I looked up the coverage afterward, I could see why I had. The foreign press had been told that the woman was mentally ill, and that she had in no way been a protester. Aside from some tut-tutting about the security breach, that left nothing for anyone to say.

Foreign journalists also took a different approach to press conferences from that of domestic media, Madame Wang said: "They normally did a lot of background research, the foreign journalists, and it's like they'd already thought about it very carefully, and in a very detailed way. And they come to a conclusion, and they would ask you whether this conclusion is correct or not. I think it's quite a challenge, but at the same time I actually enjoyed it. I think it's a quite interesting exchange."

The trouble, she said, was that some of the foreign reporters would come in prejudiced against China, because they had only been exposed to one side of the story in their preparations. "But it's my job to explain to them, time and again, patiently, what is true and what is not true."

The anti-China bias was disheartening. This was important to convey. Madame Wang paused, sitting up straight, then launched into a story: "*You yi ci yi ge Meiguo jizhi . . .*" "One time there was an American journalist . . ." She leaned forward in the big chair and tapped her chest for emphasis and kept talking. The wind whistled outside. Finally she turned to her interpreter. "*Tai chang!*" she said, smiling. Too long! "So sorry." The interpreter went back to the beginning: "That journalist asked me about eleven questions. None of it was related to the Olympic Games, they are all political, negative questions, and I answered all of them. At the end of the interview, I asked the journalist whether you would like to hear something, know what I thought, as ordinary staff of BOCOG, and that journalist said yes, so I told that journalist a story.

"The world is like a village and there are some rich residents, for example the United States, the UK, Germany, and China is—"

"A poor family," Wang Hui interjected over the translation, with a chuckle.

"—a poor villager, a poor villager in that village," the translator continued. "And the Olympic Games is like a party, and many rich residents hosted these nice parties for the whole village, but China had never had a chance to do so, because China is not developed so well and has so many children, so many people to feed. And later China grew and the economy is better, and finally the rich residents said, 'Okay, now we can ask China to host this party for us,' and China is very happy to have this opportunity, and we ask all the neighbors and all these relatives to come to help. We built a bigger house and we planted all the grasses and some people say, 'You are using chopsticks, and we are not used to it,' so we bought knives and forks, and we have also learned these languages, foreign languages, that our neighbors use"—"*Zhunbei hao duo dongxi,*" Wang prompted—"and we prepared many nice food and we welcome, we sincerely welcome all these villagers to come, but when they come they ignore all the nice things, the nice food that we put out, put on the table. They go to the"—"toilet," Wang said—"the restroom, they go to the garbage bins, and they ignore all these nice preparations that we had put up, and so at the end of my story, the journalist said to me, 'I'm so sorry, Madame Wang.' And that was, that interview took place during the torch relay that was the most difficult time for us, because we had the Tibet issue and the Darfur issue and all these disruptions overseas of the torch relay. And I told that journalist that what you did really hurt us, really hurt the Chinese people's feelings."

I asked her about the reporting that had come out after the Olympic Opening Ceremony—the replacement singing, the fake procession of fireworks footprints on Beijing, the crippled dancer. The substitutions, she said, were standard for television. For any big event, you have the option of cutting to the rehearsal tape if something goes wrong. "It's the same practice in Seoul, in Athens, in Sydney, Atlanta," she said. This did not seem exactly true, but it was hard to object on behalf of American epistemological standards, given that NBC's Matt Lauer and Bob Costas had coyly described the fireworks as "almost animation" and "quite literally cinematic," then tried to take credit for that almost-honesty.

What is real, in an entertainment production? "I read the stories about the girl, the little girl," Wang Hui said. "It's not lip-synching, because she actually also sang, but we used the voice of another girl. And also the footprints, these are all common practices in TV broadcasting. And when I saw those stories, I thought the Western media were just trying to play up these issues."

But then the chief information officer took a different tack. "I can understand why they used the prerecorded ones, but I don't think that the story is a bad thing, because it shows that people, the viewers, expect what is really happening. They expected to see what is true, and they do not want to see the prerecorded ones."

She was, she said, a documentary filmmaker. "I think people have some misunderstanding about what is true and what is authentic," she said. A director like Zhang Yimou wants to have perfect sound and lighting. "They want the sound to be pure and clear, but they did this based on true things, true performances. So I think this is quite a small issue, it's an issue of which technique you use. But some people interpreted it as 'We lied to the world,' but it's not true. But I think, in the future, maybe the artists should strive for purity, pure things, and true things. Maybe in the future, people should go in that direction."

What sort of documentaries had Madame Wang made before she went into the official information business? "I did many documentaries, many of them about ordinary people," she said. "For example, I did a documentary on fifty mothers, how they live their dreams, how they treat their children, and how they live their dreams through their children. There was a mother who was an amputee, and I did that documentary in 1994. At the time, I started to give some financial support to this mother because her husband died and she had to raise two children. Now her two children are in the university, but I'm still giving to the family."

She had also done a series on Chinese students in foreign countries. "I still remember that when I was editing the tape, I had to stop because I had to cry, because I had to go outside the studio and cry, and then come back to work, because the stories are so moving. And I think making documentaries changed my views about life and about society, and I saw that many ordinary people are great in their own right. And I wanted to tell their stories so that more people know how great they are."

Her own parents were from Beijing, she said, but she was born just to the west, in Datong, in Shanxi Province. They were government officials, but they lost their positions to the Cultural Revolution when she was in primary school. So her father "did not do anything," she said. "He stayed at home."

Another foreign reporter, she said, had once asked her a question that supposed that despite China's pursuit of Olympic championships, there was no interest in sports among the Chinese people in general. "So I told him a story from my childhood," she said. China did not have many sports facilities then, so when she wanted to play table tennis, her father made her a paddle by hand, from wood. "It was rough, it's not very smooth, but even that—I brought it to school and I showed it to my friends, my schoolmates, and at that time, even this wood table tennis paddle was the envy of many children." This was in the mid-sixties, after China had won a world championship at ping-pong. "At that time, the school made a table tennis table of cement, and there was no net in the middle, so some people placed a piece of wood in the middle to use it as a net. So we played on this cement table tennis table."

She said she had visited Beijing often when she was young. Now, she said, "I think the buildings are taller and streets are wider, and everybody's talking on mobile phones. But I think the biggest changes are not material. I think the biggest changes are that people have new ideas—their way of life, and their dreams, and what they want to achieve . . . When I'm walking on the streets, I always look at the crowds that I'm passing by, and I want to catch the smiles on other people's faces. I think decades ago, people did not smile, but now they smile. People smile a lot."

We were on message; the message was good. "You didn't ask me about my biggest impression of the Olympic Games," Madame Wang said. "I think many people would say that the lighting of the cauldron in the opening ceremony left them impressed most, but I have another story. I was working in the stadium during the Games, and every time I walked out from the Bird's Nest, normally I walk out from the basement floor." She held up sheets of paper to model the slope of the land. "So when I walk out of the stadium, I see many people in the Olympic Park taking photos, smiling, and making funny gestures and taking photos of each other, and I think the smiles on their faces, and kind of joy and satisfaction that these people are enjoying left me the most impressed. And every time I came out of the stadium I stood there for ten, fifteen minutes."

Time was up. "Thank you," Madame Wang said, in English. Would I like to stay for lunch? I would. Good. She gathered her things and headed for the door. Her assistant would take me to the cafeteria.

X.

回家 GOING HOME

28.

发射升空 Liftoff

And now it was time for Beijing to say good-bye to the world. Until we meet again. There were empty seats on television for the closing ceremony. The cameras followed Hu Jintao as he entered, then Jiang Zemin, the past and present leaders on the road to prosperity and the Olympics. Fireworks formed numerals in the sky to count down to the beginning of the farewell.

On the ground of the Bird's Nest were drummers, these ones wearing painted bicycle helmets. Had someone decided to add safety equipment? There were advancing columns of people in yellow with bells on them. Flying drums. The belled dancers made an insectoid chattering as they closed in. People were riding around inside lighted hoops, and bouncing around on stilts. In place of the solemn, intimidating synchrony of the opening ceremony, there was the spectacle of imperfect mass human movement, doodads and gewgaws. The athletes came running in, in chaos. There were tiny children on drum kits, and a female drum corps in red leatherette.

Representatives of the roughly 100,000 Olympic volunteers were brought out to be honored, accompanied by children, most in colorful dresses and pigtails. Jacques Rogge and the head of the Beijing organizing committee, Liu Qi, entered. Rogge waved to the crowd as if he were a head of state. They entered on a red carpet, with red-gowned women arranged along it as a decorative fringe. The committee chief's dye job was dark and impressive.

"Through these games," Rogge said, "the world learned more about China, and China learned more about the world."

On came the rest of the world, then, with its part of the program: a prop double-decker omnibus representing London 2012, with a multiethnic, multicultural dance troupe swarming over it, the stale Cool Britannia rebranding left over from the last century. The bus opened out into topiary and David Beckham of the Los Angeles Galaxy emerged to kick a soccer ball nowhere in particular. The pickled remains of Jimmy Page played a song that was new thirty-nine years before. The British press would trash the London segment the next day as a national disgrace, a painfully feeble showing next to all the Chinese spectacle; the Chinese press didn't disagree. A pair of performers dressed as suitcase-toting Britons climbed a staircase up into the air, presumably toward their future, to a platform high on a cherry-picker. Then they were left there and forgotten.

The host country handled the rest of the show. A tower framework appeared, covered with performers, like a *croquembouche* made of people instead of creampuffs. Or like an ear of corn swarming with bugs. The people wore two-sided suits in red and silver, making pictures as they turned one way or the other. They formed the Beijing Games logo on the tower.

A musical number: *"Beijing, Beijing, wo ai Beijing . . ."* That was what years of songwriting competitions had yielded: "I love Beijing," as a rhyme for "Beijing, Beijing." Then more music: someone singing in Peking Opera style, then a tedious operatic duet, and then a Big Windup: Jackie Chan in a volunteer's polo shirt, complete with a credential around his neck; Andy Lau. The human mass on the tower waved Fuwa dolls, and costumed mascots appeared around the pop-singer collective. The Fuwa had made it into the production.

We Are the Champions" played on the radio; Beijing Television ran a montage of all fifty-one Chinese gold-medal victories, in the order in which they were won. But the Olympic banners were already gone, replaced by Paralympics banners in less than a day. Roving volunteers had switched to wearing Paralympics shirts, in a plainer pattern than their swirly Olympics ones. Old people played hacky sack, the first sign of normal street life I'd seen in weeks. A news-stand clipped up a China Mobile sign to replace the one that had been covered over. Bootleg DVDs were available. Crews set out with crates of fresh flowers, replacing the blooms along the roadways. Fu Niu Lele, the Paralympics cow, made her entrance: on a four-part banner down the side of the Poly Plaza tower, and in floral figures on the road north toward the Olympic Green.

On the lane outside the Imperial Academy, a new facility had opened, the De Xian Ge Sweet Home for the Disabled. It was in a refurbished courtyard house, with the front room set up as a shop to sell arts and crafts made by disabled citizens. Even among the disabled artists, the Olympic mascots were evidently more popular than the Paralympic one. The Fuwa were variously rendered in thread, cloth, paper, paper cuts, and beadwork; Fu Niu Lele was restricted to a few ornaments in the corner. Also among the mer-chandise were small boxes containing little humanoid figures, assembled out of insect parts with something furry like a pussy willow for the torso. One of the shaggy-bodied creatures stood on a tiny teeter-totter, holding a tiny sign over its gleaming chitin bug-head: *"Beijing Huanying Ni."*

A passage lined with calligraphy led to the rear of the building. A tag in the corner of each calligraphic work described the creator's specific disability—there were a lot of amputees—and sometimes the cause. Electrical accidents seemed common. In the back was a life-training area, where the disabled could practice cooking and other domestic skills. On a wall in the courtyard was a Chinese rendering of a quotation attributed to Goethe, with an English version below it reading "People of happiness lies in the heart happy."

Translation was an ongoing struggle. Outside the Sweet Home, a sign with Fu Niu Lele offered an attempt at one of the Paralympics mottos: "Beyond, Integration, Sharing." Officially, it was supposed to be "Transcendence, Integration, Equality." At its most mangled, it showed up as "Surmounting Fusion Sharing."

The other motto was "Two Games, Equal Splendor." It was one of those slogans whose existence undercut its own message—nobody needed to assure able-bodied Olympians that their games would be equal to the Paralympics. Still, equality was important. A press conference was held to promote the new Sweet Homes. The Olympic media workrooms were empty and ravaged-looking. Officials, accompanied by a "representative of disabled persons" in a wheelchair, were in the press hall to report on the progress that Beijing had made in securing integration and opportunity for the disabled. But they could not admit that there had previously been any mistreatment or denial of opportunity. As with the food-safety briefings, the problem had been solved, but there had never been a problem. "I would like to say, I have never encountered any discrimination after I became a disabled person," the representative in the wheelchair, a woman named Li Nan, said. "I receive more caring and more support."

So what sorts of complaints from the disabled did the city's office for disabled advocacy deal with? The question drew a perfect, timeless specimen of the procedural answer: "The protection of the rights of the persons with disability is an important part of the law of the People's Republic of China for the protection of the rights of people with disability. In Beijing, the municipal government has also come up with the implementation regulations for implementing that law for the protection of the rights and interests of the people with disability, both for the rights, education, and the jobs, also for the transport and for the laws used once their rights have been infringed upon. The government has a very detailed implementation regulation." There.

At the back of the neighborhood, instant parks had been built in the demolition zone by Moma: an open green vista framed by undulating rows of flowers, for the benefit of passing cars. There was nothing there for pedestrians to walk to or from. Up close, the grass was sparse, with dried mud showing between. Chunks of brick, concrete, rock, and pipe were strewn on the hard surface—left scattered behind, or coming unburied. The concrete had paint on it. From the field, there was a clear view all the way to Sanyuan Bridge and the banner of the field hockey player.

Electrical poles were still standing in the patchy green blankness, leaning at angles. Their tops were a tangle of chopped-off wires, splayed like Medusa hair—lines for powering an entire neighborhood. The surviving trees were tapered low down, their branches only spreading out above the invisible line of the alley walls and courtyards that had surrounded them.

To the east, by the river, a London-style taxicab was parked on the street, in white-and-gold Beijing livery. It was a Chinese-made TX4; the badge on the rear said "The London Taxi Company." Thirty of them had just been added to the city fleet, as handicapped-accessible vehicles. Maybe London would buy some for 2012.

As I went into the study to get my things for English class, one of the overhead lightbulbs exploded again. Glass, some of it scorched, scattered out into the hallway, all the way to Mack's bedroom door. Glass shards lay on his play mat. It had blown the circuit breaker, and I fumbled for flip-flops in the darkness of the vestibule so I could go out on the landing and turn the power back on.

They were writing the words for numbers on the board when I got to the classroom. Lesson 51 was "What's your room number?" If you were telling someone your room number, 1288, you could say "one two eight eight," or you could say "twelve eighty-eight." I hadn't thought about this before.

This time, during the break, the students started asking me to autograph their books. Then they asked for my autograph in Chinese. I had to check my own business card to remember how to write my transliterated name.

One man brought over a drawing of something—a sort of rounded box on wheels, with something sticking out the top. What was it in English? Well, first, what was it at all? It was a vehicle that drew electrical power from overhead wires, but had no tracks below it. One of . . . those things. Electric-bus things. You could call it a "trolley bus," I declared. If it had tracks, it would be a trolley.

More questioning: Why would you choose to say "I'll call you tomorrow" instead of "I'll call you in the morning," or vice versa? Why the "in"? And the "the"?

Then it was time for me to read to the class, from Lesson 52, "What's your mobile number?" I had been figuring that as long as I policed my natural tendencies to drawl or be mushmouthed, my fairly neutral American accent would serve the students. But as a fairly neutral American, I say the word "mobile" as "mo-b'l." And Chinese people are taught to say "mo-BILE." "Mo-BILE," I said. "Have a nice day . . . I'll talk to you tomorrow." The class was delighted. I was a *ming xing,* someone told me, a star.

Our family was heading to a new hamburger place, supposedly a good one. The cabbie on the way there told little Mack not to suck his thumb. Then, hygienic standards having been established, he spat repeatedly out the window. The burgers were on Sanlitun, near the new kitchen-goods shop. We stopped by there, looking for kitchen shears, to help cut up food into baby-sized bites.

There was no cutlery in sight. A sign on the wall where the knives had been, dated two days after the stabbing at the Drum Tower, announced that knife sales were suspended through the end of the Paralympics. It was a citywide ban. Kitchen scissors were also included. As we were digesting the news, the store staff opened a drawer and surreptitiously produced a pair of shears.

The cheeseburger was credible. I had eaten worse ones, served with greater fanfare, in America. It was also possible, at the burger place, to buy a sandwich of wagyu beef and foie gras.

City cops and the People's Armed Police were out again to mark the opening night of the Paralympics, but the streets stayed full of people and traffic. We skipped watching the ceremony to go out to a Spanish restaurant, run by a self-taught Chinese tapas chef, in a

courtyard house near the Lama Temple. Downstairs, a wedding was
going on and on.

The Fuwa had been around too long and too pervasively for me to
let go of them, or for their influence to disappear, overnight. Even
Pan Pan, from the 1990 Asian Games, was still lurking: after Big
Mack had brought him to my attention, I noticed I had been walking by him every day, on a manufacturer's sticker the downstairs
neighbors had left on their steel security door. Later I would spot
him on the back of a China Southern Airlines boarding pass and,
most confusingly, on the side of a truck in downtown Taipei.

Before entering the mascot afterlife themselves, the Fuwa would
remain on sale until March 2009, the Fuwa designer Chen Nan said.
Big Mack and I had come to Chen's office suite, in an aging apartment tower in the northeast part of the city, for a final accounting
of where the mascots had come from and where they were going.
He wore a black shirt, jeans, and silver sneakers; his hair was styled
upward. Where the Han Meilin Museum had been a shrine to some
artistic concept of Chineseness, Chen's office was a bazaar of global
iconography. On a crowded cabinet top behind him, two fu lion
sculptures with gilt on them stood on each side of a white bust of
Mao, with old-fashioned paper-cutout puppets and figurines of
Robocop and Boba Fett nearby. A row of stuffed Fuwa stood across
the back of a couch, accompanied by the Euro-flesh-colored, floppy
mascots of the Athens Games, Athenà and Phèvos. Shelves were
filled with jumbled cartoon or science-fictional armies: more *Star
Wars* characters, the alien from *Alien*, blank-faced custom-painted
vinyl bear figures, old-fashioned windup toys, prototypes of the
Fuwa themselves. "Often, during my work time, I would sneak into
my room and play with my toys," Chen said.

One of Chen's assistants brought tea in paper cups, the office's own blend of jasmine and oolong. A fresh breeze blew in through south-facing windows. The names of the Fuwa, spelling out *"Beijing Huanying Ni,"* had been Chen's idea, he said. Besides his work on the Fuwa, he had helped the Olympic committee design Olympic merchandise. He got out a notepad shaped like a ping-pong paddle, with a screw-out pen as the handle; a wooden baseball bat that opened up to reveal a little baseball-bat-shaped pen. And now, he said, he was also helping the China Duty-Free Corporation design a set of cartoon characters to star in tourist merchandise once the Fuwa were gone.

"In the past," Chen said, "China has been predominantly involved in manufacturing, not design." His ambition, he said, was for "Designed in China" to surpass "Made in China" as a reference point for goods. He taught commercial design at Tsinghua University, where he had come to college after growing up in Tianjin. His parents had both worked in artistic fields—his father in woodblock prints and lithography, his mother in decorative design for ceramics. "She's now focusing on Buddhist painting," he said.

Chen was thirty-six years old. His birthday, he said, had been two days before the opening ceremony. "I just had a bowl of noodles," he said, miming hasty eating—there had been last-minute souvenirs to design.

What about the riot of other cartoon mascots in the city—I Participate, I Contribute, I Enjoy, the two different Dongdongs, and so on? Wenwen and Mingming urged people to act civilized (*wenming*) on the subway. Weiwei and Shengsheng promoted sanitation (*weisheng*). A line of notebooks with the official Olympic-sponsor logo on them, from the Beifa company, had a grinning monkey named Beifa Winny on them, and the promise of more characters, his friends Ooh, Jiji, Xiangxiang, and Woowoo. Even the Public Security Bureau had a set of keychains with its own cartoon figures: a riot cop with big cute eyes behind his plastic face guard, clutching a shotgun; a saluting man in the dress greens of the People's Armed Police; an officer in uniform at a computer terminal, busily policing the Internet.

If the Fuwa had come out sooner and been kept less secret, Chen said, "you might see cheering Fuwa as well." And perhaps they would have been integrated into the medal presentation and the opening ceremonies—one of Chen's main regrets, he said.

Now it was the era of Fu Niu Lele. The Paralympic cow, Chen said, was not his design. But he was pleased about the name. The organizers had chosen "Lele" because *le* meant "joy." But with a different character and a neutral tone, *le* could also fit at the end of a sentence, marking a completed action. *Beijing huanying ni le*. Beijing Welcomed You.

China was winning the Paralympics medal count even more handily than it had won the Olympic one, but not in the events I was seeing. My first glimpse of Lele on the hoof came at a wheelchair-basketball game. With the United States beating China, 43–14, a pair of inflatable Leles, one of them with a sagging, underinflated head, came out to dance. They did an oafish ballet routine, and then one of the arena volunteers bullfought them, brandishing a Chinese flag folded over into a red rag.

Ding Hai, the best Chinese player by far, ended up with 21 points and 14 rebounds, and hit a late three-pointer that sent the crowd into pandemonium. The shot cut the U.S. lead to 79–34, on the way to a 97–38 final.

In seven-on-a-side soccer, in the field hockey arena, Ireland was handling the host country easily. A little girl in a white dress was tossing and catching a Lele doll as she went up the north stairs, smiling.

In quad rugby, Japan's team sported a blond mohawk, spiked hair, blue hair, a shaved head. The Chinese mostly had their hair cropped conservatively. Four fluffy Leles were dancing around. The Japanese players were too fast in their wheelchairs for China's defense to stop them.

On the way home, in the midst of Paralympic events, I stopped for dumplings at a Manchurian restaurant near home. There was a "No Smoking" sign on the wall beside me, and an ashtray on my table.

Something was wrong with the milk supply now. Or with the powdered milk supply, at least, for starters. It had been adulterated with industrial melamine, which allowed inferior or diluted milk to pass for the regular product. In factory testing, that is. If you actually drank the milk, it was poisonous.

Little Mack had moved on to solid food and regular milk, but we had fed him plenty of formula powder before, from the Carrefour market. We had bought an American brand, or what was packaged as an American brand, but who knew? Top Chinese brands were tainted, and the details were still emerging. Officials had reportedly discovered the contaminated milk powder weeks before and kept it quiet, so no food-safety scandal would break during the Olympics, while infants were falling sick and dying of kidney failure.

So a slow-motion run was unfolding on imported foreign milk. One brand after another, the boxed ultra-pasteurized imports gradually disappeared from the shelves of our nearest expat market—first the French, then the New Zealand. The locally produced organic milk remained in the cold case, presenting a challenge. Organic milk was exactly the sort of product that should be encouraged in the Chinese marketplace. It represented the hope for safe, high-quality foodstuffs in a country where no one had pursued such a thing till recently. But with the food-supply system as corrupt as it was, what if the organic milk itself was fake?

Zhang Yimou, for one, had taken the Paralympic promise of equal splendor seriously. Philip Craven, the Paralympics president, seemed, in his final press conference, to be still a bit awed that Beijing had filled up the Bird's Nest with spectators and special effects for the second round of games. "We had tears in our eyes," Craven said.

A crowded delegation of Chinese officials followed Craven, reporting that "the Chinese team has established a very proud result." China had won 89 gold medals, and 211 medals overall; the runner-up, Britain, had 42 golds and 102 total medals. Surmounting, indeed.

In the closing ceremony, on television, a blizzard of red leaves fell and fell and fell and fell from the top of the Bird's Nest, forming drifts on the track. Dancers in full-body flower costumes formed the outlines of an envelope, a "Letter to the Future," from Beijing to the world. Performers in bulbous brown shoes tottered around stiff-legged. Were they supposed to be children? They had wigs and false eyelashes—they were dolls. A middle-aged woman stood in among them, directing traffic. A glowing tangled something-or-other was held aloft—trees? False eyelashes? A girl on a park bench, wearing a Paralympics cap, clutched an envelope, as metallic-painted men posed behind her. She got up, walked over flower petals, and dropped the envelope in a clear China Post mailbox.

A flute played. Pink flowers suddenly emerged through the fake turf. The flutist seemed to be blind, being guided around the set.

Dancers came out with a crowned hat in each hand, slapping them on their heads, passing the hats down the line one head at a time. Under the hats were headscarves. World-music music and world-music costumes. Insects kept flying into the camera. Performers on wires rose and fell in a wave around the stadium. People stuffed envelopes into the mailbox, moving robotically. Podlike parachute-balloons, floating cloudlike, had people hanging from them. Hanging by their feet. Upsetting. Inexplicable. Zhang was holding nothing back.

People acting as human mailboxes, wearing skirts made of letter boxes, were in the aisles, collecting letters from people. A choir sang "God Save the Queen." Your show, again, London. Fireworks went off in the shape of an envelope. An army of Leles appeared. Fireworks boomed outside, again.

Now it was all over. Day by day, the regular Beijing was coming back, or the improved version of the regular city. A horse-cart of melons was out on Outer Dongzhimen Avenue. By the Dongzhimen Bridge, slats were being installed for a variable-ad billboard. Commercialism was reemerging, large and small. Signs for new developments returned on the fences—"Seducing Modern and Romantic Emotion," one promised. A cargo tricycle carried coal cakes. Men in hard hats were down in the pit; clanging sounds rose. The yellow boom crane was in action, picking up a wire cage full of pipe segments and setting it down a little ways off.

I stopped by the United States embassy to apply for absentee election ballots. George W. Bush had officially opened a new embassy compound on August 8, but the president was simply another peri-Olympic Potemkinist: the facility wasn't really open, and the old embassy was staying in business till October at least.

The periods of clanging from the pit grew more frequent, till they lasted through the night, while green-tinged floodlights shone into the apartment. A guard at the gate had told me that the project was a twenty-eight-story residential tower, due to be finished in 2009. There would be three underground levels for parking. The new building would be for both Chinese people and foreigners—"*youqiande ren*," he said, rich people.

The air turned gray, the sun white and wan, till a downpour came and flooded the streets, heralding another clear spell. The roadside flowers, in the local portion of the 40 million flowerpots, were still plentiful and flourishing. The old bank on the corner was being gutted, behind a curtain of red-white-and-blue-striped utility cloth. A beggar with a blue jacket and a long goatee reappeared outside the imported-foods market on Sanlitun.

One day the courtyard felt different: there was empty space where all the parked cars had been. The odd-and-even driving ban was over—though it had been deemed such a success that a modified version, barring plates with certain specified digits every weekday, would eventually take its place. The Second Ring was jammed, irritating but also familiar, the usual old feeling of being part of a crawling mass of cars. The north wind turned over leaves and made the Paralympics banners, lingering longer than the Olympic ones had, billow southward. At sunset, the mountains were spectacular against a sky like hammered metal; clouds cut in sharp diagonals behind them, like a greater and more distant range. "*Shan wai you shan*," a provincial official had once told me, introducing a Chinese aphorism: Beyond the mountains are more mountains.

The news was on: a typhoon had hit Guangdong, killing six people; the earthquake site in Sichuan was swamped by torrential rains, killing thirteen. Liu Xiang had held his first public training session. Sun Yue of the national basketball team had signed with the Los Angeles Lakers. Wax statues of Olympians had been added to the National Museum, preserved in history. And astronauts were preparing for liftoff of the *Shenzhou 7* rocket.

The rocket launched on live TV. Had I watched a space flight in the last twenty years, since the United States stopped trying to go anywhere new? *Shenzhou 7* had a space-Moorish aspect: a needly nose, then a cone with a flaring bulge to it, and then the long body of the rocket with a ring of four boosters around the base. The astronauts lounged around the inside of the capsule in their spacesuits, helmets off, waiting while mission-control personnel in tan suits with red or yellow armbands worked at terminals. The control room looked exactly like the Beijing traffic-control bureau.

The spacesuits were white, with blue trim and dark-green knee joints. The green knees jiggled as the astronauts fidgeted. The crew put on their helmets and waved at the camera, their lounging posture still intact. A voice from ground control began speaking, loudly and commandingly. Four crane arms pulled away from the rocket, and the countdown came in Chinese: *"Jiu! Ba! Qi! Liu! Wu! Si! San! Er! Yi!"* One! A dark orange billow, like a pumpkin, appeared under the rocket, followed by a white flame. The whole thing lifted off, moving slowly.

The camera cut to a view looking down the rocket from its nose, at a burn with yellow-green edges. Then it cut to a glowing white blob against a cloudy sky. Then the view looking down the rocket again, turning purple and pixelated. One screen at mission control showed two diverging trajectories, as the booster rockets fell away.

After a while, a computer rendering of what was left of the rocket appeared: two beer cans, or a beer can and a squat thermos, nuzzling each other. Over on Phoenix TV, the flight was on a split screen. On one side, Wen Jiabao was addressing the United Nations about global poverty alleviation; on the other side were the astronauts, in their capsule, one of their notebooks floating weightless up toward the camera.

Chen Yanqun sang songs to Mack around the house, as she worked. "*Wo ai Beijing Tian'anmen*," she sang:

> *I love Beijing Tian'anmen.*
> *The sun rises above the Gate of Heavenly Peace.*
> *Great leader Chairman Mao*
> *Leads us toward the future.*

She had another song, which she called "Tibetan Plateau":

> *From the golden hilltop in Beijing, brilliant light radiates*
>   *to the four directions.*
> *The shining golden sun is Chairman Mao.*
> *How warmly, how kindly, the rays illuminate the hearts of us*
>   *serfs.*
> *We are marching on the blessed path of Communism.*
> *Hey, ba zha, hey!*

At least, those were the official words; as Chen Yanqun sang it, "the four directions" became "the Fourth Ring." Mack would dance happily to the music. My wife, meanwhile, was teaching him a rhyme she had learned from her parents—or what she could remember of it:

> *Yi, er, san, dao Taiwan.*
> *Taiwan you ge Ali Shan.*
> *Ali Shan shang you tielu . . .*

One, two, three, to Taiwan.
On Taiwan is Mount Ali.
On Mount Ali is a railroad . . .

Later, her parents would fill in the rhyme she'd forgotten:

Mingnian zhunbei hui Dalu!
Get ready! Next year, back to the mainland!

By the end of September, the air outside had the smell of Beijing again—a bit of burning, some exhaust, and plenty of dust. It was not that it was overpowering, but it was the complete familiar scent returning, in all its polluted roundness. And it was a Beijing day again, a comfortable fall day that would have been pretty but for the generalized haze lying on it.

Inside the floral starburst by the entry ramp, the Paralympics logo was slowly disappearing into new foliage, just as the Fuwa had before it, the greenery continuing to grow even in its pots and cages. The banners were finally down from the Second Ring, and the yellow and white stripes of the Olympic lane dividers had been repainted, so that they were alternating bright white and faded white. The front page of the *Beijing News*, the *Xin Jing Bao*—"*Bao! Bao! Bao!*" Mack cried—showed an astronaut planting a Chinese flag in space.

29.

路上 On the Road

If I was ever going to drive before leaving Beijing, I would have to do it over the National Day holiday break, the anniversary of the founding of the People's Republic, before my final Olympic visa expired. I called the BOCOG one-stop center to make sure it was still in business. It was. The swooping headquarters building by Chaoyang Bridge had been attached to its next-door companion, now unscaffolded and almost in use, by a glassed-in umbilical cord or corpus callosum.

The Olympic driver's-license clerk remembered me. We paged back in the ledger of licenses to find my name, the first entry in the book. Had he seen any of the Olympics? He said he had spent the whole time in the press center, eight a.m. to ten p.m., seven days a week. Before BOCOG, he said, he had been working at Fesco, the employment agency for foreign companies. Maybe he'd go back afterward.

As I was finishing up, it occurred to me that I still didn't know any of the city's actual traffic rules. The license clerk handed over a copy of "Traffic Safety Handbook for Drivers from Abroad," with the Beijing 2008 logo on the cover. Outside, up the street, a poster displayed cartoons to discourage such behavior as littering or illegal stopping in traffic. "May we remind you: Please be self-restraint and be a good tourist to mold a well-mannered imagination," the English translation read, next to a cartoon policeman scribbling in some sort of ticket book.

We could take a day trip, nothing too strenuous. Now I had to get a car. For months, I had had my eye on an Avis office just inside the Second Ring, right by Dongzhimen Bridge. Calling Avis, I reached an agent in Shanghai, who gave me the number for the rental office down the street. Could I reserve a car for tomorrow? Yes, I did have a Chinese driver's license. A small car? How small? I pictured us out on the open road, my wife and child crammed into the back of a Volkswagen Polo, or something even more developing-world and tinier. But Avis in China, it turned out, was speaking the same language as rental-car companies back in the United States, where "compact" means "normal-sized": she meant a Volkswagen Bora— the sedan known as a Jetta to twenty-first-century Americans. I could handle a Bora. The Bora would be fine. The Bora would be great. I would take it first thing in the morning and bring it back at night.

Oh, she said. But there was a special holiday policy. I would have to rent the car for at least four days. I contemplated stretching out my car driving status beyond the one road trip and clear through the weekend—popping out on errands . . . cruising around the city's byways . . . struggling up the crowded on-ramps . . . searching helplessly for parking . . . pushing my luck. The gleaming Bora receded into the distance.

The last time I'd brought up my intention to do some driving, Big Mack had mentioned that I might be able to rent something from the guy who fixes his Jeep. I was in luck: when he checked, the guy had something available. A four-liter Jeep Cherokee. I barely listened to the specifics. The Jeep guy had a Jeep! It was 400 yuan, or about sixty bucks, and I could pick it up in the morning. He promised to give it a mechanical checkup, which was less reassuring, not more.

That left only the question of where to go. We'd already been to the Great Wall, though not by our own driving. But farther out, beyond the municipal boundary in Hebei Province, there were the Qing Tombs—divided, thanks to some ancient argument over usurpation, into one set on either side of the city. The Western Qing Tombs sounded more bucolic, and seemed like an easy but substantial drive, the sort of thing you would gladly do if you had a car to yourself.

So I needed a road map of Hebei. I hailed a cab to the Wangfujing Bookstore downtown. Thick, white haze blanketed Chang'an Avenue. The store was overrun; people jostled in the aisles of the map section. The road atlases were shelved in no identifiable order: a batch on this side with the city maps, a whole section on the opposite side with the country atlases, some around on another aisle entirely. To simplify things, I just tried to find the Western Qing Tombs—if I couldn't turn them up quickly, I probably had the wrong map for my needs. I squinted at tiny characters, trying to get the basics of provincial geography straight in my head.

That was probably when I should have felt expat frustration coming on. Or when two girls stopped dead at the foot of the escalator, blocking everything, because you could hardly expect anyone to understand how an escalator works or how to behave around one— or when the woman in the check-out line was too engrossed in her book to protect the space from the people crowding in from the sides—or when I popped by the children's section, and the floor was covered everywhere with little ones sitting reading books, and bless their hearts, but you could really sprain an ankle.

But I made it outside, with the plastic flaps over the doorway hitting me in the face on the way, and then it was time to get a cab home. There were cabs all over the place—straight in front of the bookstore at the taxi stand, and more of them directly across the street. And the drivers, lounging against their cars or sitting inside, would not take me. A man with a supervisory aspect said to try across the street. Across the street, the drivers said I should try back across the street. The drivers pointed at their meter signs, which were switched from "vacant" to "pause," begging the question. Why was everyone refusing to drive? *"Lei le,"* one said. I'm tired.

These were the people I had to depend on for transportation every day because I was living this stupid alien life without a car. These, and now this: a slickly dressed man sidled up and offered me a ride, suavely rolling a shiny cell phone around in his hand. *"Bashi,"* he said, dropping his finger and thumb into the inverted V of the character for "eight." Meaning eighty. *"Bashi?"* I asked. He affirmed. Irresistibly—enough of this, enough with the language—I slid into English: "You're fucking kidding." If the man understood, he didn't care. I told him it should be *shiba,* eighteen—not even haggling, just making the point.

Finally I jumped into a cab that had just dropped a passenger, as it tried to roll away. The driver protested, but I refused to get out.

Back home, I studied the driving manual I had picked up. A round blue sign with a big red X meant "No long or temporary stopping for vehicles is permitted." I had dimly assumed that the X meant "Do not enter," and that everyone was habitually ignoring it. The real "Do not enter" was a red circle with a white bar across the middle, a text-free version of the U.S. sign. Most of the rest was familiar, or at least unsurprising: road narrows, falling rocks, men working, no U-turn, bicycles only. The sign for "One way" pointed up, and it was blue and white. Then there was the round blue one, with a picture of a horn on it. "The sign in the picture means a honk is required when a motorized vehicle reaches this sign."

The pollution disappeared overnight, leaving black smudges when I blew my nose and a bright, clear morning. I hailed a cab around seven-thirty on the alley; the cabbie was smoking, holding his cigarette low by the open window. I glimpsed the hills off to the west as we headed out Dongzhimen Avenue toward the Third Ring and up toward Mack's neighborhood, in Wangjing. I tried to view the road like a driver: right turns meant swinging wide across the access lanes. I would have to pay attention to oncoming cyclists, even if no one else did.

Cell-phone numbers had been scrawled on a Fuwa billboard in Wangjing—the traditional advertising format for document forgers, another part of Beijing reasserting itself. One number was still showing; the rest were painted over with dripping gray bars. We found Big Mack in his own Jeep Cherokee at a wide, barren stretch of roadway. I got in, and we headed for the auto shop. As he drove, he declared that Beijing driving was much improved nowadays. Now, he said, it was 70 percent civilized—"in the city," he added, as a warning about what I might face out in Hebei. We drove along the Fourth Ring Road, passed under a red inflated arch near the Siyuan Bridge, and wended our way into a complex of alleys lined with auto-repair and parts shops. This was the market that had been shut down for the Olympics, now back in business.

There was, Mack said, one problem. The particular four-liter Jeep we'd talked about was missing. The shop owner had lent it to one of the managers of the auto-repair park, and the borrower hadn't brought it back last night as agreed. But a substitute vehicle would be waiting.

And so it was. Next to the door of the repair bay stood a hulking, dark-blue Great Wall–brand SUV: battered, dented, and covered with a thick coat of dust. The left rear fender was mashed and fraying fiberglass; the spare-tire cover was a mismatched electric blue, its metallic paint crazed and peeling to show chrome underneath. The hood ornament—an oval around the stylized outline of a Great Wall watchtower—drooped toward the passenger side.

Well, it was about the size of a Cherokee, Mack said. We would test drive it. Visibly concerned about my lack of local driving experience, he offered to take the wheel. I clambered up into the passenger seat—a long way up—and cautiously we backed out of the parking space and worked our way out of the complex. The morning sun, striking the dirt on the windshield, reduced the view out front to a blurry glare. The side windows, where the dirt was overlaid on the customary Chinese tint job, were nearly opaque. The needle on the gas gauge was on *E*. Mack honked. "The horn works," he said.

We took a big loop through the neighborhood—past liquid-natural-gas storage tanks, along a weedy asphalt lane, out onto the wide dusty boulevards, and back around to the edge of the Fourth Ring. Somewhere on the last leg, a red warning light came on. We pulled into the car-repair bazaar again and raised the subject with the Jeep-shop crew. They lifted the hood and frowned at the engine. Someone cranked the ignition, and the whole motor lurched in its frame as it jumped to life. One of the shop guys peered into the car to check the light, then studied the engine again. It just needs a little more oil for the brake pump, he told Mack.

Who would I call if the thing broke down on the road? Mack said I should call him, and he'd get someone to help—or, better yet: "You take my Jeep," he said. He would take the Great Wall for the day. I waved him off. He persisted. No, no. I could not deprive him of his car. The lead repairman, a young guy in a striped long-sleeved

T-shirt, dribbled a little oil into a reservoir and gave it a thump. He checked the dash, then stared at the engine with a look of grave suspicion or concern. Then, after a long pause: *"Keyi le!"* he said. It's okay! He dropped the hood. It bounced up, ajar. He slammed it down again. It popped up. He tried again. The hood jiggled to a rest, still not shut, the Great Wall hood ornament heeling over even further. He went into the shop, got some lubricant, worked on the latch for a while. It closed.

Mack was chuckling, somewhere between alarm and amusement. Every few minutes, he revised his estimate. On closer inspection, the Great Wall was maybe a little bigger than his usual Jeep. No, it was considerably bigger. "The whole thing is just . . . rough," he said. "It's a rough machine. But they think it's a good car."

We took it out again, and the warning light stayed off. Halfway through the lap, we stopped, and I switched over to the driver's seat. The walnut-toned plastic on the door handle was chipped, and there was something gritty and sticky on the steering wheel, and when I looked over my shoulder for traffic, I could see nothing but the truck itself, the rear window half covered by the spare tire. Years before, I had driven, as a repair-shop loaner for my aged Honda Civic, an elderly Oldsmobile Delta 88—a vehicle like a rectangular midwestern county on wheels, its corners somewhere far off in the lonesome distance. But I never had had to steer the Delta 88 down an alleyway crowded with microvans and motor-tricycles and people carrying their breakfast.

Still, the Great Wall drove okay. The clutch point was tough— about an eighth of an inch above the floor mat—and the thing never seemed happy in second gear. I'd driven worse. (Hadn't I? Yes, a twenty-four-foot U-Haul with bum steering and an uninsulated engine cowling. Definitely worse.) I'd take it.

Now gas, and a car wash. There was a station just outside the gate, with a one-lane car-wash canopy in front of the pumps. The fill-up overflowed the tank—evidently the gauge was wrong and it hadn't really been empty. A four-man car-wash crew scrambled over it, the team leader climbing up the frame of the canopy to work the Great Wall over with a pressure hose. A gray BMW pulled up and honked to get us out of the way, so the driver could sit and wait for his car wash ten feet closer than he was currently sitting and waiting. It was important for me to remember to use the horn, Mack said. "Do use it," he said. "A light touch. Get their attention. Otherwise, they'll ignore you."

The crew waved the Great Wall out, for a wipedown and interior cleaning. The BMW owner sauntered around, clutching a little black man-purse. The surface had a shine to it now, so that the scratches and dents stood out. The hood ornament still drooped. A lot of drivers, Mack said, swapped out the Great Wall emblem for a Toyota one, since the Great Wall was a Toyota knockoff.

The steering wheel was unsticky. I flipped on the air conditioner, and a puff of dust came out. Big Mack volunteered to lead the way back to Outer Dongzhimen Side Street. As he turned out of the gas station, two buses were coming. I hit the horn and gunned the Great Wall out in front of them. A few turns later, Mack changed lanes and a red Volkswagen Santana tried to force its way between us. I nudged the Great Wall over to cut it off, drawing an impotent fit of honking. At a stoplight, I caught myself gazing wistfully at a trim silver Mazda 6, but the Great Wall had its own vehicular logic and in Beijing traffic that logic was persuasive. I tried the radio. It was dead.

I parked in the biggest space I could find, down the block and around the corner, by the gates of a mental hospital. Mack supervised the parking. "This is a monster car," he said. Then, in a mock-stentorian instructor's voice: "You passed the test. You can drive in China!"

But not to the Western Qing Tombs. Just getting the truck had used up most of the morning, and Little Mack was in no state to hit the open road without lunch. By the middle of lunch, he was sleepily rubbing his eyes. So while he went down for a nap, we searched the maps for an easier destination, something in the near outskirts of Beijing. Maybe we could just go out to the Fragrant Hills, northwest of the Fifth Ring. We had seen something on television about the changing leaves there. Or right before Fragrant Hills Park, the Summer Palace. I still had never been to the Summer Palace.

Car!" little Mack said, from the backseat. "Car! Car! Car!" The cars he was seeing were moving, for the most part. Traffic was light as we worked our way north and west from top of the Second Ring. My notebook sat on the passenger seat. At the top of the page was a scrawled "Legal??"—the question had come up as I followed a line of traffic making a left turn through the gap where a lane divider opened for a crosswalk. We followed the Third Ring around to the Badaling Expressway, out to the Fifth Ring. The mountains were solid-looking and green, wrapping around us on two sides. The baby whooped with glee. We passed a disabled car in the middle of the road, a truckload of scrap, another truck piled high with old quilts. I cut off a black Audi. A different black Audi, with a warning buzzer-siren, passed us on the right shoulder. There was a sign for the Summer Palace exit. It seemed a pity to stop so soon, and so short of the mountains. We passed the Summer Palace and headed for the Fragrant Hills.

As soon as we took the exit for Fragrant Hills Park, the open road closed up again, with creeping traffic and hordes of pedestrians. We crawled past the Beijing Botanical Gardens, with a rare joint display of Huanhuan and Lele accompanying the sign, and the gift shop of the Bee Research Institute. Pedestrians flowed into the roadway, around the slowly passing cars. There were tourist shops, and vendors selling candied fruit on sticks. Bullhorns squawked.

A flagman waved us into a parking-lot entrance, and a young man in a red visor and leatherette jacket, shirtless underneath, led the way to a parking field of stubbly brown grass, evidently a former farming plot. Once there, the leatherette man made a pitch: for 100 yuan, plus the ticket price, we could drive to the gate of the park and go right in. He hopped in and guided us up an even more crowded uphill lane, through a left turn, and into a parking space in front of a conversion van that was even bigger than the Great Wall.

The first fragrance that the Fragrant Hills presented was that of urine. We had parked just outside a public toilet. The man in the jacket, who said his name was Yang, produced two adult tickets, led us through the park entrance, and murmured something to the ticket-taker as he passed. We thanked him and rolled the baby's stroller on into the park. Paths split off upslope, leading to stairways for hiking up the mountain, and downslope, to the cable-car station. We headed for the cable car.

The paths were swarmed; a constant chatter filled the air. Except for a tint of yellow here or there, the foliage was all in summer green. A family with two babies in strollers passed us in the opposite direction. The babies were covered in some sort of penny-sized sores— dark and weeping sores on one baby, paler and crusty sores on the other. The family's holiday mood seemed intact.

The cable car was a chairlift, with open two-person benches. We bought tickets, left the stroller at the base station, and lined up for the ride. Fortunately, little Mack was in the mood to be held. I clutched him tight and let the car scoop us up from behind.

Behind us, the city stretched east across the plain, looking white in the afternoon light. We could see the spire of the old CCTV broadcast tower on the west side, and the loop of the new CCTV building all the way over on the east. The ridges of the mountain enfolded us. We rose over the treetops. Someone had dropped an empty box of Pocky candied pretzel sticks into the upper branches. The stairs up the mountain ran close by the cable car route, and we could see hikers below us, looking ever wearier as we went higher. Where the steps paused at observation platforms, there was a rim of litter below, like what's left by high tide.

A soaring bird passed below the chair. There was haze far off to the east. We rose higher and higher, and then the chair deposited us on the mountaintop, back in the thick of the human element. People clogged the paths and clambered over the rocks between; they swarmed souvenir stands to buy red leaves, presumably left over from the previous autumn, pressed in laminated sheets. The air was dense with babble and cigarette smoke.

Then we saw the line for the cable car back down the mountain— not just all the passengers who'd already ridden up, naturally, but an uncountable number of people who'd hiked up and wanted a ride back down. The line doubled and trebled back on itself, then stretched off down a long path. We wouldn't be off the mountain for an hour.

Just as the predicament was sinking in, I looked up and saw Yang, in his leatherette jacket, lurking by the cable-car line. He had a van available for a ride down the mountain, he said. It would be 60 yuan per person, down to the north gate of the park. We only had to wait until he could round up enough passengers.

Within five or ten minutes he had assembled about a dozen. He passed the group off to another young man in a red shirt, and we set off south along the mountaintop, then down one of the stepped pathways. Looking down the hill and off to the right, we could see a strip of roadway through the trees with some vans or minibuses parked on it. Getting to there didn't look too bad. But instead of angling along the slope to the right, we kept going straight downhill, and for much longer than I'd thought we would. Our van was not one of those vans. Then the pathway made a sharp turn along a ridgeline. On the right-hand side ran a wall, eight or ten feet high. Our guide walked ahead for a while, then stopped, seemingly nowhere in particular. Another man was sitting on top of the wall, waiting. In a minute, the guide explained, they would have the ladder.

It was a bamboo ladder, in the old-fashioned Chinese style, wider at the bottom than the top. The men handed it down over the wall and braced it at an angle. I would go first, because I had the baby. Holding Mack in one arm, I climbed up to the top. Another ladder led down the other side. Somehow I got from one to the other and down without losing the child. I was standing on a narrow unpaved path along the outside of the wall, with a yellowish thicket pressing in on it. The growth was too tall to see over.

The others followed. There was a pair of plump boys, somewhere around ten years old. *"Hao war!"* one of them said, going over the wall. Fun! Tiny dates were growing wild, and people began to pick them and hand them around. When the last passenger was over, we set off through the thicket, following the blind windings of the path out—at last!—to the edge of a roadway, where a rattletrap van was waiting. The padding in the seats had been beaten flat, and the inside reeked of fuel. An argument broke out about crowding—the guides wanted to make the plump boys sit in their parents' laps, because they were only half price, and to go find more passengers to fill the van. The driver didn't want to add any more weight. Maybe because he was the one who had to get the van down the mountain, his view prevailed, and we were off.

We passed more men climbing over the wall, loading bundles of trash from the park onto blue three-wheeled Jin Bei minitrucks. The roadway was pale concrete, a long series of curves and switchbacks with a sharp drop on the outside. Not only was there no rail, but the edge of the concrete was beveled, as if to help ease any errant wheel over the side. Before long, we found ourselves face-to-face with a Santana coming uphill, with no room to pass. The driver slipped the van into reverse and retreated to the most recent hairpin turn, where there was extra room for the car to slip by. "Scary! Scary!" the little boys yelled from the back, as if they were on an amusement ride. I still had a date pit in my mouth and was slowly grinding it to crumbs.

On and down we went, through curves banked like skateboarding half-pipes, with the children screaming. Eventually we reached an arched tunnel that looked barely wider than the van. By the roadside was a bulldozer, abandoned and overgrown with vines. The driver pulled up to the arch, backed off, and then somehow shot the gap. As soon as we were through, he announced that it was time to switch to another van. The new van—new to us, but emphatically not a new van—was waiting by the roadside, with a new driver. It had blackout-tinted windows and it smelled like skunk inside. I was not sure what in the Beijing mountains would make a smell like skunk. The original driver said that the switch was necessary because his van needed a rest from driving. No sooner had he explained this and gotten us settled in the other van than we looked out the window to see him turning the empty van around and zipping back uphill through the tunnel.

The new driver was wearing a neat yellow shirt and seemed more mild-mannered than the rest of the crew. He cranked the ignition and nothing happened. We sat there in the skunk-smelling dimness. Would the cable car really have been so bad? Resignedly, the driver dug out a tool kit and reached behind his seat to take the cover off the battery, which happened to be where our feet were, directly below the baby. He fiddled with it, and a spark popped. Then he tightened something with a wrench. The van started.

This lower stretch of road had concrete posts along the downhill side, and a less menacing aspect all around. The boys behind us started talking about what they wanted to eat for dinner. "Curry noodles!" We guessed that the other van was working the uphill leg because it had better brakes. Just as we were getting used to the new one, the driver stopped. This was it. We would be walking the rest of the way to the park gate. It would take only about ten minutes, the driver said.

The roadway was still a steep grade for walking down, especially while carrying a twenty-two-pound baby. The evening was getting cool. The stroller—the stroller, we had realized, was still at the base station for the cable car, where we'd left it. We walked past rural lanes and courtyards. There was a small hill's worth of coal, then a grazing nanny goat. Turds lay on the pavement. One of our traveling companions saw the baby sucking his thumb and launched into a lecture: He had to pull it out. If we let him do it, he'd need to do it to fall asleep. Well, yes, he would.

Twenty minutes later, we reached the bottom. The stroller was still where we'd left it, and the park hadn't quite closed for the day. Dusk was falling fast. The Great Wall was also where we'd left it. I swung it out of the space and tried to remember how I had gotten to the parking lot. A right turn to start with, for certain. I crept down the darkening street, through the people massing around the storefronts. The smell of cooking meat skewers was on the air. The parking lots along the way were emptying; we were in a thickening line of traffic, slowly oozing downhill. The next turn was a mystery to me. When in Beijing, do as the masses do: At the next intersection most of the cars were turning south; I followed.

By now it was thoroughly dark. We were on a two-lane road, under deep-suburban, if not rural, lighting conditions. Somewhere, up ahead, we would definitely meet up with an expressway if we kept going. This was a familiar thought pattern for the part of my brain that does the driving. The darkness, the traffic on the narrow country road—this was how I always felt looking for the highway in Pennsylvania.

And Pennsylvania was the next-closest thing to home. My wife and son were asleep in the car. The lights got brighter; we passed a set of the Golden Arches. At a stoplight, I checked the atlas under the dome light. The Fourth Ring should be coming up soon. I only had to be in the right lane. I swung the incontestable bulk of the Great Wall over, drawing impotent honking.

The rest was automatic, as if I'd been doing it forever. The Great Wall looped around the North Fourth Ring. This was not suburban Philadelphia, after all: now waves of colored light accompanied us, floodlights and patterned LEDs along the bridges and retaining walls. "One World, One Dream," was spelled out in green. Then, in characters, *"Huanying Ni Lai Dao Beijing."* Welcome to Beijing. Illuminated yellow hoops adorned the guardrails. The plain streetlights, even, looked like some decoration strung out on the road ahead. I passed the Ikea, took Jingshun Road, found the signs (in Chinese) for the Sanyuan Bridge. Then would come Xindong Road, and the right-left jog onto Outer Dongzhimen Side Street. I was driving on memory, making no wrong turns, automatically heading for something like home.

30.

回忆 Memory

The city plunged deeper and deeper into autumn. The ivy on the wall of the expat compound began to turn red, and the smell of burning coal was in the air. The municipal collective heat would not come on till November—November 1 for hospitals and kindergartens; November 15 for everyone else. Even then, the target would be a thrifty 16 degrees Celsius, or about 61 degrees Fahrenheit. Meanwhile the chill was seeping up through the apartment floors again, as it had each spring and fall before.

Progress marched on: in less than a month, the concrete work in the pit had reached ground level, with the rebar stretching higher than that. A stoplight went in at the mouth of the alley, and a tea shop opened on the corner where the bank had been. The roving newsstand moved a few more yards up the street to make room for it. Then the newsstand itself was replaced by a new-model stand, with a glass canopy and fluorescent lighting, paid for by the postal

service. Over by Moma, the insta-parks had been taken out as fast
as they'd gone in, and the land was walled off by new construction
fencing. Peach-colored dust floated in the sunlight. The taxi drivers
kept their uniforms and added blue waist-length jackets that said
"Taxi" on a tag at the back of the neck. A crane was lifting pieces of
a crane.

Smog pushed into the city, wind pushed it out again, and the
smog pushed back. On Old Drum Tower Avenue, a stretch of renovated buildings was being re-renovated. Where the front wall had
been cut open, the layers showed: three inner rows of ancient,
rounded, gray bricks; two more rows of modern red bricks; and on
the outside, a thin layer of lighter-gray brick-shaped veneer. The
north wind threw dust around.

There were still thirty or so students in English class, though Sha
Meiyuan said that interest had waned since the end of the Olympics.
The teacher now was another college student, named Jennifer; she
wore a bias-cut plaid shirt and jeans with sequined hearts on the
back pockets. I led the class in reading Lesson 55, about the Sawyer
family, who lived at 87 King Street. Mr. Sawyer went to work, the
children went to school, and Mrs. Sawyer stayed home and did the
housework. She usually ate lunch at noon, and her friends often came
over for tea.

After the lesson, the Three Represents man presented me with a
sheet of English he'd written out: "Marxism's core is capitalists
exploit workers' 'surplus value.' In @ other word they exploit workers' labour. So. It calls that the proletarians of the world unite up!
Knock down [wipe out] the bourgeoisie." It ran through the history
of China after the defeat of the Kuomintang; it included the Three
Represents; and ended with the declaration: "Our great mother land

is ~~going~~ marching forward to ~~powerful~~ ^the^ prosprous and strong ^and^ harmony society."

Once I'd had a chance to study it, he came back to quiz me on the words. Did I know "surplus value"? Did I know "exploit"? Did I know "bourgeoisie"? He kept pronouncing "bourgeoisie" with a hard *g*. I worked on straightening that out. Did I know about the global economic crisis? He pointed out "crisis" in the dictionary: *weiji*. Did I know that word in Chinese? This was, unknown to him, the word immortalized in the old saw about how the Chinese word for "crisis" contains the word for "opportunity." *Ji* does sometimes mean "opportunity"; this fact becomes less profound, however, once you realize that it also means "machine," or, given its semantic elasticity, something more like "doohickey." (Did you know the Chinese word for "crisis" contains the word for "thingamajig"?)

At the end, more students clustered around with a final set of word questions. A man in a blue blazer and a tan porkpie hat said he wanted to know how to write "microphone." But then why was he asking, if he already knew the word? He clarified: the word he wanted was the word for "concealed microphone." We settled on "bug" or "listening device." But if it's on the telephone, I told him, you can say the phone is "bugged," but you would probably call it a "wiretap." I wrote out "wiretap." Or "phone tap." The senior citizens noted it down: wiretap.

October 29 was overcast and drizzling. It would not rain again till long after we were gone—more than a hundred days, the longest drought since 1971. Only one brief, dirty snow flurry, an unmeasurable trace, would fall in that time.

Christina and I were on our way to see a dance competition, down by the Altar of Heaven. Five kites were high in the air over Chang'an

Boulevard. An ad on a bus was for Watson's Bird's Nest facial cleanser; a store had been selling Water Cube bottled water, from Canada. We drove along the north side of the Altar of Heaven park. Crumbling squalor showed through the openings in a beautification wall—semi-demolished but still functioning alleys. The aspect outside was gray and timeless, the ordinary, grimy, lived-in Beijing.

We were meeting Christina's ballet classmates at the dance theater, a pink-and-gray box with a gilt ballerina floating over blue-tinted glass above the entrance. Amateur classes like the ones at the coal-mining academy had been growing into an ongoing business for their teacher, Dong Chang, a former dancer with the China National Ballet Company and the Guangzhou Ballet Company. In a country where dancers had been selected and trained from a young age, people were beginning to study dance on their own, with their leisure time. "Now younger people, middle-class people, white-collar people have taken it up," Dong told me in an interview over coffee, with Christina translating.

You Di, one of Dong's students, who worked in public relations, was helping to organize and put on the classes. He was an earnest balletomane, with a shorter and chubbier build than a professional male dancer, and he kept notebooks in which he had written every dance combination they'd done. Interest in dance had grown wildly in the last three years, You said, and the dancers were shifting to "something closer to the core of what ballet is"—wanting to perform, rather than thinking of it as a mere form of exercise. "You need men to be with women to have performances," he said.

And those dancers needed dancewear. Dong and You had found a manufacturer that Chinese professional dancers used, and had ordered up a line of clothing for their hobbyists. There were opportunities within opportunities. Outside the competition hall, You was carrying newly printed catalogs.

The show was the semifinals of the Second Beijing International Ballet Invitational for Dance Students. We took our seats in the second-level balconies, and then a flood of wispy young ballet students came washing in around us.

The competition began with classical ballet routines, one from each of the eighteen entrants. There were three Chinese Prince Siegfrieds from *Swan Lake*, two of some character named Philippe from something called "The Flowers of Paris," three of Franz from *Coppélia*—one Chinese, one Japanese, one Korean. The performances varied from dutiful or wobbly to inspired, but all were lit the same and briskly timed.

Then came the modern-dance segment. Up first was a Chinese dancer in black trunks who had been an indifferent Siegfried and who was now crawling and contorting himself across a blue-lit stage with precision and intense focus. This half of the program would have production values.

The next number, according to the hard-to-read video screen, seemed to be called "Let's Go to Shoot Together." The lights shone on a pile of colorful cloth at stage left—a collapsed lion-dance costume?—and Contestant No. 2 entered, wearing a school uniform, a red scarf, and a backpack. He approached the pile and started pawing at it, lifting the bright cloth objects to reveal some sort of outsized brown straw hat—or volcano?—underneath. No, I had misread the title: it was not "Shoot," but "Shool," meant to be "School"; the Chinese was *"Women Yiqi Qu Shang Xue,"* We Go to School Together. And what the dancer was pawing at was a bunch of abandoned child-sized backpacks, and the pile was a burial mound, and what we were seeing was someone's choreographic reaction to the Sichuan earthquake. With great gestures of grief, the dancer hoisted and clutched at the empty bookbags (they were still visibly stiff and new), then finally gathered them up, not without difficulty, pulling the multiple straps over his arms and then—with a brave gesture of farewell—marching determinedly off under the burden of them all, presumably to school.

The lights went off, plunging the whole theater back into darkness. The next competitor was announced. The stage lights came up—on the pile of backpacks, returned to the burial mound. Contestant No. 3 would also be presenting "Let's Go to School Together"—writhing, grieving, the whole bit. The backpacks would reappear for No. 9. The Sichuan tragedy was a hit. None of the dances commemorated the Olympics.

Workers hacked up the flower beds by the Second Ring and raked away the remains. The palm trees on the Third Ring were tied up, with trucks waiting to carry them off. A scaffold went up on the new Uniqlo store on Sanlitun, improving the improvements. What would it even mean, to preserve Beijing? If the work stopped, the city would cease to exist.

In the kitchenware store, a thickset man with glasses and a mustache was looking at pots and pans. The salesclerk pointed out for him that one pan was more expensive than the others he'd been looking at. If it wasn't expensive, the man said, he wouldn't buy it. "Remember, I am a rich person!" he said. *Wo shi youqiande ren!*

A week into November, the building in the pit was higher than our window level, with rebar pointing even higher. The *youqiande ren* were taking away the sky. The days were grayer and chillier. Chen Yanqun told Christina that we were special because even though we were educated, we still made things. Made things? Like breakfast. And cake. In China, educated people didn't learn to do things like that.

The supply of foreign milk recovered, then faltered again. Now there was melamine in the eggs, too, because there was melamine in the chicken feed, because there was melamine anywhere people could find a chance to fake the protein content of something. The eggs at the expat market had a notice on the carton lid, and on a pamphlet inside, declaring that they were melamine-free.

A Chinese cousin nagged us over lunch: Don't let the baby drink milk when he has a cough. Don't let him suck his thumb. Don't feed him with a fork, it's dangerous. Don't take him outside without a hat.

Our lease would be expiring on December 21. I needed one last visa to get to the end. Earlier in November, Wen Jiabao had announced that the expanded freedoms for foreign journalists would continue, even after the Olympics. But to get a journalist's visa required an invitation letter from one's interview subjects. The Dongsi English learners demurred; press freedom or none, registering with the government as interview subjects was still too alarming for the class's organizers.

Eventually the Gong An agreed it was possible for me to go out as a tourist, on a spousal tourist visa. All I needed, a Gong An officer said, was a marriage certificate.

By now we had our own homemade version of a Chinese citizen's identity file in the desk in our apartment. When I came back with the marriage license, the officer on duty said I would also need an official seal from my wife's office on the application. There was no way to get one before the weekend, when my visa would expire. That was okay, the officer said. I could come in on Monday, it would be fine.

Nothing at the Public Security Bureau had ever been fine. The notion was so implausible, I wrote down the officer's badge number. At last, I had made a wise tactical decision. When I returned on Monday, another officer took my paperwork, flipped through it, and put on what I recognized as the rejection face. There was no copy of my wife's foundation's registration certificate, she said.

That was not what the officer had told me last week, I said. Officer 013025 had told me that I needed only the office seal, not the certificate. Officer 013299 considered what I was saying. What was that number again? I showed her my pocket notebook: 013025. She took down the number. Well, then, my application was all set. She handed me the yellow pick-up receipt. With only a few weeks left in my life in China, I had cracked a part of the bureaucratic code—once the officer was able to shift responsibility to someone else, she had no more incentive to block me. I had won an argument with the Public Security Bureau. Tourist visa? They should have awarded me a residence permit for that, on principle.

By late November, the Uighur peddlers were back, selling their candied-nut loaves from the back of their cargo tricycles by the bus terminal. It couldn't be a very good business model, having a half-dozen or more people trying to sell the same thing one right next to another; it's hard to say who would even buy a slice of nut loaf at all. Presumably the Uighurs were happier hanging out where they could see other Uighurs, rather than plying their trade alone in the ocean of Han Chinese.

Even the cabdrivers complained about the cabdrivers. The economy was slowing down, one cabbie told Christina, and old cabbies weren't renewing their licenses. New drivers were tested on map knowledge and on customer service, not on driving; there was a training car for them to learn their way around Beijing, but the trainees would just take it out for joyrides. The cabbie said he had gone out drinking himself one night, and at three a.m. he had hailed a cab. The driver told him he had been out on the road all night and the whole day before, since dawn—because, he confessed, he couldn't figure out how to get home.

We took one more trip to Hong Kong, then flew back into Beijing for the last time. Once more, we landed without benefit of a jetway. The sky was clear for December, but after the Hong Kong sea breezes, the Beijing air arrived like a punch in the lungs. While we were away, the view from the living room window had disappeared altogether. The apartment tower project was now taller than our building, seven or eight stories, covered in new scaffolding and green mesh cloth. Temporary wooden stairways led from floor to floor, up the outside. Noise from the pit shook the bed in the middle of the night.

Our landlady was getting ready to clear us out. She was very unhappy about the broken toilet in the second bathroom that she had never fixed, and about a dowel that had broken in the old dining table top when we disassembled and stored it, and about a cracked window. But if we left her the big oval dining table and our couch, and she kept our deposit, she was willing to call it even.

Chen Yanqun was visibly rankled at having to witness this display of middle-class high-handedness. When the landlady raised some concern about the television, she cut her off. They don't even watch TV, she said. It's bad for babies to watch TV before age two. Chen had never seemed particularly invested in the teachings of the American Academy of Pediatrics before. In passing, the landlady rebuked us for letting the baby walk around in stocking feet on the cold floors. The baby, Chen said, is used to walking around in his socks.

The movers arrived—three men riding in a completely bare truck, without even rags for padding. The company had assured us that we didn't need to pack anything, that they would handle all that themselves; nevertheless, we had put things up in boxes ourselves. They took the cartons, the armchair, and the desk. Spurning the landlady's offer, we had the movers take the couch. She could keep the dining table. We haggled our way to a partial return of the deposit.

The couch would arrive in America loosely wrapped in cardboard, one sturdy leg completely sheared off. Some of the boxes had been opened and reshaped into larger boxes, using scraps of orange cartons. Other boxes were so crushed they slumped into puddles, incapable of being stacked; two or three had simply been annihilated, leaving loose books and clothing in a shallow cardboard tray. Three boxes failed to arrive, having been impounded by Chinese customs on the suspicion they contained cultural artifacts. We were mystified: our newly made wooden lattice? the knockoff contemporary paintings? We hadn't owned anything, as far as we knew, that could be mistaken for Chinese cultural patrimony.

We had a week left. A team of plainclothes policemen showed up at the door to check passports and registrations. The leader was a round-faced man who wore his jacket zipped all the way up. Was I going home soon? he asked. Yes, I said. "Merry Christmas!" he replied.

Big Mack dropped by, and we went down to the gatehouse to talk to Wang Jiashui, one last source to interview before I left. Wang had added a gasoline motor to his cargo tricycle, for 850 yuan. The tricycle itself was three years old, and had cost him 750.

Wang was dressed neatly, as usual, in a black sweater with the Izod crocodile on it and olive wide-wale corduroys. He told us he had come to Beijing in 1987, following old friends from his village. "It was okay, the city," Wang said, "but I was nervous, because I didn't know how to make a living." He worked at a factory producing chicken and pig feed, then at a refinery making gasoline. "I've done a lot of different things," he said, "but I just can't make money."

He settled on the scrap trade in 1998. "I don't have other skills, so I have to do this," he said. In an average month, he said, he would make 1,000 yuan, after paying for food and accommodation. He lived outside the Fifth Ring, on the east side, and sold his scrap outside the Third Ring, where bigger collectors would buy it and take it to still-bigger collectors in the suburbs. "It's like an onion," he said. "Every person involved takes a peel, till you're left with nothing."

If he had a full load of scrap, he would commute on his tricycle, so he could drop it off along the way. Otherwise he would park it and take the bus, for 8 mao, eight-tenths of a yuan. It was a half-hour bus trip. Now that he had the motor, the tricycle ride was fast enough to rival the bus, forty minutes, but it burned 4 yuan worth of gas.

The neighborhood had been Wang's collecting territory for ten years. He had started coming by, he said, to get scrap wire from the construction site here, where our building was. Our shabby, beaten-down, cream-and-brown building was only a decade old. "Some clothes look old, but actually they're new," Wang said. "People have their own tastes. This particular organization likes this paint."

Before the apartment was built, he said, there had been a factory making aluminum products on the site. The rest of the area—the construction site, the suburban-style expat compound, the other apartment towers—had all been cheap, low-slung, *pingfang* alleys till the end of the nineties, like the little surviving patch to our east. "This whole street used to be a vegetable market," he said.

The past was even shallower underfoot than I'd imagined. I had been right about the scrap of *pingfang* that was left, though: developers wanted regular lots, Wang said, and it was too small and oddly shaped to be worth demolishing. The big vacant lot where the building was rising had lain fallow for so long, Wang said, because the land had been owned by the former mayor, Chen Xitong, who was arrested for corruption. So developers were afraid to touch the site. If not for its troubled past, he said, "the building would have been completed already."

The new building wouldn't help Wang's share of the scrap trade, he said. Other collectors already had lined up friends on the inside, and they would keep anyone else from gleaning things there. Scrap was slumping overall, along with everything else. Business had been bad during the Olympics, when trucks couldn't get into the city, and now the global downturn was keeping prices depressed. Iron and copper were the best salvage materials, but their prices were plummeting, too. Copper had gone from 50 or 60 yuan a kilogram down to 10 or 20. Plastic water bottles had gone from 14 fen, Chinese pennies, each down to 4 fen. "This financial crisis is so big," Wang said.

Still, China had an appetite for scrap. Wang said he had heard about discarded computer monitors from abroad coming into China for free. "Nobody wants those monitors, and here you can sell them for money." What's good for reselling? I asked. *"Dou yao,"* he said. People want it all. Wang said he had heard from people who had traveled abroad that there were rules against throwing things away— you could be fined if you threw out your garbage on the wrong day. People didn't know how to get rid of their unwanted things.

"You can sell all those things in China," he said.

Our own things had been picked up, but were still waiting for the movers to ship them, and we had accumulated a few additional boxes in the meantime. Downstairs, as evening was falling, I found Wang again. Could he help me bring them over to Christina's office? He loaded the cartons onto the back of the tricycle and tied them down with a dark-stained rope, wrapping the stack methodically. He laid a plastic garbage bag on the slates of the flatbed—my seat—and told me to hang on. Then he put it in gear.

We putt-putted around the far side of the courtyard and out the gate, into the sunset. There was a pink tinge of haze in the air, but Venus shone clearly in the darkening sky. The day had been relatively mild, and the air was cold but pleasant rushing by. A *chuan'r* grill on the alley gave off billows of smoke. Behind us, cars honked impatiently. We crossed the intersection, past the new tea shop and the new stoplight, continuing along the other half of Outer Dongzhimen Side Street. There was brown-looking ice on the Liangma River beside us. Then we made a jog out onto Xindong Road, the north-south thoroughfare. Ahead, in the haze, were the buildings of the new city. Poplars and willows stood over the service roadway. Over my shoulder was the big modern complex at the head of the road, not yet dripping with its nightly light display. All around the bed of the garbage tricycle stretched the dome of the world.

And then we were leaving, out the airport expressway for the last time. The little poplars had long since grown and filled out into a wall of green, no more or less dishonest than the strips of woods that conceal American suburban subdivisions and the eight-lane interstate from one another.

The great imposing hall of Terminal 3 was frigid, its heating system no match for the cold north wind. You couldn't warm up that much space. The attendants at the front desk of the Air China lounge were bundled in coats; the skin on one of my knuckles was split open from the cold. Little Mack, in my arms, was coughing and wheezing again, violently. He would pass the flight clinging to us in misery, and he would get off the plane to spend a week, including Christmas, hooked to a hospital oxygen monitor, with a diagnosis of acute asthma and pneumonia. Something for him to remember his birth-place by.

The New York Times reported that the International Olympic Committee had issued a final write-up on the Beijing Games: the event was an "indisputable success" that had "brought many tangible and intangible benefits to China." The elderly would-be protesters, though not mentioned in the IOC report, had been spared house arrest after all. Actual punishment was unnecessary. The protesters had wanted to give the government a message, and the government had given them a message in reply. Beijing had opened up as far as it needed to open.

Chinese exceptionalism was flourishing, even as being American was not as impressive or secure as it had once been. In 2004, a dollar had been worth more than 8 yuan. Practically 10 to 1, if you were converting prices in your head—just move the decimal point and call it a bargain. What came out of the ATM was Monopoly money with Mao on it. By the end of 2008, the exchange rate was barely over 6 yuan to the dollar, and we could feel the purchasing power ebbing, as if stricken with incurable illness.

Beijing and China would go on without us. It was time to go to the boarding gate. Where we made the turn, there was an airport shop decorated along the top of the wall with pictures of the Fuwa— Huanhuan playing handball, Jingjing boxing and shooting, Beibei and Beibei doing synchronized-swimming together. The Fuwa merchandise itself was gone. Instead, shelf after shelf was given over to stuffed panda bears, pandas upon pandas, in monotonous black-and-white rows. On closer look, they weren't all pandas. For variety, some were white teddy bears dressed in panda suits, peeking out from under panda masks. One last calculated revelation: Had you, the souvenir-shopping traveler, considered the possibility that China was no different from anywhere else? The future had already begun.

Epilogue

The air at the gate to the Olympic Green was sweet with flowers. There were dense beds of them, lush bands of pink, red, yellow, purple, leading from North Pole Star Road toward the Bird's Nest. The sky above the Bird's Nest was blue, with clean white clouds.

It was May 2010, nearly a year and a half after we'd left, and we were back in Beijing for the month. Christina had one last project to wind up. This time around, we had caught up with the surge of progress: we were staying on the twelfth floor of a plush hotel apartment at the southwest corner of Dongzhimen Bridge, a tower sprouting from the top of a five-story shopping mall, next to the big four-legged bronze *gui*. We had seen the building go up, but it hadn't opened till we were gone. The façade was decked out in irregular glass facets, black-and-white graphics, color-shifting LEDs, and video screens. In the hotel lobby was a bronze of a reclining mother holding up her child, the baby with an adorable curling forelock, that I immediately recognized as the work of Han Meilin. Little Mack, now almost three years old, liked to sit by the living room's full-length windows in the evening and look down at the roof of the mall part, through the angled skylights to the shoppers and the hotel swimming pool below. "Night is falling," he said. He wanted to be told and retold the story of how one would get to the hotel: onto the airport expressway and through the great expanse of city, past the Fifth Ring, the Fourth Ring, the Third Ring, to the Second Ring and Dongzhimen.

Diagonally across the bridge from the hotel was the Dongzhimen transit station, still missing parts of its glass skin, the construction not visibly advanced since 2008. Christina asked a cabdriver when it was supposed to be finished. *"Shei dou bu zhidao,"* he said. Nobody knows.

Some things were as they'd ever been. We had been back in Beijing for forty-eight hours before I even realized that our windows faced the mountains in the west. The usual yellow-brown pall had been there to greet us when we arrived; the blurry cityscape faded out in the middle distance. Then, on the second full afternoon, there was thunder and a bit of rain, and suddenly we were looking at the old CCTV tower—not the twenty-first-century Koolhaas loop, but the 1990s broadcast tower, a spike like a lacquered souvenir, all the way across town, with mountains upon mountains behind it.

The more celebrated CCTV building, to our south and east, was still empty. Two more Spring Festival Galas had come and gone, and the would-be studio space had yet to host one. During Chinese New Year in 2009, its companion building, the Television Cultural Center, went up in flames—a fireworks accident, investigators said—days before a luxury hotel was supposed to have opened there. The blackened hulk of the TVCC building remained there, next to the unopened architectural masterpiece. Officially, it was structurally sound, but nobody appeared to be in any hurry to renovate it and move in. From a certain angle, driving past the complex on the south, you could see the scorched form of the second building framed perfectly in the silvery loop of the first, like a gigantic and useless art installation, or a monument to the space between intention and reality.

I was prepared for more desolation at the Olympic Green. The monumental construction rarely holds up well in any Olympic city, once the event is gone, and I had heard about fumbling attempts to make use of the empty venues: there'd been a water-ballet version of *Swan Lake* at the Water Cube, and over the past winter, someone had pumped artificial snow into the Bird's Nest to make a bunny-slope ski park. The posts holding up the flowerpots on the road north to the Green were rusting, but they did have flowers in them, even snow.

And the way into the Green had never looked so good. Dozens of tourists were ambling around the site, spread out and uncrowded in the open space. The trees around the Bird's Nest had grown and leafed out; grasses were tall and thick; the fences and gates and barriers had been scaled back. Water lilies bloomed in the reflecting pond beside the stadium. "The Grass Is Smiling at You, Please Detour," a sign advised. Pedestrians stopped on the footbridge to admire the view. "Lean Against the Guardrail with Care," another sign warned. A booth offered to print photos of people posing in front of the scene: a six-inch print for 10 yuan, a twelve-inch print for 30. Beside the pathway were rolls of new sod, bundled in red-white-and-blue-striped tarps.

At the ticket windows outside the Bird's Nest, signs and banners announced that it was hosting the "Unlimited Sky Adventure" of Ahdili, an endurance tightrope walker from Xinjiang. He had been walking back and forth on a cable across the open top of the stadium for three weeks, five hours a day, and would keep going until July. I tried to buy a ticket, and the clerk asked me if I spoke Chinese. My Mandarin had faded badly, but it had begun coming back. If it was too windy, she said—the clean north breeze had been blowing all day—he wouldn't walk today. At 50 yuan a ticket, it seemed wiser to wait for a return visit.

On the plaza west of the Nest, peddlers were selling replicas of the Olympic gold medals, complete with inset imitation-jade rings. A mute woman sketched the price in the air: 15 yuan. I haggled down to 10, which was still five times too expensive, then went ahead and bought one. It would fall apart by the next day.

The ethylene-tetrafluoroethylene bubbles of the Water Cube looked rumpled and a little baggy in the sunlight. The Cube itself was fenced off for its renovation into a water park, but the gift shop next door was open: blue-on-white-on-blue merchandise with bubble-cell patterns. Your Chinese zodiac symbol in blue glass, on top of a rippled glass box. There were some leftover Fuwa pencil sets, but mostly the Water Cube had become its own brand. I bought an inflatable swimming ring, in the standard pattern, for Mack to wear in the hotel pool.

Loudspeakers on the plaza were playing the old Olympic songs in surround sound. "One World, One Dream" thrummed over the pavement, and then, unavoidably, the now familiar opening notes. Back in America, the summer before, a Chinese-American toddler friend had shown Mack the video on YouTube, on her parents' iPhone, and he had kept asking to see it thereafter, over and over, the song that would never fade or end. *"Di ji ci lia mei guanxi,"* the voices sang, *"you tai duo huati. BEEEI-JINNG HUANYING NIII . . ."*

On the way home, I asked the cabdriver to circle the whole Green and the Olympic Forest. Undergrowth had filled in the bare ground, until it almost looked natural. Something else had come in, too, on the east side—a cluster of rooftops, peeking up behind the treetops. All the new greenery made it hard to tell what they might be.

The new city had plans for an even newer city. Reports had just come out that the heart of the Drum Tower neighborhood, the gentrifying hutongs north of the Forbidden City, would be torn down and would be reinvented as something called "Beijing Time Cultural City," anchored by a museum of timekeeping and an underground shopping mall.

Along Outer Dongzhimen Side Street, the new towers across from the old apartment had reached their full height. Glass and brown stone panels were going on the outside, and high up in the interior shadows, welding sparks were shining. Down at the corner, where the restroom had been, the new stretch of blank wall was already chipped and begrimed to match the rest of the alley. Somehow a fecal smell still hovered there. Cargo tricycles passed: watercooler bottles, old quilts, a mixed cargo of baby cabbages and flattened cardboard.

Wang Jiashui and his cargo tricycle were still inside the gate of Yard No. 26. He was binding together a fresh load of scrap. How was business? In this line of work, he said, you won't starve.

Moderate prosperity. The world economic crisis had set the new Chinese era off to a wobbly start, even as the United States seemed lost and stagnated. Migrant workers had been put out of work by the tens of millions. Around China, there had been a string of haunting, vicious attacks: crazed lone men with knives invading well-to-do kindergartens, killing the innocent children of the moneyed class. Workers in a factory that made iPhones were killing themselves. The murders were suppressed in the official media; the suicides were played up—a symbol of China's refusal to be exploited, or its refusal to be seen as being willing to be exploited. The provinces were raising their minimum wages; in Beijing, the minimum would go up 20 percent, to 960 yuan a month.

China was on the top of the pile and on the bottom, all at once. Inside our mall downstairs was an H&M, a brand built on cheap Chinese-made fashion exports, now selling direct to Beijingers. China could now exploit China all on its own. The cars on the streets were bigger and shinier than before. The young men and women gliding through the logo-glow of the shops in the Village at Sanlitun all seemed to be six feet tall. They moved as if they owned a piece of the century to come.

The Dongsi Community was still holding English classes. Some three dozen students were there when I dropped in. The Olympic countdown sign still stood outside, its numbers blank. "When did you go to Athens?" the lesson on the chalkboard read. "I went to Athens last week. When will you go to Beijing? I will go to Beijing next week."

I led the class through a reading of a lesson about train tickets. Two travelers duck into a pub by the station to wait for the 8:19 to London. "We've got plenty of time." But the station clock is ten minutes slow, and they miss their train. When's the next one? "In five hours' time."

The Three Represents man came by my seat to welcome me back. Beijing has changed since 2008, he told me. "Rule of law more and more," he said. "Democracy more."

This was a debatable interpretation. In 2008, a few hundred intellectuals, caught up in the Olympic-year notion of internationalism and liberalization, had signed a document called Charter 08, calling for government reform. Discussion of the petition was banned in the media, its authors were detained and harassed, and one of them,

Li Xiaobo, was arrested and sentenced to prison for subversion of state power. In the fall of 2010, he would win the Nobel Peace Prize, an item of news that was first censored, then denounced, in China. The metaphoric zone of freedom accompanying the Olympics was as much an illusion as the free-speech zones had been. Ai Weiwei, the designer-turned-denouncer of the Bird's Nest, had become a public crusader for the rights of earthquake victims, and local police in the earthquake zone had beaten him into a cerebral hemorrhage for it. As the government pushed back ever harder against its critics and would-be reformers, not even Ai's stature could protect him; in April 2011, he would be seized at the Beijing airport and taken into detention. The riots of Lhasa had repeated themselves in Urumqi in 2009, with Uighur mobs and Han Chinese mobs beating each other to death. The government blamed "splittists," again, and cut off all Internet service to Xinjiang.

China was proving too large to be conquered, by the social and political reformers or the inquiring press. The walls of Beijing had held; the spectacle of the Olympics had served its purpose. No one had been obviously poisoned by the air or the food. The tanks had not rolled in. The ambition and nationalism behind the show was implied, not expressed. China was a phenomenon the world believed it could absorb.

Who could deny that China had joined the world? Something was circling the world, drawing us all together. But after my time in modern, international-minded Beijing, I had trouble believing the unifying force was liberal democracy. Growth, development, security—these were the values that marked a nation as a twenty-first-century power. Maybe that was all it had taken to mark a twentieth-century power, too.

The Olympics were going on to London, and then, for 2016, the International Olympic Committee had chosen Rio de Janeiro—a city that wore its internal contradictions even closer to the surface than Beijing did. Christina and I had been to Rio in 2007, with Mack in the womb; the week before we got there, grenade and gun warfare between gangs and police had killed nineteen people. Buses had been burned. Yet the IOC, fresh from its triumph in Beijing, expected that Brazil could tidy up the city to its satisfaction. Among the other finalists, stable, reliable, all-American Chicago was rejected on the first ballot.

Liu Xiang was nowhere to be seen. I ate three scorpion skewers at the Donghuamen market and then walked up and down the Wang-fujing shopping street, looking for a single billboard or poster of him. The Nike store, where the hurdling mannequin had been in the window, was full of World Cup gear. The Olympic merchandise flagship store was now the flagship store for the Shanghai World's Fair, Expo 2010. Copies of the Shanghai Expo's blue wave-shaped mascot, Haibao, stood where the rows of Beibei, Jingjing, Huanhuan, Yingying, and Nini had been.

Late in the month, Liu appeared in a track meet in Shanghai. He had been racing for a year, but he was still trying to recover from surgery. He had not threatened a world record in a long time, and was not expected to do so this time around. I watched on the hotel TV as he burst from the starting blocks in the final. David Oliver of the United States surged ahead, decisively, the way Liu had once surged ahead of the field. Liu staggered wildly as he headed for the finish line, battling a Chinese teammate for second place. He lost even that, in a photo finish, by a hundredth of a second.

If you looked closely enough around town, the silver panels on the store façades were grimy with age. Poplar fluff still swirled in the air; the city had redoubled its efforts to hormonally suppress it, and had somehow only prolonged the fluff season. But at the bus stops, people in jackets with the Line Up Day 11 logo were herding the crowd into more orderly lines.

I met Soojin Cho at a Starbucks in Jianwai Soho. She had closed her dance studio in the downturn, and a rival cheerleading company had poached a batch of her dancers. She had sued one of them for making off with some of her cheerleading costumes, after seeing a photograph of the wayward dancer wearing the uniform at an event at Hooters. "I called her up and the girl refused to apologize," she said. "So I sued her." After two rounds of litigation, Cho was waiting to find out what the judgment would be.

But Cho's plan to become a media personality was working out. She was hosting a talk show on Hunan Television called *Her Village*, a Chinese equivalent of *The View*, and she was serving as a celebrity judge for reality-TV shows in which women competed to become cheerleaders for the Chinese Basketball Association or the upcoming Asian Games. In the latest edition, the winners would dance as a team in the United States, at an NBA game.

Cho was engaged to a fellow foreigner, an American named Nicholas Krippendorf, who had helped bring the New England Patriots cheerleaders over for cheerleading camp in the spring of 2008. He had proposed to her during *Her Village*, on camera, at the end of a segment about older women who hadn't married yet. The producers were talking to the couple about having the wedding itself on TV.

Big Mack was tired of Beijing, he said. His neighborhood out at Wangjing, which had been towers in empty bulldozed land when he bought his apartment, was now noisy and bustling at street level. Beijing's official population, residents and migrants together, would be announced at 20 million over the summer.

I had come by for a lesson in cooking Beijing noodles, *zhajiangmian*. Ginger, leek, garlic; two kinds of bean sauce. Ground pork. Dry tofu and garlic shoots for texture. The kitchen counter was installed higher than normal, so Big Mack could work comfortably. He wanted to unload his apartment before the real estate bubble burst—that there was a bubble, and that it would burst, was a given; the government had just tightened loan regulations to make it harder for speculators to accumulate second and third apartments—and move somewhere more peaceful, a nice seaside city of a few million.

Ahdili, the tightrope walker, was a tiny red-clad figure, moving back and forth across the sky. There were something like two hundred people in the Bird's Nest to watch him, but the pixel pattern of the tens of thousands of empty seats kept it from feeling deserted. At one end of the rope, on the edge of the stadium's eye, was a little hut where he stayed when not walking. Every now and then he would wave, or sit down on the rope, or do a little heel-toe dance.

Because of the nature of his project, Ahdili was not available for an interview. In a basement room, with Christina translating, I talked to his wife of sixteen years, Yebaguli Abedurizake. Her husband was getting blisters on his feet, she said, and it was lonely for him up there. Over time, his tightrope was sagging closer and closer to the cables that were still strung across the stadium from the opening ceremony. Every day, his three daughters would call him on the phone. "For him," she said, "the Bird's Nest is what all Chinese people look to, the heart of the country."

The concourse of the Bird's Nest was lined with large color photographs, a historical record of the Games. On the inner side were pictures of Olympic athletes; on the outer were portraits of construction workers. There was a gallery of wax figures of IOC presidents—Jacques Rogge, looking solicitous, hands clasped; Juan Antonio Samaranch, who had died the month before, smiling from a chair carved with golden dragons. A gift shop farther around the concourse had leftover Olympic merchandise. For 100 yuan, there were little boxes of turf from the stadium field itself, "rapidly collected and processed" as soon as the Games were over. One rack was filled with souvenir countdown pins: "900 Days to Go." 800. 700. 200. 100. 3. 5.

This time, the sky was gray and drizzly. Up close, the silver columns were streaked with dirt, and patches of paint had fallen away. The damage seemed less a defacement than part of a natural process, the climate of Beijing marking the stadium as its own. Birds chattered inside the structure. The curving bulk of it was still engrossing, even its new state of pointlessness. I stood on the plaza for a while, letting it loom over me once more.

Across from the Planning Exhibition Hall was yet another new luxury complex. Banners announced it as "Ch'ienmen 23," using the old Western-imperialist-era transliteration of the name Qianmen, for the emperor's south-facing Front Gate. I went into the museum, heading for the third floor. The escalators were motion-activated, and attendants waited beside them, stepping out to trip the sensor in advance of each visitor. I rode past the bronze city of 1949, with its expanse of tiny rooftops, and made my way for one last look at the Planning Model.

I had not been back since my first visit. Now, as I surveyed the miniature city, I could follow the plan, reading the model in space and time. I drifted around the room, taking it in from every angle. There was the gleaming Egg, the concrete-and-glass Danish at the

Dongsi Bridge, the White Dagoba rising above Xicheng. The undulating dragon's neck of the 7 Star Hotel, with a tiny cutout for the giant video screen. The Altar of Heaven and the Altar of Earth. The Drum Tower and the Bell Tower, and the low gray roofs that spread out around them, for now. I could look west over our little hotel tower to the CCTV spike across the room.

It was the city, and it was not. The *gui* at Dongzhimen was absent. The wavy municipal information building was missing its mate. The TVCC building was undamaged. Throughout the model were buildings done in colorless plexiglass, representing the next round of development. Dongzhimen Station was still in plexiglass. More ghost buildings marched south along Fuxingmen, west of the Egg; they occupied the space south of the Asian Games complex; they filled in the east side of the Olympic Green, where a science and technology museum had just opened.

In the miniature Olympic Forest, I found the buildings I'd glimpsed from the taxi, some four dozen in all. These were not plexiglass, but solid, finished works. A Chinese tour group was passing through, and I asked the guide what they were. *"Biesu qu,"* she said. Villa development. The more-than-moderately-prosperous class had claimed a piece of the Olympic site all for itself.

By the escalator, I studied the 1949 bronze relief map, the city of the buried past. Dongzhimen, to the far northeast, was high up, almost out of view. I zoomed my camera in on it and snapped a few pictures. Later, back in the hotel, I enlarged them more on my computer. There was the tower of the gate and the fortification in front of it. The hutongs of Inner Dongzhimen were packed inside the city wall, while the land outside—beyond the old city limit—sat almost empty.

Almost. A cluster of buildings, forming a sort of crooked wedge, led away from the imperial gate. There was a narrow gap running through the middle of them: a sagging east-west line. I knew that line. I had picked out its angle time and again, on pocket maps and road atlases, on Internet satellite photos, on the floor of the planning model. I had walked it every day, steered the Great Wall SUV along it, ridden up it in a taxi with our newborn son.

I e-mailed the photo to a friend, an expert on the layers of Old Beijing, to make sure. Yes, he wrote back, that was Outer Dongzhimen Side Street. Back then, it was just Outer Dongzhimen Street. The reason our old alley fit awkwardly into its surroundings was that it had been there first, before the boulevard, before the embassies, before Workers' Stadium. On that side of town, it was the oldest thing outside the Second Ring Road.

From the Planning Exhibition Hall, I walked west and south, toward Qianmen proper, at the foot of Tian'anmen Square. There, at the south end of the capital's ceremonial axis, was the renovated Beijing, the twenty-first-century city, the ragged old commercial district remade into a wide pedestrian shopping zone, Chinese and international all at once. The surface roads approaching it were fenced off to foot traffic and choked with cars. A surviving Fuwa sign welcomed me to Beijing as I descended the stairs into a network of grim underpasses. In the tunnel, a beggar was doubled over on the floor, facedown by a metal cup.

At the head of the Qianmen shopping zone were a polychrome quintuple wooden arch and a fountain blowing spray. Before I entered the pedestrian mall, I veered west, toward the side lanes where I had seen eviction notices posted four years before. In less than a minute, passing a Porsche Cayenne parked with two wheels on the sidewalk, I had reached a galvanized metal construction wall and a rubble zone.

It was two years since the new Qianmen had opened for business, right in time for the Olympics, but the neighborhood here was frozen in mid-demolition. Walls or corners of buildings were still standing, even as the rest of the structure slumped into piles of broken bricks, or twisted steel and concrete. Dirt and debris spilled out of empty shopfronts into the street. There was still a little work going on; a demolition crew was perched on the ruins, having a snack of ice cream. But mostly there were mounds and mounds of rubble. Someone had scrawled graffiti in dripping white characters on a wall: *Those who litter here are donkey cunts; those who piss here are pig cunts; those who litter here are dog cunts.*

A sign said this was Langfang No. 1 Street. I rounded the corner, reversed direction, and found Langfang No. 2. Here, the redevelopment had stopped halfway: the south side of the lane had been redone in carved wood and gray brick veneer; the north side was walled off and partly demolished. Roasted ducks hung behind plate glass in a new restaurant, while a dog wandered through the wreckage across the way.

Where Langfang No. 2 Street approached the Qianmen shopping zone, a vendor had hung out a row of T-shirts. One of them had the Beijing 2008 logo, and another had the Water Cube pattern on it. Alongside were shirts featuring Mao, pandas, a dragon, the Great Wall, a red star, and Peking Opera masks. Five thousand years of civilization. More vendors had set up in a crowded, narrow corridor running north and south, parallel to the main street, their stalls filled with everyday Chinese merchandise—clothes, trinkets, luggage. Mandarin pop songs played. It all looked the way things had looked in 2006, before anyone tried to improve it.

Then I was out in the wide, smooth new Qianmen Avenue. A strip of white marble ran down the middle of it—the center line of the capital, of the world—in imitation of the marble path in the Forbidden City, reserved for the feet of the emperor.

Trolley tracks flanked it. The buildings were gray brick-look, trimmed in carved stone, and were mostly two stories, in a reproduction of the early-twentieth-century Republican style. Security cameras were everywhere. A four-sided clock tower bore the Rolex logo on every face. There was a Uniqlo, a Swatch store, a Häagen-Dazs, and also a shop called Sweet Sweets Family and a shop selling China Intangible Cultural Heritage, which seemed to mean snack food. There was a Starbucks done up in green and gold and lattice-work like a parody of the high Chinese manner, the beached double-decker pleasure boat of a degenerate aristocrat.

Everywhere on the street, if you looked, there was something odd about the details. A wood-paneled trolley went by, its overhead brushes reaching into empty air, where electrical wires would have been. The shop signs were rendered in elaborate pre-Revolutionary characters, but they read from left to right, in the modern manner. The manhole covers identified the street in English as "Qianmen Emperor's Avenue," then said "Hundred-Year-Old Street" in Chinese—both claims couldn't simultaneously be true, since the emperor had been gone for more than a century.

A store called Me & City covered an entire block—nine different façades of two or three stories, each with its own "Me & City" sign, were grafted onto an enormous beige box. It was a feat of bullshit architecture that would have done any post–New Urbanist American mall developer proud. It was fake as fake could be, this China. A revolutionary Communist state gone over to luxury consumer goods. Incoherent, ahistoric, self-contradictory, all-devouring.

But if you walked twenty yards away from this glib prosperity, you could stand in the rubble, graffiti, and squalor, the Beijing of ruins and unfinished works. Ten yards back, and there was a crowd of people getting along with their ordinary business, buying and selling. These three Beijings—the moneyed artificial one, the wretched and broken one, the live and bustling one—stretched on in parallel, just out of sight of one another. You could stand in each one, any one, and believe you were seeing the true thing.

Acknowledgments

This book is a work of reported nonfiction; the people in it are all actual people, and the events happened as described and in that order.

I wouldn't have dared to write a book about Beijing without the help of an ad hoc work unit of expert friends and friendly experts, of which the leader was Zhang Xiaoguang. Phil Pan, my college roommate, was already in the city when I arrived, and his guidance and wisdom were all over these pages before there even were any pages. Gady Epstein and Sarah Schafer were likewise there for the book's beginnings; Susan Jakes and Evan Osnos did me the honor and favor of reading the manuscript. To the extent the facts are straight, credit goes to them, and to Jeffrey Prescott, Mayling Birney, Alex Wang, Hyeon-Ju Rho, and Glenn Tiffert, who kept me supplied with information and companionship. Jodi Xu's reporting and translation skills saved the day at least twice. Alex Pasternack, Adriane Quinlan, Joe Kahn, and Jim Yardley all gave me crucial help at one time or another. Eric Abrahamsen (and his *Beijing by Foot* guide) supplied vital and obscure information. Pan Deng provided able research and translation. The teachers

of the Taipei Language Institute did wonders in getting my Mandarin up
to a passably rudimentary level.

Nor would there have been any book if the subjects of it had not been
so generous with their time, especially Ma Jian, Soojin Cho, and the Dongsi
Olympic Community English class. Zhang Qiang of the Weather Modification Office went out of her way to explain the cloud seeding. The staff of
BOCOG was patient and professional; Jeff Ruffolo put in extra effort to
keep me in the ever-shifting loop.

In the United States, I owe thanks to Peter Kaplan for bringing me to
New York to work for his *Observer*, and for then letting me shuttle back
and forth to the far side of the globe. Once I was gone from the *Observer*
office for good, Tom McGeveran and Josh Benson kept finding ways to fit
foreign dispatches into a New York–centric newspaper. Gareth Cook and
Steve Heuser at *The Boston Globe* and David Plotz and Josh Levin at *Slate*
also kept me in assignments through lean times in the industry; so did
Anuj Desai at the late *Plenty* magazine and Mark Bryant at the late *Play*,
while they could. Portions of this book got their start in those
publications.

Larry Weissman, my agent, persuaded Sean McDonald at Riverhead
to publish the book. Sean, Geoff Kloske, and Laura Perciasepe edited the
manuscript, with Ed Cohen copyediting it.

Choire Sicha was a good-enough friend and adviser to read the first
pile of words, before it even qualified as a manuscript; he and Suzy Hansen
absorbed the worst side effects of the writing—complaints, drafts of paragraphs in progress, more complaints.

I thank Ting and Lily Ho, my father- and mother-in-law, for all their
help and kindness, whether joining us in our travels or welcoming us home.

Jane and John Scocca, my first readers and editors, supported and sustained this work to a degree that could be called extraordinary, were it not
of a piece with thirty-nine years of the same.

The first word and the last, and everything in between, go to Christina
Ho and Mack Scocca-Ho.

A Baltimore native, Tom Scocca lives in New York with his wife and two sons (one born in Beijing, one in New York). He is the managing editor of *Deadspin*, writes the "Scocca" column for *Slate*, and contributes to *The Awl*.